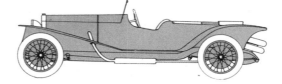

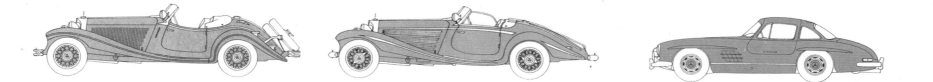

MERCEDES·BENZ

PORTRAIT OF A LEGEND

MERCEDES·BENZ
PORTRAIT OF A LEGEND

INGO SEIFF

GALLERY BOOKS
An Imprint of W. H. Smith Publishers Inc.
112 Madison Avenue
New York City 10016

Text Copyright © Ingo Seiff, 1989

First published in Great Britain in 1989
by Macdonald and Co (Publishers) Ltd
London and Sydney

A member of the Maxwell Pergamon
Publishing Corporation plc

First published in the United States in 1990
by Gallery Books, an imprint of W.H. Smith
Publishers, Inc., 112 Madison Avenue,
New York, New York 10016.

Gallery Books are available for bulk purchase
for sales promotions and premium use. For
details write or telephone the Manager of
Special Sales, W.H. Smith Publishers, Inc.,
112 Madison Avenue, New York, New York
10016. (212) 532–6600

Typeset by Flairplan Phototypsetting Ltd,
Ware, Hertfordshire
Printed in Italy by OFSA SpA, Milan

Editor: Roger Tritton
Copy Editing: CW Editorial Ltd
Art Director: Linda Cole
Designer: Alan Gooch
Translator: Oliver Dielewicz

ISBN 0 8317 5859 7

CONTENTS

CONTRIBUTORS

Ingo Seiff, born in 1928, has a commercial background in the power production industry. Having been in show business for ten years he started working as a freelance journalist and PR consultant. Although his specialist field is writing about motoring history, he is also an accomplished photographer. His books include *The Great Classics* (1982) and *Porsche-Portrait of a Legend* (1985).

Hans-Otto Neubauer was born in 1929, has written several books about the history of the automobile and works for various specialist magazines in Germany and abroad.

Dr Paul Simsa, born in 1924, studied ethnology, early history and classical archaeology at the University of Maine. Besides his academic education he worked for a motorcycle factory in Frankfurt and during this time he was a contributor to a number of specialist publications. Since 1955, he has worked for Motor Presse Stuttgart. Until 1973 he was chief editor of *mot* and later *PS* magazine and has published several books.

Stanislaw Peschel, born in 1948, studied geography, geology and sport at the University of Heidelberg. He is employed by Daimler-Benz AG in the archives department.

Hans-Karl Lange, born in 1962, is an editor of the leading German motor magazine *Auto-Zeitung* and is a specialist in the automobile history of Britain and Italy since 1950.

Richard von Frankenberg, born in 1922, was killed in an accident in 1973. He was a renowned German motor sport journalist, writer and racing driver. From 1953 to 1960 he was a member of the Porsche racing team, becoming German sports car champion in 1955. He was awarded the silver laurels.

Professor Hans Scherenberg, born in 1910, joined Daimler-Benz in 1935 as a newly qualified engineer. Between 1935 and 1945 he was involved in various development projects, including motor and aerospace engines, as well as diesel engines and fuel injection.

In 1952 he became director of passenger car construction at Untertürkheim, and by 1965 took over from Fritz Nallinger as head of the overall research and development function for passenger and commercial vehicles. His influence was responsible for the 'new generation' models of 1968, including the new S-class and the SL (W107).

On his 65th birthday he was presented with one of the highest awards of the Federal Republic of Germany, the Distinguished Service Cross.

Professor Werner Niefer was born in 1928 and after the completion of an apprenticeship as a machine-tool maker at Daimler-Benz, he studied to become an engineer. In 1952, he took up the position of engineer for the manufacture of large engines at the Daimler-Benz plant in Untertürkheim, later becoming plant manager. His career included various key positions until he was appointed to the board of Daimler-Benz AG in 1976, with responsiblity for production. Since 1 September 1987, he has been deputy chairman of Daimler-Benz AG and in 1989 he took on the additional role of chairman of the newly created Mercedes-Benz AG.

In 1987, the Technische Hochschule Darmstadt awarded Werner Niefer an honorary professorship for his special involvement in education and science and for his efforts to encourage management trainees.

PREFACE

The putting-together of *Mercedes-Benz* was hugely rewarding. It was not my ambition to give a detailed and complete account of the history of this most famous of marques, nor did I intend to compete with the topicality of specialized motoring journals: Instead I planned the book from the point of view of an observer; one who wants to get to the bottom of things, and who, in this particular case, wanted to know what is the source of the fascination about the brandname Mercedes-Benz and its predecessors.

I am delighted that my expert colleagues (Hans-Otto Neubauer, Stanislaw Peschel, Dr Paul Simsa and the late Richard von Frankenberg) could supplement my work with their contributions.

Without the support of the members of staff of the public relations department and in the archives of Daimler-Benz, it would have been impossible to complete this book on time. For this reason I extend my special thanks to Untertürkheim.

Above all, I would like to thank Professor Werner Niefer (Deputy Chairman of Daimler-Benz AG), Professor Guntram Huber (Head of Bodywork Development for cars at Daimler-Benz AG) and Karl Kling (former Grand Prix racing driver and, until his retirement, head of the Mercedes-Benz racing department) for their creative collaboration and assistance.

My particular thanks go to Stanislaw Peschel from the archives department at Daimler-Benz AG. For many months he accommodated my requests for written and photographic material with endless patience, and assisted me with much valuable advice.

During the compilation and drafting stages of this book the Daimler-Benz Group underwent important restructuring. Within the new organization there will be a holding company (Daimler-Benz AG) at the head of the group. Under this holding company three independent companies will operate: the new Mercedes-Benz AG for the automobile sector, AEG and Deutsche Aerospace AG. For 1989 the total turnover of the technology-group may lie in the region of 80 billion marks (=£27 billion), 75 per cent of which is derived from the automobile sector alone.

Ingo Seiff

The Three-pointed Star

The badge of Mercedes, one of the classic commercial emblems of the modern world, has been greatly modified over the course of this century, always influenced by changes within the company and by the spirit of the time.

In 1909 the managing board of Daimler decided to find out whether a three-pointed star, enamelled in white had been previously registered as a trade mark. It had not. The Daimler sons Adolf and Paul had proposed the star. They remembered a photograph from 1873 which showed the factory of Otto and Langen in Deutz, where their father was a director and had a house. On this print Gottlieb Daimler had marked a biblical morning star and his sons recalled that he had made the remark:: 'From here a star will rise and my hope is that my family and children will benefit from it.'

Not only the three-pointed star (A) was patented in 1909. There was also a star with four points but it was not used. In 1916 a three-pointed star within an outer ring which itself contained four stars appeared (B).

1909 was also the year in which the Benz Company applied for a trademark for their own insignia, the word 'BENZ' surrounded by a laurel wreath (C). When in 1926 Daimler and Benz merged to use the name Mercedes-Benz, a new emblem was designed, the Mercedes star surrounded by the Benz laurel (D). The exact form that the new badge had to take was established in the merger contract and it is still seen today on all Mercedes-Benz passenger cars.

In 1933 a highly impressive abstract three-pointed star (E) was registered as a trademark, and since that date that image too has acted as a guiding star to all drivers of Mercedes-Benz.

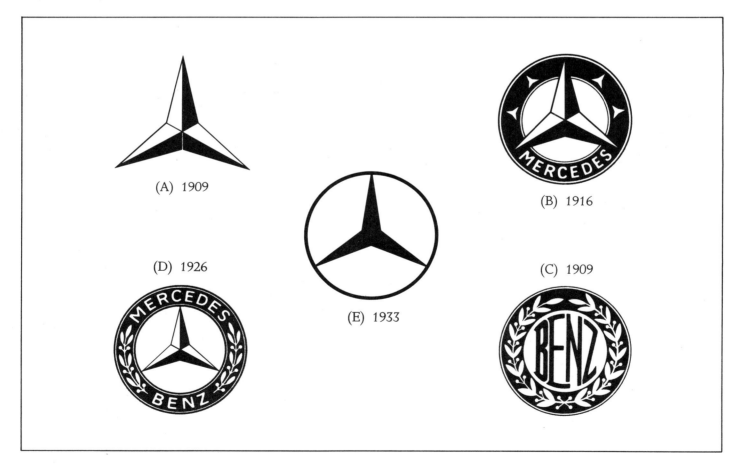

(A) 1909

(B) 1916

(D) 1926

(E) 1933

(C) 1909

Previous page: The Benz Patent Motor Car 1886. The patent for Benz's motor car, No. 37435, dates from 29 January 1886. This 'gas-driven engine' – as the patent calls it – fulfilled Karl Benz's revolutionary idea of a new means of transport. Unlike Gottlieb Daimler, Benz had a motorized road vehicle in mind in which both the engine and the chassis were conceived as a single unit. The car body and its driving system were in harmony with each other.

Technical data: 1 cylinder, four-stroke engine, capacity 984 cc, output 0.9 bhp, maximum speed 16 kph at 400 rpm.

Above: The flywheel of the Benz Patent Motor Car 1886. The large flywheel of the engine was fitted horizontally as Benz was afraid that if it were positioned vertically it might adversely affect the car's stability on corners.

Above: The Daimler Motor Coach 1886. It was the world's first petrol driven four-wheeled car. Its small engine was mounted between the front and rear seats. The Motor Coach was based on a so-called 'American Coach Car' into which Daimler implanted the 462 cc engine, the gear belt, rear drive and steering.

Technical data: 1 cylinder, four-stroke engine, capacity 462 cc, output at 700 rpm 1.1 bhp, maximum speed 16 kph.

Overleaf: Benz Racing Car 1899. Although Karl Benz – unlike Daimler – did not think much of racing cars for sport and underestimated their potential in marketing, he did build a sports car before the turn of the century which, at the time, was considered to be one of the most beautiful and reliable. However, with its 10 bhp it was inferior to Daimler's 'Phoenix' of the same year by some 17 bhp.

Technical data: 2 cylinders, four-stroke engine, capacity 2 714 cc, output at 1 000 rpm 10 bhp, maximum speed 50 kph.

Above: Daimler Riemenwagen ('Belt-driven Car')
1894. The two cylinder engine positioned behind the
rear axle, completed by Maybach in 1892, was
considered at the time to be a highly modern unit. It had
an output of 2 bhp at 700 rpm. The fuel was supplied by
a revolutionary jet injection carburettor. The four-gear
belt-drive transferring the power from the engine to the
rear wheels ensured a gentle shift when changing speed.

Technical data: capacity 762 cc, maximum speed 20 kph.

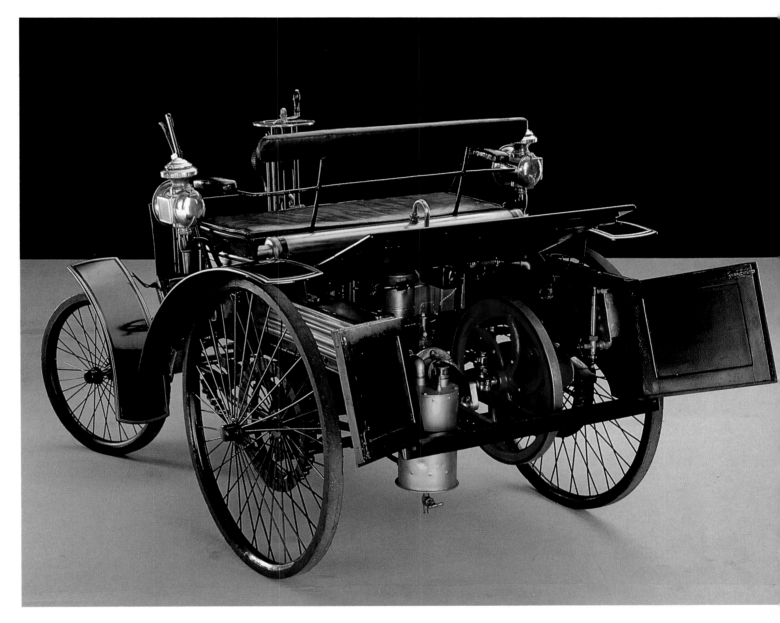

Above: Benz Velo 1894. The 'Velo', built from 1894 to 1899, ranks as the world's first serially built automobile. 381 were produced between 1894 and 1897. The 'Velo', with its removable semi-top, cost 2 200 Goldmarks.

Technical data: 1 cylinder, four-stroke engine, capacity 1 045 cc, output at 450 rpm 1.5 bhp, maximum speed 21 kph.

Overleaf: Benz 12/18 bhp Parsifal 1903. The 'Parsifal' was the car that was meant to help the Benz company out of its crisis at the turn of the century. A team of French engineers led by Marius Barbarou produced a wealth of ideas which in turn inspired Benz's German engineers. The result – a counterpart to the Daimler Simplex – was the 'Parsifal' with its several engine variations. It was presented at the Paris Salon 1902, was a great success with the public and helped the Benz company establish a great standing.

Technical data: 4 cylinders, four-stroke engine, capacity 2 413 cc, output at 1 200 rpm 18 bhp, maximum speed 60 kph.

HANS-OTTO NEUBAUER

The Making of Mercedes-Benz

When Karl Benz was born, on 25 November 1844, what we now know as Germany was made up of numerous kingdoms and duchies which jealously guarded their privileges. A variety of interests led various German states to enter into coalitions and to fight each other to achieve their aims. By 1871, however, the Second Reich had been created, in which the kingdoms and duchies could, to a large extent, retain their rights.

KARL BENZ

Benz was born in Karlsruhe, the capital of the grand duchy of Baden which had a reputation for trade and craftsmanship and especially for its attention to education, from which Karl Benz was to benefit. His father was a train driver with Badische Eisenbahn, an occupation which eventually brought about his demise. In helping to put a derailed locomotive engine back on the rails he caught a cold which led to pneumonia and a few days later he died. His wife and her two-year-old son were left with just a small welfare payment of 24 Kreuzer, not sufficient to support a family. To make ends meet she took up a position as a cook, which enabled her to send Karl to a good school in the capital: a grammar school, which specialized in science.

The young Benz then transferred to the *Polytechnikum* in Karlsruhe, one step on from schools of engineering and higher technical institutes. One of Karl's teachers, Ferdinand Redtenbacher, introduced him to the internal combustion engine for the first time, and it is perhaps this which gave him the idea of looking for an alternative power source to steam, a search which was to become his foremost objective in years to come.

In 1864, Benz left the *Polytechnikum* and held a number of different positions before setting up his own business, together with a partner, in Mannheim in 1872. This company was called Benz & Ritter, but it was not long before his partner, having asked Benz to buy him out, departed. Even as sole proprietor, however, Benz

17

found it difficult to earn enough to keep the young family he now had. In 1878, he began to concentrate on the two-stroke engine and two years later the first working unit appeared. In 1881 the company Gasmotorenfabrik Mannheim was registered, but the engines did not sell very well and Benz was obliged to look for new financial backers. Even this newly created shareholding company did not prove to be a great success, however, and Benz finally left his partners.

In 1883 two men appeared who were to determine his destiny. These were Max C. Rose and Friedrich W. Esslinger, who together provided the money for Benz to found a new company, the Rheinische Gasmotorenfabrik, in Mannheim.

The new engines sold well and allowed Benz to follow up an idea he had had in mind for quite some time. This was to create a vehicle to be propelled by his engine – a type of vehicle that had never been built before.

GOTTLIEB DAIMLER

Gottlieb Daimler was born more than ten years before Benz, on 17 March 1834, the son of a baker in Schorndorf village in the kingdom of Württemberg. After finishing school, where his main interests were maths and geometry, Gottlieb began an apprenticeship as a tinmaker, following which he enrolled at the Polytechnikum in Stuttgart to complete his education. The Polytechnikum was associated with the Maschinenfabrik Grafenstaden in Alsace which enabled Daimler to gain a better theoretical and practical engineering background. By the time Daimler left the Polytechnikum in 1858 he had formulated particularly strong ideas on the internal-combustion engine, based on the work of Lenoir.

Having spent some time in France and in Great Britain with Armstrong-Whitworth he returned to Germany in 1862. In that time, not only had he increased his knowledge of engineering but he had also learned how to manage a business. The next three years he spent at Straub & Söhne in Geislingen, and they were a turning point in his life: it was there he met Wilhelm Maybach.

From 1869 to 1872 Daimler worked first at the Maschinenbau Gesellschaft Karlsruhe and then as technical director for Gasmotorenfabrik Deutz, where he could finally devote himself to the internal-combustion engine: Deutz being the builders of the Nikolaus August Otto engine. Deutz's facilities exceeded all Daimler's expectations; neither of the Gasmotorenfabrik partners, Eugen Langen and Nikolaus Otto, was an engineer and the company was in desperate need of someone to consolidate their technical success. Daimler was soon able to surround himself with an excellent team and appointed Wilhelm Maybach as chief engineer.

The relationship between Daimler and the self-taught Otto was, however, ill-fated. Daimler demanded considerable privileges for himself; Otto the inventor felt pushed back. The relationship further deteriorated when the four-stroke engine appeared in 1875. It was Otto's invention, but Daimler had developed and produced the actual engine. The four-stroke engine became known as 'Otto's new engine', a description which Daimler took as a personal insult. During the following years tension between the two did not improve, and ultimately the Gasmotorenfabrik was obliged to part with Daimler in order to keep Otto and his patents.

Daimler had devoted a great deal of energy to Otto's engine, trying to develop it into a light and, for the time, high-revving unit which would be suitable for all types of vehicles. He continued with the experiments after he left Deutz, setting up his workshop in Bad Cannstatt, near Stuttgart, and taking Wilhelm Maybach with him.

The quest for the high-revving internal-combustion engine became the main concern of both men and in 1885 they reached their goal. Reichspatent number 34926 was granted on 3 April 1885 for a *Gas-bzw, Petroleum-Kraftmaschine* ('a gas or petrol engine'). This was the first upright Daimler engine and the basis of all further development. Daimler's dream of creating an engine capable of propelling a vehicle had been accomplished. Practical proof that his idea was feasible came in the same year, when he introduced the first vehicle with an internal-combustion engine, his *Reitwagen* – the forerunner of the motor bike. Using this pilot model, Daimler attempted to put his ideas into practice. Nevertheless he had no plans to pursue the development of this type of vehicle any further: to him its only role was to prove that he was able to create a workable engine which was light, space efficient and could be used to power other vehicles.

THE FIRST MOTOR CAR

Karl Benz's approach was quite different to that of Gottlieb Daimler. He did not want to build *Einbaumotoren* (mounted engines) – his plan was to combine engine and vehicle to form the first motor car. He was confronted with the task of designing not only a suitable engine but also an appropriate vehicle and drive mechanism. In 1885, Karl Benz's 'self-propelled vehicle' became a reality in the form of the *Fahrzeug mit Gasmotorenbetrieb* ('vehicle with a gas engine'). On 29 January 1885 Benz was granted Deutsches Reichspatent number 37435 the number now thought of as the 'birth certificate' of the car. Benz not only built the engine and all its components but also the chassis, the differential and the electric ignition.

Even today it is unclear exactly when Benz completed the vehicle. However, it does seem that the first test drives were carried out by the end of 1885. By mid 1886, the newspapers of Mannheim were carrying reports about the first public demonstrations.

The Benz Patent-Motorwagen was a three-wheeler. Benz had chosen this type of vehicle because the construction of a steering system for two wheels represented an insurmountable problem at the time, and the traditional cam-and-peg steering was considered to be too heavy. The main problem faced by Benz in the development of his new concept, the motor car, was not a technological one but a commercial one. How could he sell an idea so different from what had gone before?

Unlike Benz, Daimler did not pursue the creation of a motor car but was eager to equip various kinds of vehicle with engines. At first he mounted an engine in a boat and then in 1886 he converted a carriage and created the first four-wheeled motor vehicle. Unlike Benz again, Daimler did not see that cam-and-peg steering would present any obstacles. Indeed there was initially only one vehicle built which was not developed any further by Daimler.

WORLD EXPOSITION

In 1888, Karl Benz demonstrated the prowess of his Model 3 at the Munich Agricultural Exhibition. Not long before, his wife Berta had impressively proved the reliability of the Benz vehicles on a long trip from Mannheim to Pforzheim and back.

By this time even Daimler was coming round to the idea that a vehicle and an engine should form one functional unit, and he was convinced by Maybach to build such a vehicle. Maybach's influence could clearly be seen on the car which was eventually exhibited at the World Exposition in Paris in 1889. The *Stahlradwagen* (literally 'a car made of a tubular frame') had a two-cylinder vee-engine and four wheels. Its graceful form made a great impression.

The French industrialists Levassor and Peugeot soon became interested in this vehicle. They agreed to build Daimler engines under licence in their factories which had already helped create the fast-growing French car industry. In 1890 the Daimler Motorwagen Gesellschaft was founded in Bad Cannstatt. Daimler's partners were Wilhelm Lorenz and Max Duttenhofer, who assured him of a completely free hand in all technical matters: a promise which was soon broken as his influence was systematically curtailed. Daimler's partners favoured the construction of boat engines, whilst Daimler thought that the manufacture of lighter engines for motor vehicles would have better prospects. Since they were unable to agree on this point Daimler decided to terminate his contract at the end of 1892 and resigned from the company.

In a rented building which used to be the Hotel Hermann in Bad Cannstatt, Daimler set up his new workshop with an atmosphere more conducive to creative work. Here he was very successful and Daimler later described the period as 'the happiest time of my life.' Of course, it goes without saying that Wilhelm Maybach went with him. There, among other things they created the new N-engine (better known by its French name of 'Phoenix'), which was notable for its revolutionary spray carburettor and honeycomb radiator. Daimler's old partners soon realised that they could not be guaranteed a prosperous future without Daimler and negotiated his return. Thus, in 1895, Daimler's workshop closed down and Maybach also returned to the Daimler Motoren Gesellschaft to be appointed technical director. They had now made production of motor vehicles the prime objective.

The years which Daimler spent in dispute with his partners had meanwhile been exceptionally good for Karl Benz. In 1890, he found two new partners, Friedrich von Fischer and Julius Ganss, who devoted all their energies towards the development of the company, and, as a result, the sales of the stationary engine, powered by gas or petrol, were excellent. Apart from the engines themselves Benz also concentrated on building motor cars. It was the details of his designs which in particular fired his imagination, his most significant achievement being the 'steering device' patented in 1893, which became known as axle-pivot steering. The fact that this seemingly new invention had already been produced by Georg Lankensperger in 1816 should not overshadow his achievements.

In 1893, the first four-wheeled Benz car, the Viktoria, was introduced. The improved steering allowed it to become a huge success and further models followed, such as the light Velo in 1894, which became the first mass-produced car in the world.

In 1897, the new two-cylinder engine, the Kontra-Motor was introduced, featuring horizontally opposed cylinders and, in 1899, Benz completed his first racing car, which could reach speeds of up to 70 kph (43.5 mph). In all Benz models – as in the first Benz three-wheeler – the engine was rear mounted. By the end of 1900, 2317 motor cars had been produced and the Benz company could proudly call itself 'the oldest and largest motor car works in the world.'

With the return of Daimler and Maybach to the Daimler Motoren Gesellschaft meanwhile, the production of motor cars resumed and in 1896 forty-three vehicles were manufactured. In 1897, the first Phoenix appeared, with a front-mounted engine and chain transmission. One year later the first four-cylinder engine was launched. Daimler's influence on the company, however, remained as small as ever. He owned only 19.8 per cent of the equity, but Maybach told him that the company would like even this holding to be further reduced. In

1898 their partners sought financial backing to form a wholly new company, the Motorfahrzeug und Motorenfabrik Berlin, to build motor vehicles according to Daimler patents. Daimler protested, but in vain.

By this time Daimler's health was failing. Since his time at Deutz he had suffered from heart disease and he had now lost his fighting spirit and was unable to cope with the arguments he had with his partners. Even a spa cure in 1899 did not produce a lasting improvement. He failed to recover from a heart-attack and died on 6 March 1900. In time the influence of his heirs was reduced to insignificance. In 1902, the Motorfahrzeug und Motorenfabrik Berlin was taken over, given the name Werk Marienfelde and produced commercial vehicles for Daimler Motoren Gesellschaft.

Some historians do not wish to accept this astonishing fact, but, although both pioneers lived only 120 km (75 miles) apart, and introduced the motor car at the very same time, Daimler and Benz never met.

THE MERCEDES ERA

At the turn of the century, production at the Benz works was about six times greater than at Daimler, although both company's cars were rated amongst the best. Their superb reputation had reached the French Riviera, where the automobile was already an established form of entertainment for the rich who wintered there. Horse racing no longer satisfying them, they began to organize car races, too. The Austro-Hungarian consul general in Nice, Emil Jellinek, was one of those who was absolutely fascinated by motor cars. He was a financial wizard and had become very rich as a result of his business transactions in North Africa. He owned and raced a Daimler and when racing used his daughter's first name Mercédès as a pseudonym. He soon realised that Daimlers were totally unsuitable for sport and, in 1900, proposed that Daimler build a completely new car. Jellinek also offered some technical expertise for this new project.

The engine should have 35 bhp and was to be mounted closer to the ground than usual to lower the car's centre of gravity. With a firm order of over thirty-six cars Jellinek convinced the Daimler works to start production of his new model. Wilhelm Maybach was in charge of the project, which soon gave him the title 'king of car design'. Jellinek insisted that he, Jellinek, should be granted the trade rights for the Austro-Hungarian Empire, France, Belgium and the United States of America, as well as being allowed to trade the car under the name of Mercedes. In Bad Cannstatt they agreed, albeit reluctantly. Although the new model failed when introduced at the Grand Prix of Pau, near Toulouse, in 1901, the high quality of Mercedes cars was demonstrated at the Nice races which took place soon afterwards. All the important races during the 'Nice Week' were won, and even the French newspapers showed great approval. 'We have begun the Mercedes era' was just one of the comments which greatly encouraged Jellinek and Maybach.

The name Mercedes soon became universally known, and Daimler adopted it for all of its cars. In 1902, 'Mercedes' became a registered trade mark (the two accents were actually retained until 1926).

In 1903, the company suffered a set-back due to a fire in its Bad Cannstatt works. However, just before the fire a new site had been acquired in Stuttgart-Untertürkheim, as Daimler had outgrown Bad Cannstatt and so the fire prompted immediate construction of the new factory. Unfortunately, the racing cars which were due to go to the 1903 Gordon-Bennett race in Ireland had fallen victim to the fire, but several private owners lent their Mercedes to the company and Belgium driver Camille Jenatzy drove to victory. This success consolidated the Mercedes reputation, and the company found that it could look ahead with confidence.

CRISIS AT BENZ

Developments at Benz proceeded quite differently. Their cars enjoyed an excellent reputation, but the progress of the Mercedes had set completely new standards. Benz cars still had rear-mounted engines, for example, and Karl Benz himself did not believe at all in looking for high speeds or in motor racing.

It was only in 1902 that Benz followed Daimler's lead, producing its first car with a front-mounted engine and contracting the French designer Marius Barbarou. Benz now had two design departments which worked separately but pooled their ideas. Benz, as a trade name, lacked the desired impact, and so the company followed Daimler's example and settled on the name Parsifal.

Karl Benz strongly disapproved of this whole development and without a moment's hesitation left the board of directors. The Benz company soon began to deteriorate, and in 1903, only 172 cars were sold. They survived this all-time low, however, and by 1905 the company's books showed a considerable profit. Benz regained its earlier market position and the name Parsifal was abandoned. The Mannheim works once more rose to full capacity, so when the opportunity arose in 1907 Benz took over the Süddeutsche Automobil-Fabrik in Gaggenau, which had specialized mainly in producing commercial vehicles. From then on Benz's activities in that field concentrated on Gaggenau, with the main works in Mannheim being replaced by a new plant in the Waldhof district of the same city.

The following years brought great prosperity to both Benz and Daimler. Racing successes gave both companies much publicity, at the same time as proving the cars' outstanding reliability and solid construction. In addition to car engines, Benz began to manufacture aircraft power plants, production rising to great heights during World War I. The post-war period, with its political and economic difficulties, however caused both Benz and Daimler no end of trouble, although there were still some moments of triumph. Benz applied itself to developing a diesel engine for vehicles, using the pre-combustion method of Prosper L'Orange. The first diesel-engined vehicle, the Benz-Sendling-Motor plough, appeared in 1923, and in the same year, Benz introduced the first diesel-engined truck.

Daimler tried to regain the prestige lost during the war through success on the racing circuit. Their sport models boasted supercharged engines using the technology developed for aircraft engines during the war. With Germany impoverished, however, customers were demanding small and economical cars, cars which were not part of Benz's or Daimler's production schedule.

For both companies, car production had settled right back at the levels of 1910/11. The end of runaway inflation and the consequent stabilization of the currency eased the situation somewhat, but future prospects remained gloomy. In 1924 car exports dropped by a full fifty per cent compared with the previous year, and imports rose by about four hundred per cent. Immediate action was called for.

Mergers were obviously on the cards. Both Benz and Daimler had strong links with the Deutsche Bank, and it was this institution that first tried to amalgamate the two. In 1924 the companies finally agreed to pool their resources. The first step was to shorten their product lines and to integrate research and development as well as sales and purchasing. A complete merger followed the agreement signed on 28 June 1926.

MERCEDES-BENZ

The new company was called Daimler-Benz Aktiengesellschaft. The Mercedes star surrounded by the Benz wreath of bay leaves became their trade mark, and the cars were marketed under the name Mercedes-Benz. Commercial-vehicle production in Berlin-Marienfelde and Gaggenau was also included in the contract and administration was centralized at the head office of the Daimler works in Stuttgart-Untertürkheim.

After 1923, technical development at Daimler had been largely influenced by director Dr Ferdinand Porsche, who was mainly responsible for the construction of the supercharged models. Porsche did not entirely approve of the merger with Benz, but he continued to work for the holding company until 1928.

Car production was continued in Mannheim as well as in Untertürkheim, although only the six-cylinder models were produced at Mannheim. In Untertürkheim, the eight-cylinder Nürburg and the successful supercharged models were added to the production line. The Sindelfingen works, which had been built during the war, concentrated on car chassis production, while the Gaggenau plant was relegated to producing commercial vehicles and that in Berlin-Marienfelde was converted into a car repair workshop.

Since they could not compete on price, Daimler-Benz concentrated on quality cars. The company was slow to adopt all the new mass-production methods pioneered by the Americans and it was only in 1936 that Daimler-Benz started to manufacture their cars on a moving line. With the introduction of a big sheet-metal press in 1928, however, the Sindelfingen works had begun again to look ahead and were already setting new standards in chassis construction.

The two founders of the company died in the same year, 1929; Karl Benz on 4 April and Wilhelm Maybach on 29 December.

THE GREAT DEPRESSION

The German car industry was very badly hit by the Great Depression. Domestic sales and the rates of production of the remaining twenty-six German car manufacturers reached their lowest level in 1932, exceeding everyone's worst fears. Strict trade barriers were imposed on German exports and it was cold comfort to the manufacturers that no more than 4600 foreign cars had been sold in Germany in that year. One in ten of the six million people now unemployed had been made redundant by car manufacturers. Meanwhile, numerous well established firms were hit by their own financial problems – Brennabor, Stoewer, Hanomag and Hansa Lloyd went into liquidation, and the Saxon car manufacturers Horch, Audi, DKW and Wanderer only saved themselves from bankruptcy by merging to become Auto Union AG.

During the disastrous year of 1932, Daimler-Benz had to cut its labour-force by half, to 6860 employees. Remarkably, however, the company did not give the impression of being discouraged by the depression. They even presented a luxury car, the so-called Grosser Mercedes, and launched the new 170 at the Paris salon of October 1931. This showed impeccable timing. There was great demand for this relatively small six-cylinder-engined car in Germany and, according to motoring journalist Werner Oswald, 'It helped Daimler-Benz a great deal to overcome the problems which were caused by the Great Depression'.

The 170 was the first car with all-round independent suspension and it emphasized the three most important features of Daimler-Benz cars: performance, safety and comfort. The 170V, which was launched in 1936, was to become a real success and showed that Daimler-Benz could finally market an economical medium-size car, offering different types of attractive bodies.

THE RISE OF HITLER

Daimler-Benz managed to weather the Great Depression and re-emerged strongly when Adolf Hitler rose to power after January 1933. Millions of people were electrified by the cunning showmanship of this demagogue: Hitler promised to eradicate unemployment and to revitalize the economy; he kept his promise, but at what cost! The new wealth of the German nation went hand in hand with the atrocious activities of the Gestapo, the persecution of the German Jews and the denial of all democratic rights. But industry was back in full swing and so was Daimler-Benz. In the car market it had a share of eleven per cent, ranking third after Opel and Auto Union. As with all the other German car manufacturers, Daimler-Benz benefited from Hitler's rearmament programme and the car industry boom stimulated by the government. From 1 April 1933 every German who bought a car, was exempted from road tax, which led to a vast increase in car production, and the capacities of the Daimler-Benz's works in Untertürkheim, Sindelfingen and Gaggenau proved insufficient to cope with the greater demand.

Hitler, who was fascinated by cars, was offering the German people the automotive equivalent of bread and circuses. It was he who initiated the construction of the 'Silver Arrows', the Mercedes-Benz and Auto Union racing cars which dominated the world's circuits until 1939. Hitler favoured too the production of luxury cars such as the 540K Mercedes, the Maybach Zeppelin and Horch 853A. He also instructed Ferdinand Porsche to design the Volkswagen or 'people's car'. Daimler-Benz undertook some of the development work and thirty test cars were built in the Daimler-Benz Sindelfingen chassis plant. Daimler-Benz did not show much enthusiasm for this project, however, not believing that the VW would prove a success.

Hitler's motivation for encouraging the production of the people's car was to prepare them for the imminent *Blitzkrieg*, because every *Blitzkrieg* requires reliable transport . . . . The original Volkswagen was itself transformed into the legendary VW-Jeep, which Field Marshall Rommel used in North Africa.

The outbreak of war did not come as a surprise to German industry. As German historian Hans Pohl put it in a documentary about Daimler-Benz, 'Hitler's four-year plan of 1936 and the outbreak of war in 1939 forced German industry to switch to war production; which reached its peak in 1942 when Albert Speer was Minister of Defence. At the Daimler-Benz works, preparation for defence production had begun prior to the beginning of the war. They sold some of their premises, extended individual plants and even built new works, like the one for aircraft engines in Genshagen near Berlin . . . . Within the framework of general rearmament they increased in particular their production of large engines; aircraft and ship engines. By order of the Reich's Ministry of Aviation, Daimler-Benz began the construction of jet engine plants as early as 1941, although production was never started.'

Even though the Daimler-Benz board of directors eagerly participated in Hitler's armament race, not all of them were committed National Socialists. In 1942, Dr Wilhelm Haspel, who was not a party member, was appointed chairman of the board. Since he had a half-Jewish wife, the Nazis did not trust him and his links with the Jewish community soon created trouble. If he had not been of such vital importance to the running of the company, he would soon have fallen victim to the Gestapo. Indeed, at one point he was nearly committed to the Wolfenbüttel concentration camp. His wife was only spared because his expert knowledge was considered to be indispensible. Members of the supervisory board and the board of directors who had great influence protected him, and the Minister of Defence, Albert Speer, could not have managed without him . . . .

Today young Germans growing up are keen to know if industrial giants such as Daimler-Benz were guilty of supporting Hitler's rearmament efforts or of financing his devastating plans . . . .

Henry A. Turner, Jr, a Yale professor and a leading

expert on the the Third Reich confirms in his latest book that '. . . the Daimler-Benz AG, for example, acted in a reserved manner when it came to financing the National Socialist Party. The executives of some of the biggest corporations, such as the Mannesmann steel firm and the Daimler-Benz automotive works, conspicuously abstained from any political activities and even from an active role in the major national trade associations . . .'.

Daimler-Benz suffered considerable damage throughout the war and in 1944 eighty per cent of the Untertürkheim and Sindelfingen works were destroyed by the massive Allied bombing offensive that took place by day and by night at that time. Nevertheless, the much-vaunted rapid reconstruction of Germany after the war has become for the student of economic history the example of the classic economic miracle. The post-war history of Daimler-Benz bears this out since in May 1945, just after the end of the war, the company employed 2860 people, whereas in 1988 nearly 170,000 employees helped produce a turnover of nearly 55 billion Deutschemarks (roughly £15 billion).

INGO SEIFF

Berta Benz and Louise Sarazin
Mothers of Invention

The woman driver is an eternal topic of conversation among men. Since the invention of the motor car, men have claimed to be the only truly competent drivers. It is men who have made and related the history of the automobile and therefore it is no surprise that the important role played by women during the development of the motor car is usually only briefly chronicled. However, during the early development of the car, there were two women – Berta Benz and Louise Sarazin – who provided a real driving force.

The story of Berta Benz begins with her husband Karl, who went into bankruptcy in 1877 when his iron foundry and workshop failed. This was just after the Franco–Prussian War of 1870–1, which culminated in the fall of the Second French Empire and the founding of the German Empire and brought a period of unprecedented industrial upswing in Germany. So when Berta and Karl Benz found their lives in ruins, they decided that only something out of the ordinary would guarantee them a reliable source of income.

In 1876, the year of Benz's bankruptcy, the four-stroke Otto engine was patented, with Deutsches Reichs-patent number 532. The great era of steam as a means of power was already over, and the world of science had become highly tuned to improving the ratio between energy expended and power output achieved. Karl Benz himself decided to embark upon a bold plan: he began to develop his own internal-combustion engine. Rather than acquire a licence to use the Otto principles, however, the economically minded Benz decided on a two-stroke engine.

As millions of people prepared for New Year's Eve celebrations in 1879, Karl and Berta Benz returned once more to their small workshop to subject their two-stroke engine to another test, as it was still not working satisfactorily. After dinner, Berta Benz had encouraged her husband by saying, 'We've got to go to the workshop and try our luck just one more time. There's something that bothers me.' So Karl started the engine. Later he recalled, 'The engine answered phut, phut,

phut. The beautiful, even, alternating rhythm of the beats of a sound of the future. For more than an hour we were captivated by its monotonous song. No magic flute in the world could achieve this, but the two-stroke engine was now capable of it. On this New Year's Eve we did not need best wishes from other people. We had had a stroke of true good fortune. Our poorly equipped workshop had become the birthplace of a new engine that evening. Suddenly, the bells began to ring. The New Year's bells! For us it was as if the bells were not ringing because of the New Year, but to herald a new era, an era which was to receive a new rhythm; that from the car engine'.

The shared experience of Karl and Berta Benz is reminiscent of the results of Henry Ford's experiments with his first engine. On Christmas Eve 1893, he decided to test his construction in the kitchen of his small house in Piquette Avenue, Detroit. His wife Clara was busy changing the nappies of their small son Edsel and preparing the turkey, when Henry put his metal machine into the sink and muttered: 'Darling, this is my first engine! Come on and help me to get it to work!' After several attempts the single-cylinder engine began to turn over, puffing, hissing and causing a stink, and from that moment Clara became the driving force, the good conscience, the confidante of a husband who was so obsessed with mechanics . . . .

A long and difficult road lay ahead of the Benzes before Karl could patent his engine, but patent number 37485 was finally granted on 29 January 1886. The specification read simply 'Fahrzeug mit Gasmotorenantrieb' (vehicle with a gas engine), but this was to become the first practical automobile in the world.

A 'SALES CAMPAIGN'

Although there were no buyers even two years later, neither Karl nor Berta was discouraged. However, the remarkably energetic wife embarked upon what we would today call a 'sales campaign'. She decided to take the Benz three-wheeler on an impromptu long-distance drive, to publicize their invention, and to test it thoroughly in all conditions.

Berta made sure that her protective husband did not find out about her adventure beforehand, and at five o'clock on 4 August 1888 she and her sons Eugen (15) and Richard (13½) sneaked away from the house. The Patent-Motor-Wagen (patent motor car) was pushed silently out of the garage, the three adventurers starting the engine in the yard in order not to wake Karl. The single-cylinder engine was relatively quiet, producing something of a hissing and puffing sound (silencers were already in existence to reduce the noise of the engine, partly so as not to inconvenience people and partly so as not to frighten horses).

The trio soon realized that even the slightest incline was a problem for the vehicle and there were critical moments after the city of Weinheim, the first port of call: approaching horse-drawn carriages were given due respect and speed reduced to 'dead slow' as required by law. Passers-by were aghast; a vehicle without horses, crewed by a woman and two boys (one of whom was steering) and all in high spirits – it was like something out of a Jules Verne book . . . .

In Wiesloch, the crowd of curious onlookers noticed that the vehicle was in need of 'fodder' of a very unusual type. Berta went to a chemist and bought petrol, at the same time asking for water to quench the inadequate cooling system's inordinate thirst. When the three approached the gentle slopes of the Kraichgau, one of the boys had to jump out and push, while a climb near the hamlet of Bauschlott (321 metres [1053 feet] above sea level) seemed to be the end of the excursion. The only thing the three could do was to push together with all of their strength.

In Bauschlott itself, the leather-pads of the block brake had to be replaced by a cobbler and the cooling system once again had to be refilled. Berta somehow repaired a defective carburettor with a hatpin and a short circuit in the electrical system was mended by the ingenious lady-driver using a garter for insulation.

The continuing trip was threatened by yet another mountain, but this time a detour was made via Wilferdingen, which was far less arduous. It was already dark when the intrepid team arrived in Pforzheim and, as the three-wheeler did not have any lights, they were forced to interrupt their trip. Anyway, they wanted to have a good sleep before seeing the boys' grandmother the next morning, so they looked for somewhere to stay overnight.

Berta sent a telegram to her husband from the guesthouse 'Zur Post' in the Ispringer Strasse and proudly told him about the successful 'test-drive'. Meanwhile, a crowd of inquisitive people had come to have a look at the car from Mannheim and gloomy predictions were made that all horses would now be killed . . . .

Karl felt somewhat betrayed, but was truly quite proud of his wife and sons. Although they were not mechanics, they had been able to rectify any technical faults and had reached their destination with the *Patent-Motor-Wagen*. However, Karl asked Berta to return the transmission chains by post because they were needed for the exhibition vehicle which was to go on show at a Munich exhibition of that year!

Berta did not leave the journey at that. She compiled a report for her husband on all the technical shortcomings which had led to complications on the journey. She recommended for example a further gear for the transmission in order to avoid problems with slight climbs. She might also have recommended installing strengthened block brakes and pads as well as improving the cooling system! Berta was without doubt the world's first 'test driver'.

LOUISE SARAZIN

Gottlieb Daimler too was fatefully connected with a woman, although only through business. Today the French woman, Louise Sarazin is generally acknowledged to have been the pioneer of automobile production. For several years her husband, Edouard Sarazin, was the French representative of the German company, Gasmotorenfabrik Otto & Langen, during which time he took out the Daimler patents for Belgium and France and became the intermediary between Daimler and the French engineers Panhard and Levassor, who installed Daimler engines in their vehicles. Edouard died in 1887, but Louise decided to continue his work. Even during his last hours, on Christmas Eve 1887, he had implored her, 'Keep in touch with Daimler in the interest of our

children. Don't let the relationship come to an end. Continue to work with him, and with Panhard and Levassor. Only together can you get the most benefit out of the Daimler patents.'

A document dating back to that time confirms how sensitively Gottlieb Daimler conducted his affairs with Louise Sarazin, despite the large amounts of money involved. On 4 January 1888 he wrote a letter from which we quote:

'Dear Mrs Sarazin,
The past year did not end happily for us. Your message that your beloved husband, our Dear Mr Sarazin, is no longer among us was a terrible shock. I cannot tell you how sad this loss is for me. He is constantly in my thoughts and I regret that I did not come to pay my promised visit to Paris, so that we could shake hands and meet just once in this life . . . . I reproach myself for perhaps having caused him to worry about business matters during his last days; however, I did not know about his illness and only noticed that his handwriting seemed slightly different. Perhaps you would be so kind as to let me know about his illness and the last days in your next letter.

With regard to business, there is no hurry to find a new representative in Paris and I am pleased to hear that you are on top of our current business matters and, also, that you want to take over, about which I am only too happy. Furthermore, I can see that you are in favour of my engines, just as was Mr Sarazin and I can well understand that you do not want to see someone else reap the fruits of your husband's work. I would like to express to you in these few lines that I hope I am acting in accordance with the wishes of your husband when I assure you that you will continue to remain a business partner, although I cannot tell you now in what capacity. In any case, I shall not enter into any future business arrangements without your advice . . . .

Please allow me, dear Mrs Sarazin, to express my most sincere condolences. May God give you and your family deepest sympathy for your painful loss.
    Yours, Gottlieb Daimler'.

A few months later, Louise Sarazin came to visit

Cannstatt to negotiate with Daimler. Although there had never been a written agreement between her late husband and the German, he was so enchanted by Mrs Sarazin's charm and cleverness that he appointed the widow to be his representative and licensee for France and Belgium.

The author Pierre Souvestre wrote about this fateful meeting between Daimler and Madame Sarazin in *The Story of the Motor Car* (1907): 'Madame Sarazin was never to forget the critical hour which she spent in the small office in Cannstatt. Face to face with Gottlieb'. Daimler was already a man of ill-health and often overcome by paralysing tiredness and it was under these circumstances that the French woman met the ingenious German. He sat quietly opposite her and, although he was listening, he seemed removed. Perhaps he was pondering whether it was a sensible idea to appoint this young, optimistic woman. Daimler, of course, in the end made the correct decision. Agreement was reached with a hand-shake and the promise from the elderly man that Louise would not have to pay any licence fee until she began to make a profit.

Louise had taken a Daimler engine in her luggage so that she could show it to her backers in France, but on her return a problem arose at the border, which almost led to the engine being confiscated. Fortunately, however, there was a French minister in the same train compartment who had been complimentary to Mrs Sarazin earlier in the journey and he managed to help her out of the scrape!

Panhard and Levassor broke down the German engine into all its constituent parts and soon realized that they had made exactly the right decision in working with the Daimler product. This Daimler power unit was indeed to become the prototype for the later Panhard engine.

On 17 May 1890, Louise Sarazin married her business partner, Emile Levassor, a union which also had a symbolic significance, because that year marks the real beginning of the automobile industry. The first motor cars from Panhard & Levassor and Peugeot to be equipped with Daimler engines rolled over French roads and the Daimler Motoren Gesellschaft was established. Thus began an era that would have been unthought of had it not been for the strength of mind and unceasing endeavours of Louise Sarazin-Levassor.

INGO SEIFF

Taking on the World

The Franco-Prussian War of 1870–1, in which the German troops were victorious, left deep scars in France. The two countries remained arch-enemies for several decades, particularly so after King Wilhelm (1797–1888) of Prussia was announced first Emperor of Germany at the royal residence of Versailles in 1871.

The interest of some forward-thinking Belgians and Frenchmen in Daimler's and Benz's patents was, however, not hampered by these events. As early as 1886, a far-sighted Belgian, Edouard Sarazin, had taken out Daimler patents for Belgium and France. Together with his friend René Panhard he often talked about technical developments possible for the future, about self-propelled vehicles and, above all, about steam having reached its limits as a source of power. They pondered on the ingenious inventions of Nikolaus Otto (the inventor of the internal-combustion engine, which was named after him) and of Karl Benz and Gottlieb Daimler; and how they could make use of these innovations to further the 'glory of France'.

RENÉ PANHARD AND EMILE LEVASSOR

René Panhard was a useful partner for Edouard Sarazin, as he had also been a business associate of Monsieur Périn, the inventor of the band saw. In 1872, Périn and Panhard established the company Société Périn-Panhard which, apart from constructing woodworking machines, soon began to employ more efficient methods for metalworking.

In the same year, Emile Levassor joined the company, which was henceforth called Société Périn, Panhard & Cie, and three years later this concern built its first gas engine, a diversification prompted by a fall in the demand for band saws. When Périn died in 1886, Emile Levassor took his place and the company's name was changed to Société Panhard & Levassor.

Sarazin's hour had come. He was obliged by patent law to rebuild the Daimler engine in France, according to the original drawings, and as he had known Levassor for more than twenty years he asked him to do the work. Levassor became fascinated by the work of his arch-rival in Germany, and it was 'his' Daimler engine which really represented the beginning of the French automobile industry.

Karl Benz had to overcome greater difficulties to become established in France. Cooperation with Panhard and Levassor did not materialize. Although the two French pioneers made several trips together with Karl Benz in 1888, they were not won over by the car from Mannheim. In any case, unbeknown to Benz the two had already made arrangements with Daimler.

Even the death of Edouard Sarazin, in 1887, could not harm the relationship between Daimler and his French partners. With great panache, Louise Sarazin followed in the footsteps of her late husband and, as Daimler's general agent in France, proved to be one of the great driving forces in automobile history.

THE PANHARD ENGINE

The engine she had taken back from Cannstatt became the prototype of the Panhard engine, which could be used as a built-in power unit for 'horseless' cars, boats or rail vehicles or as a stationary power source. Naturally, Daimler and Benz engines were shown at the Paris Exposition in 1889. Millions of visitors came to admire the sensation of the exhibition, the 300-metre (984 ft) Eiffel Tower; also called the last wonder of the world, and designed by the French engineer Gustave Eiffel. The other exhibits, including the internal-combustion engines by the Germans Karl Benz and Gottlieb Daimler, in the hall of 'machines et moteurs', were the wallflowers of the exhibition. This could perhaps also be be attributed to their country of origin . . . !

Only when one of the Daimler engines was started up in order to drive a generator which lit thirty light bulbs, were people drawn in; and then they crowded like moths to a flame. Daimler's power unit became almost a fairground attraction. Daimler was not too vain, however, to see that the visitors were not really interested in the engine itself, but in its effect.

THE CHARRONAGE-HALL

On the other hand, many questions were raised. What could you do with this engine and what could be propelled with it? Would horses be out of work? Was it the end of the steam engine? The answer to these questions was waiting in the so-called Charronage-Hall, where two paltry 'voitures à pétrole' were hidden between marvellously adorned horse-drawn carriages. One of the cars was Karl Benz's latest three-wheeler and the other, the second Daimler car, was the graceful Stahlrad (steel wheel). This was a four-wheeled vehicle with a vee-twin-cylinder engine that produced a power output of 1.6 hp.

The diary entries of October/November 1889 by Wilhelm Maybach show that on 29 October 1889 an excursion was made, together with a certain Mr Virot, in the Stahlrad. Apparently this was the J. Virot who had been concerned with the construction of a steam-driven three-wheeler. They drove along the Avenue de la Grande Armée, where Madame Sarazin lived. On the same day he made a trip to Argenteuil with Louis Rigoulot, a leading engineer with Peugeot. Jeanne, René and Henri, Louise Sarazin's children also took part in the drive near the Champs de Mars, which was close to the arena of the Paris Exposition. Moreover, Gottlieb Daimler, with his friend Maybach, steered the petrol-driven boats Violette and Passe-Partout up to St Cloud and Suresnes on the river Seine. Their favoured guests were Louise Sarazin and Emile Levassor.

Despite all this activity, however, the French journalist Pierre Giffard noticed during the Great Exhibition that Stahlrad demonstrations, by Gottlieb Daimler's son Paul, along the embankment of the Seine and also boat trips on the Seine, operated by Gottlieb himself, aroused hardly any public interest. 'It occurred to nobody that, in this corner of the Great Exhibition's fairground, today's technical revolutions were to be found'.

Incidentally Karl Benz was also disappointed by the public's reaction to demonstration trips carried out by his agent, Emile Roger. Had all the efforts made by the two German automobile pioneers to arouse the interest of the millions of visitors to the Great Exhibition been totally futile?

Gottlieb Daimler was not discouraged; he knew from his own experience not to panic – the Germans had been even less interested in his motor car. In France he knew three far-sighted people who would spread the transport revolution with him. These were Louise Sarazin, Emile Levassor and René Panhard and they were so impressed with Daimler's Stahlrad that they persuaded their German business associate to leave it behind in Paris as an exhibition and demonstration vehicle. On 1 November 1889 a deal was struck; Louise Sarazin received a written confirmation from Gottlieb Daimler that she would be permitted to exploit all French and Belgian Daimler patents to the best of her ability.

ARMAND PEUGEOT

Before Panhard and Levassor ventured to construct a Daimler-licensed car, Levassor and Madame Sarazin married, on 17 May 1890. At that time another, now legendary, man appeared in the small company; this was the far-sighted French automobile pioneer Armand Peugeot.

The Peugeots were a family who had established a tradition as craftsmen and industrialists over a number of centuries, particularly in the textile and metalwork industries, but now they directed their interest towards the construction of vehicles. In 1889, the Peugeots already employed 2000 people in their iron and steel works, partly thanks to the crinoline fashion of the mid-nineteenth century, which had produced a demand for tons of steel frameworks for corsets and for the petticoats used to distend skirts. They had also experimented with steam-driven cars, without success, over a period of several years.

In 1890, the first Peugeot car was introduced, powered by a Daimler engine acquired from Panhard & Levassor. It was called the *quadricyle à pétrole*. The family's background as successful manufacturers of bicycles was proving to be a substantial advantage, especially in the use of steel tubes and the achieving of cleanly welded joints. Like that of the Daimler Stahlrad, the tubular-steel framework of the Peugeot chassis was also used to carry cooling water between engine and radiator, the vee-twin-cylinder Daimler engine being mounted at the rear. The wheels were smaller than those of the Stahlrad and had ball bearings instead of bearing bushings.

Panhard & Levassor were now some way behind Peugeot, as it took time to refine the Daimler engine. The car they themselves introduced in 1890 was still built along similar lines to the horse-drawn carriage. The chassis was made of wood and had bogie-steering. In contrast Peugeot's car already used twin-pivot steering employing the Ackermann principle (Rudolf Ackermann was a German bookseller and publisher who patented the system which compensated for the tighter radius taken by the inner wheel in turning). The Panhard & Levassor was bigger and more robust than the Peugeot, something which was compensated for by a slightly more powerful, 2 hp, engine, in this case front mounted. The type of transmission used by Peugeot was also different from that of Panhard & Levassor. Levassor did not favour belt drive and was also very sceptical as to the reliability of Daimler's huge gliding barrels, so he mounted his engine, which had two gears, at an angle and decided to use chains for transmission.

THE 'PANHARD-SYSTEM'

In the history of the petrol-engined car, the year 1890 should be recorded as crucial. At that time there were five pillars on which the development of Benz's and Daimler's inventions rested: Karl Benz, Gottlieb Daimler, Panhard & Levassor, Louise Levassor and the Peugeots. Today we would call Benz and Daimler the 'brains trust', while the French were the 'masterminds' and the 'marketing experts' who brought about the professional manufacture of the petrol driven car.

Why did the French react more enthusiastically than the Germans towards the innovations of the two arch-enemies? The French were on a spiritual high borne of the impressionist movement and approached the inventions of the two Germans with much greater sensitivity. They knew that the motor car would add a totally new kind of freedom to their way of life. At the beginning of the last decade of the 1880s, the Germans could offer nothing comparable to the team of René Panhard, the Levassors and Armand Peugeot. It was no surprise that it was the Frenchmen Panhard and Levassor who in 1891 gave the motor car its current basic shape, with the engine mounted at the front. This innovation made history as the legendary 'Panhard-system'. If we investigate more closely the circumstances of this epochal innovation, however, we find that it had less to do with pioneering spirit than with practicality. Louise Levassor had one constant subject of complaint: that the motor in the rear would warm her buttocks in an unseemly way, and so her husband was obliged to move the engine to the front!

AUTOMOBILES AND PIANOS

The United States should have taken the motor car to its heart, as, until the end of the nineteenth century, there was in that country vast *terra incognita* which was without a road network. That it did not was due to a very clever lawyer from Rochester, New York, who boldly ensured by law that every car manufacturer was obliged to pay a fee to him.

In 1877, one year after Nikolaus Otto had filed a patent for his four-stroke petrol engine, George B. Selden drew *pro forma* plans for a 'horseless carriage' in which it was possible to install an engine. He filed his patent, which was registered with the number 549160 on 5 November 1895, and constant improvements on the designs were made. The crafty Selden stated in a patent specification that a stationary Brayton 'ready' two-stroke engine from 1871 (!) was to be mounted as the planned power unit and fuelled with liquid hydrocarbon. At the time, this Selden-buggy had not even been built, but on paper he was ahead of the developments of Daimler and Benz by decades! Constantly filed amendments to the designs of his patent made competition all but impossible. Because of his patents Selden considered himself the inventor of the motor car, and for more than two decades he blackmailed about thirty American car manufacturers into paying licence fees. Only a court case fought over many years by Henry Ford led to Selden being deprived of his patents in 1911.

Meanwhile, in response to the threat of what the court case might find, Selden was finally forced to construct a 'real' car . . . .

The Selden syndrome doubtlessly hindered, but did not prevent the development of the motor car in the USA, the brothers Charles and Frank Duryea being the first to construct an American vehicle. In 1892 a car with a single-cylinder power unit and friction transmission was built. Daimler, meanwhile, had entered the American market with William Steinway, a piano manufacturer of German descent. Wilhelm Maybach met Steinway, for whom his brother worked, during a visit to the Great Exhibition in Philadelphia in 1876 and when Steinway visited Germany, twelve years later, he came across Daimler and the two soon started to talk business. Steinway was very interested in exploiting Daimler's patents in the USA and, unlike the French arrangement, Daimler was directly involved this time. With half the share capital (US$10 000) represented in the form of these patents, the Daimler Motor Company was founded in 1888. First Steinway built a large workshop on his land near Bowery Bay for the manufacture of boat engines and during the '90s production slowly started to pick up. The cautious Daimler was, however, soon in disagreement with Steinway, who wanted the former to invest cash in the company. Daimler on the other hand reproached him for putting company money into his piano factory.

Reluctantly Daimler did pay $5000 but he did not participate further when the capital was increased. However, he continued to interfere in the running of the company; a situation which did not bode well. Motor car production began in 1895 on Long Island and the Daimler Motoren Gesellschaft acquired American patents. Steinway did not receive any financial support, however, and one setback led to another: the difficulties due to the Selden patents were exacarbated by Steinway's death in 1896 and meant that the Daimler Motor Company were forced into liquidation in the same year.

A major shareholder, General Electric, took over the company, which was now called the Daimler Motor Manufacturing Co., but the new owners were no more successful at selling cars to this great new market. Although in 1910 they were the sole representatives of

Gottlieb Daimler

Karl Benz

Mercédès Jellinek

Berta Benz

Louise Sarazin

Wilhelm Maybach

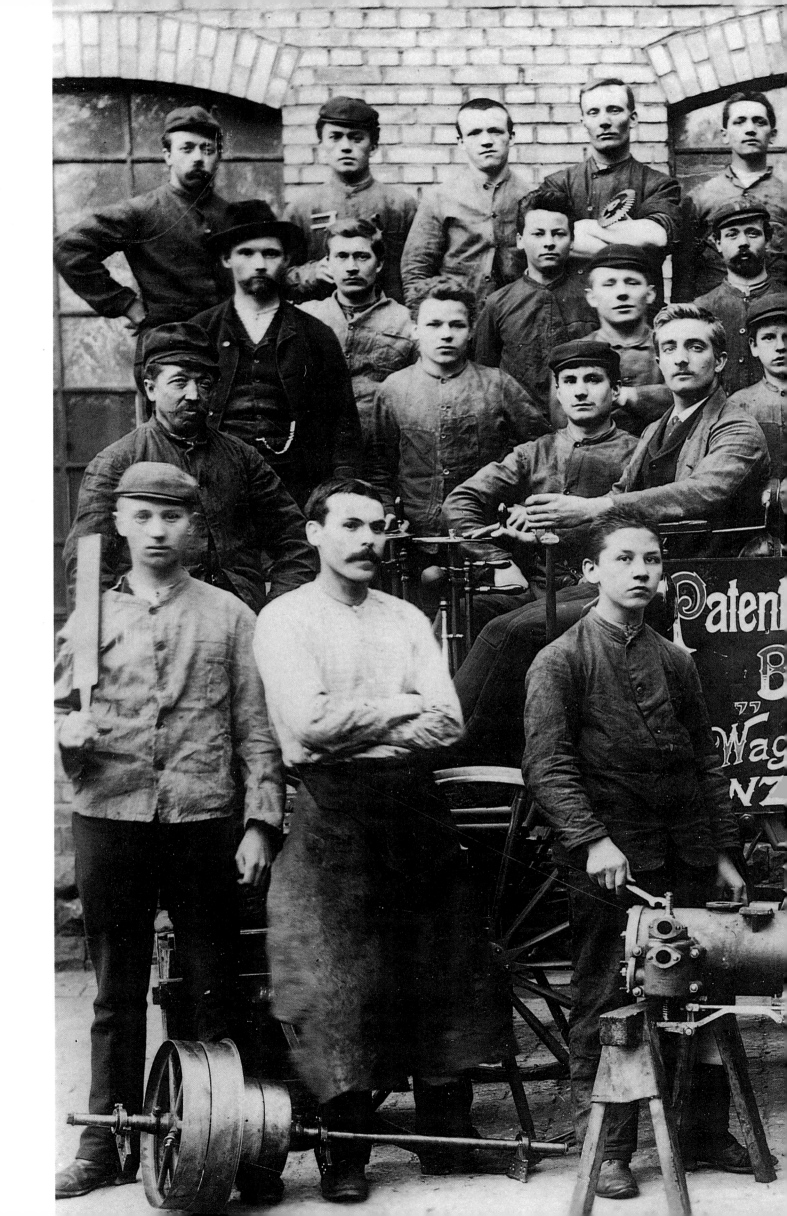

Previous page: Members of the staff of Benz and Co. in 1894.

In July of the same year the Austrian industrialist Theodor von Liebieg made the first long-distance journey in a Benz-Viktoria from Reichenberg in Bohemia via Mannheim and Gondorf on the Mosel to Reims and back.

Above: Karl Benz (right) with wife, daughter, and friend Fritz Held in 1894 in a Benz-Viktoria. Fritz Held had already become a successful racing driver in Benz cars by the turn of the century. He had won the Berlin-Leipzig Race in 1897 and the Frankfurt-Cologne Reliability Race (in 8 hours 35 minutes) in 1899.

Opposite (top): Advertisement for the 'American Mercedes' which boasted 40-45 bhp. William Steinway, the German-born piano maker, was Gottlieb Daimler's licensee in the USA.

Opposite (bottom): The Mayor of Portsmouth, Alderman A. L. Emanuel in front of the town hall of this sea-port in the south of England, 10 November 1900. He is sitting at the wheel of a 6.5 bhp Daimler belonging to Mr. Henry Edmunds. The car is equipped with a provisional radiator. Behind is a second Daimler of the same model.

THE AMERICAN MERCEDES

Is an exact copy—part for part—of the great car of international reputation, and is built here to save American buyers the heavy import duties.

The American **MERCEDES** is the car for speed, power and noiseless running. It is the acme of reliability.

One size, 40-45 H. P. One-horse power for every 50 lbs. of weight. One price, **$7,500.** *Our booklet explains all.*

DAIMLER MFG. CO., 931 Steinway Ave., Long Island City

New York City Garage, 10 WEST 60th STREET

Previous page: Car assembly in the Daimler Motor Company's Cannstatt works in 1900. The foundations for the 'Mercedes Era' were laid here as begun by Emil Jellinek and continued by Wilhelm Maybach.

Above: The Daimler Motor Company paint-shop in the Untertürkheim works, opened in 1904 and shown here in 1906. The new works was equipped well: from the very beginning it had 600 electric machines and decent working conditions. The 54-hour week was the norm and the piece work rate was 45 to 50 pfennigs an hour. An in-house lemonade factory supplied 4 000 bottles a day 'to curtail the consumption of alcohol'.

Opposite: Mercedes 37/90 1912. Cars of this type were primarily used for sporting competitions such as the Prince Heinrich rallies and so they were normally fitted with a sports or racing body. On account of its transmission the 37/90 was also known as the 'Kettenwagen' ('Chain Car').

Technical data: 4 cylinders, capacity 9 530 cc, 90-95 bhp at 1 300 rpm, maximum speed 115 kph.

Above: Mercedes 22/50 1914. Another model from the 'Prince Heinrich' category. Unlike the Mercedes 37/90 it is driven by a cardan shaft.

Technical data: 4 cylinders, capacity 5 720 cc, 50 bhp output at 1 300 rpm, maximum speed 70-75 kph.

Left: Steering wheel of the Mercedes 22/50 1914. The outer lever in the middle of the wheel allowed for fine-tuning the ignition and the inner lever was used for 'hand acceleration' in addition to the foot pedal. This can be compared with today's choke.

Opposite: Sectional view of the 12.8 litre engine of a Mercedes run at the French Grand Prix of 1908. Christian Lautenschlager won over a course near Dieppe driving a car of this model. The car had four huge cylinders and an output of 150 bhp with a capacity of 12.8 litres.

Overleaf: Mercedes-Benz 720, Model SSK 1928. Even 60 years later this is one of the dream cars of racing history. This series was given the master touch by Ferdinand Porsche when he was still working for Daimler-Benz. SSK is an abbreviation of Super-Sportausführung 'Kurz' ('Short' Super Sports-model).

Technical data: 6 cylinders, capacity 7 068 cc, 170 bhp output at 2 900 rpm, with supercharger 225 bhp at 3 300 rpm.

Pages 46 and 47: Mercedes-Benz SS 1928. Formerly owned by Rudolf Caracciola.

Page 48: Mercedes-Benz SSK 1928.

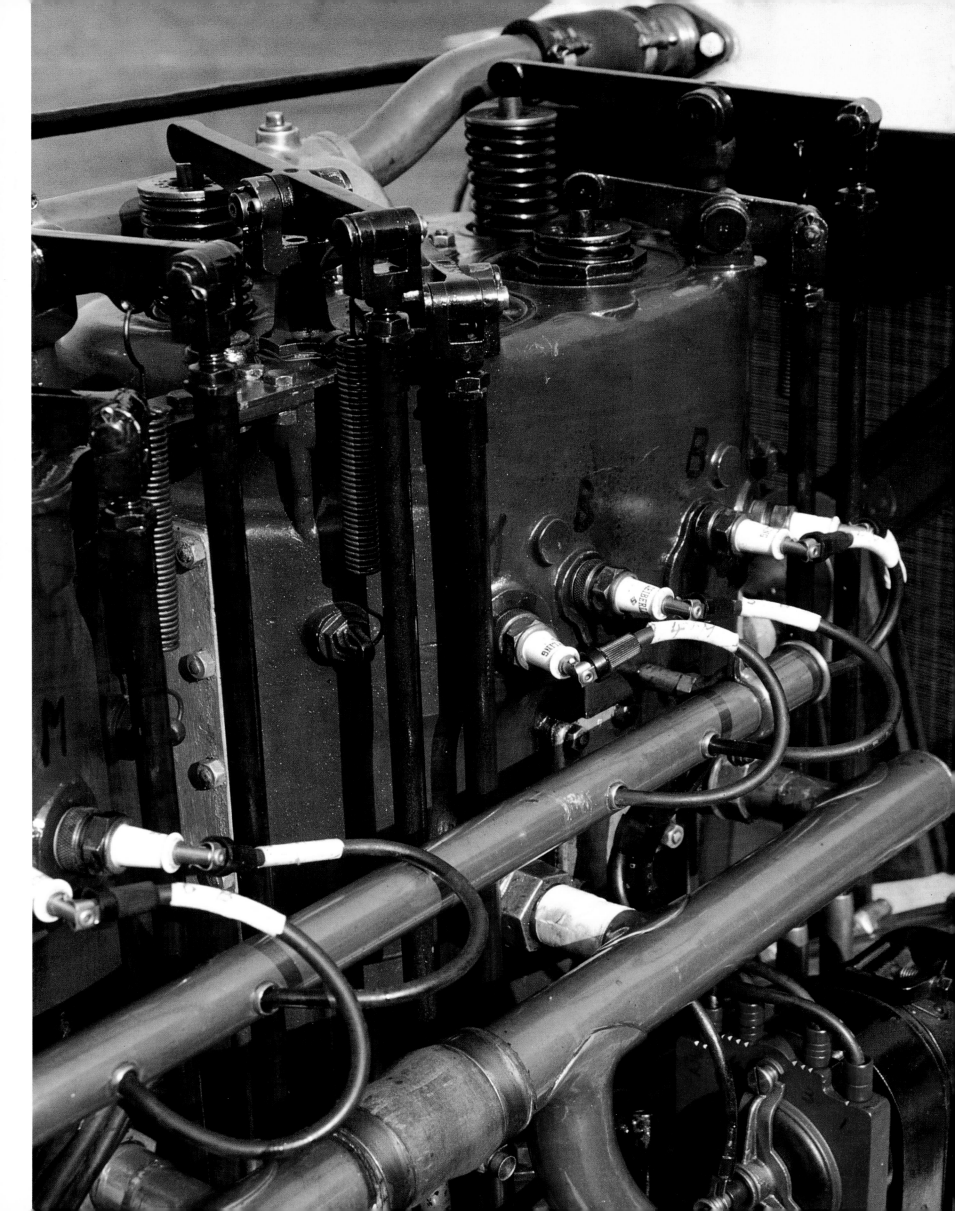

the Daimler Motoren Gesellschaft in North America, bankruptcy had to be declared and the firm ceased to exist in the following year.

JULIUS GANSS

During the 1890s, Karl Benz benefitted hugely from the marketing talent of his partner Julius Ganss. During the second half of the '90s, the manufacturing programme of Benz, which after 1897 included a highly successful new development – trucks – was unstoppable. This was no more than a reflection of Julius Ganss's marketing success. The man was a real marketing genius, and his presence was a major stroke of luck for the young company. Thanks to his efforts Benz & Co. was represented all over Europe, and in Buenos Aires, Mexico, Cape Town and Singapore. Shortly before the turn of the century he signed agreements in Great Britain and France for 200 cars each.

August Horch, who was then in the employ of Benz, described very vividly the fear of the over-cautious Karl Benz because of these large orders and his concern about the quality of his cars once they were 'mass-produced'.

Emile Roger, who was the first Benz customer, had already done a good job of selling the car – although not always in the best interest of Benz. Roger said nothing about the fact that it was Benz and not he who was the inventor of the motor car (or at least of the engines which Roger installed in his chassis, following instruction from Mannheim). Successes at the first French long-distance competitions made the cars from Baden very popular. (Daimler, on the other hand, achieved better results in racing with his engines – these events were not contested by Karl Benz, who was not remotely interested in the quest for higher speeds.)

BREAKTHROUGH IN BRITAIN

The first Benz car delivered to Britain was a Velo. However, at that time the absurd 'Locomotives on Highways Act' was still in operation and this greatly hindered the success of the new horseless carriage. It was a baffling situation, one which was described by the British journalist and historian Cyril Posthumus as 'Britain's own bigoted legislation'. Although Britain had been the pioneer of the Industrial Revolution and the example for young, striving industrial nations, with regard to traffic and transportation the nation seemed to have taken a step backward.

Even steam-driven road vehicles, a very effective British invention, were handicapped by the infamous 1861 Act. This was intended to put an end to arbitrary district rules; it stipulated a national road toll for vehicles with iron tyres and uniform regulations concerning compensation for damage to roads and bridges. The maximum weight of a steam car, or locomotive, was limited to 12 tons and the maximum speed on public roads to 10 mph and in built up areas 5 mph.

Even more curious was the Red Flag Act of 1865. Under the terms of this legislation, each vehicle had to be preceded by a man with a red flag, keeping a distance of 60 yards from the vehicles and thus being able to warn people of its approach. Road locomotives had to have three men, of which one was the driver, the second the stoker, while the third waved the flag. When a horse came into sight, the steam vehicle had to stop in order not to frighten the animal. It was also prohibited to emit steam or dirty smoke . . . . Only in 1896 was this unworkable act repealed, ten years after the introduction of the motor cars of Daimler and Benz.

During the early 1860s, the young Gottlieb Daimler had made several trips to Britain, particularly to Leeds, Manchester and London, to study industrial methods of production and he considered the British to be pioneers of mechanical engineering who were predestined to have his motor car. The Red Flag Act had, however, up to that point prevented practical motor car use.

A young engineer, Frederick Richard Simms, seized his opportunity when he met Gottlieb Daimler at an exhibition in Bremen in 1890. He was fascinated by Daimler's engines because they possessed a much more favourable ratio of weight to power output than did steam engines. Simms was an inventor and a businessman and he correctly assessed the immense possibilities for the future.

Cyril Posthumus writes, in his book *Veteran & Vintage Cars*, that Simms 'asked Daimler for the British patent rights. An agreement was drawn up and the following year a single-cylinder Daimler engine and a Daimler-powered motor launch were sent to Britain.

'In May 1893 Simms formed the Daimler Motor Syndicate Ltd, concentrating at first on boats; but by mid 1895 hopes that the severe road traffic laws might be relaxed, encouraged him to import a Daimler-engined Panhard-Levassor for the Hon. Evelyn Ellis. October that same year brought the first motor exhibition ever held in Britain, a one-day open-air affair organized by Sir David Salomons at Tunbridge Wells. The object was to display publicly the new horseless carriages and to strike a blow against the acts of 1865 and 1878.'

Simms's financial position did not, however, permit himself to take out Daimler licences. Despite the Locomotives on Highways Act, he had to convince British backers that motor cars with internal-combustion engines would be the transport of the future, and eventually he did manage to find two partners and £6000 to establish the Daimler Motor Syndicate Ltd.

Simms enjoyed a good relationship with Gottlieb Daimler, but the latter was experiencing great difficulties in his own firm, particularly with the group surrounding the shareholding manufacturer Max Duttenhofer who wanted to curtail Daimler's rights. Daimler was about to resign, and was no longer a shareholder, the idea of which seemed greatly to offend Simms. Meanwhile, the Germans were demanding 300 000 Marks for the patents to be granted to Britain. Simms realised that the deal he had initiated would be worthless if Daimler (and also Maybach) were not to return to the German Daimler company to support him, so it was important to find backers.

Following three years in which losses were incurred, the Daimler Motoren Gesellschaft urgently required money. Meanwhile, Simms had organized a new, financially strong, consortium led by the bicycle manufacturer Henry John Lawson. In November 1895 he bought Daimler patents for his Daimler Motor Syndicate for 350 000 Marks and handed them over to Lawson's newly established British Motor Syndicate Ltd. for

double the amount, at £36 250.

Naturally, Simms had made it a condition of the deal that Daimler would resume his old position at Daimler Motoren Gesellschaft and that Maybach should eventually start working there. On similar lines Hamburg merchant, Wilhelm Deurer, the longest and most important customer of Daimler had intervened to restore Daimler and Maybach. Duttenhofer and Wilhelm Lorenz, the second-largest shareholder in Daimler, had to agree; the future of the company depended on new funds.

THE FIRST BRITISH DAIMLERS

The first British Daimlers of 1896–7 used the original engines from Cannstatt, while chassis and bodywork were after the style of the French cars of Panhard & Levassor. Gottlieb Daimler was appointed a director of the British company, but this was rather an honorary title, Daimler himself not concerning himself seriously with the development of the motor car in Britain.

Lawson and his business partners were, in contrast, exploring all possibilities in this direction. Meanwhile, in 1896, regulations concerning the Locomotives on Highways Act were relaxed by Parliament. Cyril Posthumus wrote about the matter: 'Concessions were small enough, with the speed limit for "light locomotives" raised to a grudging 12 mph, but motorists were freed at last from "that man in front".'

In 1896, a significant year for the British motor industry, Lawson exhibited all his skills as a showman. He established the Motor Car Club and organized the first motor show in London, at the Imperial Institute in South Kensington. Here he displayed to celebrities interested in the motor car not only the products of his company but also those from abroad, such as the original Daimler and Benz cars, the Panhards and Peugeots, Lutzmanns, De Dions – and some electromobiles, too.

The amendment to the Act was the encouragement Harry Lawson needed to organize the 'Emancipation Run' from London to Brighton on 14 November 1896. This started at the Metropole Hotel in Whitehall and finished at the Metropole Hotel in Brighton. Leaving London, there were four Panhards, four Roger-Benzes, four Léon-Bollées, two Duryeas from the USA, one Beeston tricycle, one Pennington, two Arnold-Benzes, one Lutzmann and a number of electromobiles. Gottlieb Daimler was present and accompanied F.R. Simms in a Cannstatt-Daimler Phaeton.

Even before the turn of the century Coventry-Daimler had embarked in a different innovative direction from Cannstatt-Daimler and it was not long before the British Company was building vehicles which had nothing at all in common with the German Daimlers. The inventions of Benz and Daimler released previously unknown powers of innovation in Britain. It was not just clever salesmen who prepared the market for the big motor car boom following the repeal of the 'Red Flag Act', but British engineers, who used the concept of the internal-combustion engine and developed their own initiatives; engineers such as Herbert Austin for Wolseley, Frederick Lanchester, Walter Arnold and Sir William Arrol (Arrol-Johnson).

THE AUSTRIAN CONNECTION

In keeping with the motto of the Austrian monarchy 'tu, felix Austria, nube!' ('happy Austria – marry!'), the Austrian royal-carriage manufacturer Ludwig Lohner tried to make contact with Gottlieb Daimler. The company was at the head of its field in Europe and the worldly, multi-lingual Lohner was a far-sighted man: an engineer with international experience who was able to assess the significance of the Daimler and Benz cars. If these petrol driven vehicles were to become established, and the carriage manufacturer had no doubt that they would, his company with its outmoded technology would face great problems.

In June 1896, he decided therefore to visit the Daimler Motoren Gesellschaft in Cannstatt to get to know Gottlieb Daimler and his much praised motor cars. A test drive entirely convinced Lohner of the automobile's potential and he decided to take the motor car into his production programme. However, he was not aware of Daimler's stubbornness and his tendency

to be indecisive – Daimler was prepared to talk to him neither about a licence contract nor about a general agency. Whether Daimler did not trust the shrewd Austrian, or whether the severe illness from which he was suffering had made him avoid important decisions, or whether, again, he had already made plans with his sons with regard to Austria is uncertain and on this historians will remain divided.

The new sense of mobility that the Daimler car brought had left a great impression on Ludwig Lohner and he extended his trip from Cannstatt to Paris to meet Emile Levassor – Gottlieb Daimler having given him a letter of recommendation. He was extremely interested in what he had seen in Germany and France and in Autumn 1896 he decided to return to Paris on another reconnaissance visit. He wrote:

'On the morning of 3 October 1896 I found myself for the second time at the Gare de l'Est in Paris. This time I felt just like a grain of sand in the sea of one and half million people. Paris was taking immense trouble preparing itself for the arrival of the Tsar, and the one and a half million people had come to join in the activities which would exceed anything hitherto known.

'This coincided with the return of the competitors from the great motor car competition, Paris–Marseille–Paris, which was followed by the exhibition in the Palais de l'Industrie. Not only engineers, but also amateurs had eagerly subjected themselves to an exhausting and dangerous drive in their cars during these ten days. The enthusiasm of the whole French public was expressed by numerous bunches of flowers given to the competitors. The great numbers of visitors coming to see the motor car exhibition amidst the unparalleled hustle and bustle which followed the Russian visitation, as well as the serious study of all detail on behalf of the amateurs, has left such a deep impression that I promised myself to wake all my modest ambitions and transplant this progress in technology to my country.'

PAUL DAIMLER

Lohner purchased from the French company Lefèbre several Pygmée engines, which he mounted in his carriages, but his cars were not successful. An attempt to cooperate with Rudolf Diesel also failed. Lohner however was not deterred. He began to concentrate on the electromobile and in 1898 he hired a very young engineer who for over fifty years influenced motoring history worldwide, Ferdinand Porsche. The cooperation between Lohner and Porsche resulted in the Lohner-Porsche, the sensation of the 1900 Great Exhibition in Paris.

The Lohner electromobile was, of course, very different from Daimler's engine concept. However, in 1890 Daimler engines were represented once more in Austria by Josef Eduard Bierenz, a friend of Daimler. Bierenz was aware of a growing popularity of Daimler cars and in 1899, with the industrialist Eduard Fischer, founded the Österreichische Daimler Motor Kommanditgesellschaft, Bierenz, Fischer & Co. At first, the capital was 200 000 Goldgulden and Daimler's eldest son Paul was entrusted with the technical management. Paul did not, however, decisively influence the destiny of the company, as he was otherwise preoccupied: with the development of Mercedes with Wilhelm Maybach. The death of his beloved father on 6 March 1900 and the subsequent reorganization of the Cannstatt firm gave him even less time for his work in Wiener-Neustadt.

Finally, in 1902, Paul was able to devote himself completely to the Austrian subsidiary, which now had the name of Österreichische Motorengesellschaft Daimler. The press commented on Paul Daimler's arrival in Wiener-Neustadt and his principles on motor car construction as follows:

'It is known that both sons of the ingenious inventor Daimler have followed in their father's footsteps. Mr Adolf Daimler is working in the Daimler factory in Cannstatt, and Mr Paul Daimler works in the offices of Österreichische Daimler Motoren Gesellschaft in Wiener-Neustadt. The company owes to the latter the construction of a beautiful light car which in the factory is called the Paul-Daimler-Wagen. Although the car does not deviate in its shape from the classic type, it shows in its technical arrangement some characteristic features. Today it has become almost an accepted rule that the engine is mounted in such a way that the engine-axle runs parallel to the longitudinal direction of the car. The flywheel then rotates to the transverse direction of the journey. Mr Paul Daimler has not accepted this arrangement. He is of the opinion that rotating the engine in transverse direction to the journey would cause lateral vibrations which are transferred to the entire chassis. Indeed, these drastic lateral vibrations can be observed on racing cars whose engines are at times slowed down with a regulator. Mr Paul Daimler lets the movement of the engine coincide with the direction of the journey in his constructions by simply mounting the engine widthwise. This means that the cylinders of the engine are not arranged after one another but next to each other when seen from the front.'

Paul Daimler remained chief engineer of the Austrian Daimler company until 1905 and early in 1906 he was succeeded by Ferdinand Porsche, at the suggestion of Emil Jellinek, who had used his influence on the Riviera in matters concerning Mercedes.

Meanwhile, the Österreichische Daimler Motoren Gesellschaft had separated from the parent company. We will encounter Ferdinand Porsche again later, in the story of the Daimler Motoren Gesellschaft, at Stuttgart-Untertürkheim, where he was chief engineer during the mid 1920s.

PAUL SIMSA

Milestones in Innovation

Gottlieb Daimler and Karl Benz were inventors in the true sense of the word, who used all their resources and entrepreneurial spirit to realize their dream of motorized transportation.

Simultaneously they embarked upon the same road, completely ignorant of each other's existence. Their trains of thought were entirely different, and a partnership of two such different personalities would surely have been unthinkable. However, history ultimately did justice to both names when the companies of Daimler and Benz were joined together four decades later.

Gottlieb Daimler was an entrepreneur, the head of a major industrial force, but he remained first and foremost, an inventor: the first person to recognise the epochal significance of a small universally applicable power unit. Engineers had long been able to construct heavy stationary engines, which Karl Benz managed to reduce sufficiently in size for mounting in a vehicle. It was Gottlieb Daimler, however, who, together with his engineer Wilhelm Maybach, developed a new concept in engines and set standards for the new century.

They had to overcome various obstacles on the way. Daimler had been employed at the Gasmotorenfabrik Deutz since it was set up and had helped get the company established, but the incompatible personalities of Daimler and Nikolaus August Otto caused conflicts. The latter's inventions had been the basis of the company's formation and success: only by using the four-stroke principle of the Otto engine was Daimler able to produce his own engine. Daimler could not expect to be granted a licence because of his differences of opinion with the company and he was thus obliged to find a different way to get his own ideas patented.

What he did was to attack his opponent's weak point. Otto had declared that the key element of his patents was that: 'the gas and gas particles are burned in a certain place where combustion is continued slowly,' – an erroneous statement, because the combustion process is not slowed down at any point.

The engineer Daimler went for the throat when he

filed for his patent in retaliation. 'A combustible mixture (made up of air and gas or oil) is compressed in an enclosed area, enabling it to ignite when the pressure is at its highest and the entire mixture explodes or a rapid combustion occurs . . . .'

The four-stroke principle was perceived by Otto merely as a means to an end. He was self-taught and did not recognize the full implications of his innovative achievement. Daimler meanwhile, not only wanted to bring down the Otto patent but also to solve the problem of ignition at a high rpm in a small engine. This was a bold concept. Although Daimler was granted a patent, his was dependent on the Otto patent: the two being overlapped and the patent for the four-stroke principle still being valid.

Daimler's patent was based on the principle of heating the cylinder to the temperature of ignition, so that consequently it had no cooling. Daimler's design promised to be the ideal heat engine but his position was quickly undermined by Wilhelm Maybach: 'The gas engine with the Deutsche Reichspatent number 28022 will never be built as it cannot be practically adapted,' said Maybach.

In looking through hundreds of patents Maybach had found instead an ignition system that could be further developed for his purposes. In it a little pipe protruded from the combustion chamber with a cap on the outside which was heated by a small petrol flame. This cap was open on the inside and worked like a diesel's glow plug ignition and this system too was incorporated in patent number 28022.

Otto had ingeniously allowed the igniting flame through to the combustion chamber via a gate valve. This was however only possible at low engine speeds – around 200 rpm. In contrast, the Lenoir engine already had electric ignition in 1860. Lenoir's was the first usable gas engine but he, not unlike Daimler, was not interested in the problems of the electric system.

Karl Benz meanwhile had great difficulties with ignition. His system featured a vibrator that produced a succession of sparks, but this was unable to trigger the ignition at the right time.

For a long time hot-tube (or 'glow-plug') ignition proved to be the most reliable available and it contri-

buted considerably to Daimler's income from licencees. Only the Bosch low-tension magneto which appeared in 1895 was superior. By 1898 Daimler was convinced of its advantages; cars had become faster, while in his own system the air stream blew out the ignition flame.

Patent number 28022 was granted to Daimler on 16 December 1883. Since August of that year, trials had been undertaken with the experimental engine which reached 600 rpm with a power output of approximately 0.25 bhp. The inlet valve was of the automatic type opened by the suction of the piston descending the cylinder. The operation of the exhaust valve designed by Daimler did not use a camshaft but a slide in a curve. Engine speed was adjustable.

This engine, with a vertical cylinder and without a cooling system, was only used for stationary tests. Although patent number 28243 was granted on 22 December, 1883, the design still depended on Otto's patent DRP 532. Incidentally a group of industrialists had filed a court case against Otto in 1880, for claiming to be the sole inventor of the compression unit.

In 1884 Daimler and Maybach completed their light-weight engine with an upright cylinder and enclosed crankcase. This engine was also called *Standuhr* (grandfather clock) because of its shape. Patent DRP 34926 was duly granted for it on 3 April 1885.

There was another breakthrough in that year: the *Petroleum-Kraftmaschine* was granted patent DRP 36423 on 29 August. This was the forerunner of the motor cycle with a wooden frame and supporting wheels. Its performance was unsatisfactory but the design, conceived by Daimler as a snow vehicle with skis and spikes, showed promise!

MAYBACH'S VISION

Maybach continued to draw up plans, among which was a design for an asymmetric tricycle whose 0.5 hp engine had a displacement of 212 cc and maximum engine speed of 600 rpm. This was an astonishingly powerful design and a masterpiece of light construction notable too for an effective cooling fan.

The engine breathed through a petrol container

which then worked as a 'vaporizer' to provide fuel vapour. Maybach had already thought about fuel injection in the patent, and was years ahead in its development: 'Instead of using a vaporizer a spray pump can also be used' he pointed out and, needless to say, he had already designed one!

Otto was no longer an obstacle for other inventors. They knew that his patents would be declared null and void on many points. He had not heard of the French inventor de Rochas who had created the four-stroke engine in 1862 and that was to be his downfall.

The first Daimler car of 1886 was equipped with a more powerful engine and a water cooling system. Motor boats were frequently used as part of the engine's test and demonstration programme, which led to power units for rail vehicles and various other purposes and in 1889 the first two-cylinder vee engine was launched. The *Stahlradwagen* was the first real prototype of the motor car, rather than just a motorized horse carriage; it was, for example, equipped with the first four-speed gearbox, invented by Wilhelm Maybach. This progress was all the more surprising as Gottlieb Daimler saw the future initially in the construction of engines rather than cars.

Karl Benz was a completely different type of pioneer. His small business managed to survive difficult times, and with the advent of the manufacture of gas engines in 1883 he was able to realize his dream, the manufacture of a motor vehicle, in 1885.

First the engine. His stationary coal gas two-stroke engine was suitable for industrial applications. To begin with it had individual pumps for gas and air; the improved version used the piston's downstroke to compress the air beneath it but a patent was not granted. The patent's office concluded that Benz had used the gas stratification system originally invented by Otto. However, on 30 January 1886 Otto himself lost his patent.

Benz's smaller version of the two-stroke engine was unable to produce the required power and was also too complex. So, in 1884, Benz constructed a single-cylinder four-stroke engine in the traditional way, with an open crankshaft and large flywheel, carburettor and electric ignition. This was an improvement on the 'vibrator ignition' which gave a more rapid supply of sparks. The

vehicle on which it was mounted followed bicycle construction principles and was patented on 29 January 1886 as the *Fahrzeug mit Gasmotor* (vehicle with a gas engine).

Apparently Benz was granted the patent DRP 37435 for this machine, the first real motor-car in the world; his three-wheeler had made history. Its engine's most obvious feature was its large, exposed flywheel. Fitted horizontally, it was intended to act as a gyroscope to counteract any tendency the tricycle showed to tip over in corners, and to increase stability and road safety. Flywheels were usually installed vertically but Benz was worried that this might affect the steering. In fact the energy released by the flywheel was far too low to have caused a problem.

Karl Benz's determination to manufacture a car for everyone's use was indicated by the nature of his patented design features. Take the fuel gauge, for example, and the system by which one lever was provided for both clutch and brake so there could be absolutely no confusion between those functions.

Engine cooling meanwhile was by a radiator sufficiently novel to be included in the patent, and Benz also recognized the necessity of a differential gear in the transmission.

COMMERCIAL SUCCESS

To show to what extent he was in the forefront of automobile development Benz's wife, Berta, organized a demonstration drive in 1888. Berta successfully drove from Mannheim to Pforzheim with the third three-wheeler to be constructed. Benz, however, was not to achieve commercial success until his four-wheel car and its axle pivot steering was given patent DRP 73515 on 28 February 1893.

As Benz recalled later, 'In 1884 I wanted to construct a four-wheel car, but the steering presented some difficulties. Right from the beginning I objected to a steering system whereby the entire front axle moved, as it did in the horse-drawn carriage.' His pioneering development of hub-pivoting steering was another vital step in car development.

Although Benz, strictly speaking, concentrated on

automobiles, Daimler broadened his scope. He invented, for example, the motor boat, extending his patent for the motorcycle in 1886 to cover a 'device to power a propeller shaft of a ship via gas or petroleum engines'. His technicians were working prodigiously: in 1887 the car radiator was patented with 'a rotating pump driven by the engine', and a system of heating, using part of the air needed by gas engines' was also listed. Furthermore, in 1888, the first fire engines were patented.

The four-stroke engine had also been adapted as a boat engine in 1890 by Panhard & Levassor in France and they called it the Type P. Although the four-stroke only became established in motorcars shortly before the turn of the century, Daimler had been supplying the Type P for airships since 1895. The engine was made of light alloys with an aluminium crank case, and was an important landmark in the design of cars and later of aircraft engines.

Both Gottlieb Daimler and Wilhelm Maybach agreed that the engines of the Daimler Motoren Gesellschaft would soon propel more and more cars on the roads. However, the new shareholders Duttenhofer and Lorenz greatly restricted Daimler's activities and also those of his friend Wilhelm Maybach, who left the company. Then, in 1883, Daimler established – more or less privately – an experimental workshop, in order to continue his own development work. He took Maybach with him and it was in this workshop that Maybach worked with his greatest success. His patented 'improved steering device', for example, was a clever feature of the *Stahlradwagen* and it meant, incidentally, that Benz was unable to take legal action against his rivals for infringing his own patent of 1893.

In 1898 Daimler supplied cars with hot tube ignition and tiller-steering if not otherwise requested, but great change was on the way. As soon as the Daimler-Phoenix series appeared in 1896, Emil Jellinek ordered a Phoenix car for racing, with a powerful four-cylinder engine. This led directly to the revolutionary construction of the first Mercedes of 1901.

It was an unbeatable amalgamation of all the latest technical improvements: use of light metals, the honeycomb radiator, an improved spray carburettor and the Bosch magneto ignition. 'I can still see the surprised faces of many of the French motorists in the first hour after the engine was started,' said Emil Jellinek later. 'It was not the rumbling noise of the Panhards but a quiet smooth humming which had never been heard by anyone before.'

Demand for cars was bigger in France than in the German Empire. The booming French marques began with Daimler engines, but as for car design itself Benz's innovative technology had set the trend. Now came the 'Mercedes era', to set new international standards; Wilhelm Maybach had given the automobile both its technology and its classic form.

He had also developed the first truck which was delivered on 1 October 1896 to the British Motor Syndicate Ltd in Coventry. Meanwhile, the Daimler Motoren Gesellschaft also created the first taxi-service in the world, in Stuttgart.

Until the launch of the Mercedes, Karl Benz had enjoyed a series of successes. He developed and improved his motor cars with the utmost care and was not prepared to have any part in the new 'Mercedes' trend. When his partners wanted him to follow Daimler, however, he was soon pushed into the background and in 1903 left the board of directors. In 1904 he became a member of the supervisory board, to which he belonged until 1926 when Daimler and Benz merged.

Nevertheless the car factory C. Benz & Söhne in Ladenburg, built cars from 1906 until 1926, a strong indication of Benz's independence. Despite the presence of his highly qualified sons Eugen and Richard, however, it was impossible to establish the company successfully and to further its research and development. The company continued in being as a components' manufacturer and still exists today as a supplier to Daimler-Benz.

Gottlieb Daimler did not live to see the Mercedes. He died on 6 March 1900, by which time he had become chairman of the supervisory board. Wilhelm Maybach, his closest collaborator, left the company in 1907 and established his name making airship engines in Friedrichshafen. It was his son, Karl, who made the Maybach marque famous in the car industry. The Maybach company ceased car manufacture after World War II, but continued as a component supplier to Daimler-Benz.

The great innovator and motivator Emil Jellinek belonged to the supervisory board until 1908 when he left his position during a crisis arising from the presence of too many competitors in what was still a small market, especially abroad. When Jellinek left, Maybach lost a most valuable supporter within the organization.

Paul, the eldest son of Gottlieb Daimler, born in 1869, proved to be an important and influential pioneer with Austro-Daimler, the Austrian Daimler Motoren AG founded in 1899. In 1902 he had been appointed technical director of the company based in Wiener-Neustadt. Unfortunately, he did not succeed in further developing the Type PD for production. This venture had already failed in Cannstatt due to insufficient capacity and in Wiener-Neustadt his position as technical director took up too much of his time, so only a few prototypes were ever built.

In 1905 Paul Daimler was asked to return to the Cannstatt works and there he played a decisive role in the planning and construction of the first Mercedes six-cylinder engine to be mass-produced, in 1907. He also developed the four-cylinder Grand Prix racing car in which Christian Lautenschlager won the 1909 Grand Prix of France, beating his eternal rival Victor Hémery, driver of a Benz.

RECORD SPEEDS

Paul Daimler became head engineer at Cannstatt in 1907, while the next year the young Hans Nibel was appointed head engineer at Benz. Nibel, born in 1880, developed the four-valve-per-cylinder technology for racing cars and was also the man behind the *Blitzen-Benz*. In 1909 that became the first car with an internal combustion engine to reach a speed of more than 200 kph (124 mph), going on to set its world record of 211.267 kph (131.mph) in 1910. It also achieved a greater speed of 228.1 kph (141.74 mph) which was not recognized internationally. It was only in 1919 that the Blitzen-Benz's record was surpassed. Mercedes cars were successful on the track too; three cars with ohc four-cylinder engines won the French Grand Prix in 1914 in sensational style.

Benz launched the first diesel truck in 1924 and

Daimler-Benz produced the first diesel car in 1936. Another section of this book is devoted to the development of the diesel engine in detail, a development which began with the patent for the pre-combustion method of Prosper L'Orange in 1909.

In 1902 the Daimler Motoren Gesellschaft took over the Motorfahrzeug und Motorenfabrik Berlin AG in Marienfelde which was founded in 1898, converting the plant into a truck factory. The Benz company also expanded into building commercial vehicles, pooling their resources with the Süddeutsche Automobilfabrik GmbH in Gaggenau in 1907, to produce buses and trucks. In 1910 this became the Benzwerke Gaggenau GmbH. Both Daimler and Benz brought about important improvements in the construction of commercial vehicles, especially in the development of fire engines.

At the outbreak of World War I Benz produced more cars, while Mercedes concentrated on prestige models. Benz led the way in commercial vehicles while Daimler were in the aero engine market, having begun by supplying engines for airships.

SUPERCHARGING

Naturally the demand for aircraft engines increased rapidly during the war, as did their power output and reliability, as epitomized by the Mercedes D III and IV. Paul Daimler himself worked particularly assiduously on supercharging the engines for the high altitude-flying of fighter pilots.

In 1919 this aero-technology was applied to cars for the first time. Four steel cylinders were welded together and surrounded by a water jacket to form one block. The combustion chambers meanwhile were hemispherical with angled valves operated by an overhead camshaft. The supercharged variants appeared in racing cars in 1921 with displacements of 1.5 and 1.6 litres. The Roots blower was not constantly in operation but was activated when the accelerator was fully depressed. The increase in power, roughly fifty per cent, was only intended to be used for a short time.

The result was a demanding, expensive sports car which was not a great success, but a new era began in racing with the 1.5-litre twin-camshaft version. In response to the political and economic upheaval in Germany the company had now turned its attentions to the prestige and new trade opportunities provided by the international racing circuit.

In 1922 a new 2-litre Grand Prix formula was created and a completely new racing car emerged. In contrast, for road races such as the 1922 Targa Florio, not only were 7.2-litre, pre-war supercharged six-cylinder engines re-activated, but so were the pre-war 4.5-litre GP cars, including Graf Masetti's private 4.5-litre, which won the race. In other races, such as Indianapolis they were less successful . . . .

Paul Daimler had intended to design an eight-cylinder engine for the company's prestige road cars, but at the end of 1922 he left the Daimler company and started working for Horch.

Although Benz had a good footing in the market with their mid-range car they wasted their energies with the large number of models on offer. This was a miscalculation which proved expensive but educative.

The designers of the Benz *Tropfenwagen* (Teardrop) tried to revolutionize the construction of racing cars following the theorems of Edmund Rumpler. Rumpler had patented a streamlined design intended to smooth the airflow over cars to stop dust and dirt being sucked in. However, in Rumpler's car the engine was rear-mounted. Moving it to the middle of the ultra-light, box-shaped frame of the car allowed the car to sit very close to the ground. The 2-litre, six-cylinder engine with twin overhead camshafts was a further development from the Kaiserpreis aircraft engine of 1912. It was equipped with a welded water jacket cooling system around the steel cylinders and featured the new Mahle magnesium pistons. Rumpler had also developed the rear swing axle and Benz used the design to create the first racing car with independent rear suspension; at the front, however, they used a traditional rigid axle.

In 1923, three cars entered the European Grand Prix at Monza and were beaten, although Benz was awarded an honorary prize for the most exceptional cars in the race. The sports version was also very promising, but in 1924 the ambitious streamlined cars were abandoned when the economic situation led to Daimler and Benz

pooling their resources. As forerunners of the modern racing car, however, they remained unforgettable.

FERDINAND PORSCHE

When Paul Daimler left to go Horch he was succeeded by Ferdinand Porsche. He had been the head engineer at Austro-Daimler and was just as interested in the supercharger as his predecessor. Porsche sent three new 2-litre, eight-cylinder super-charged cars to the Targa Florio in 1924. These were to be driven by Alfred Neubauer, Christian Werner and Christian Lautenschlager. Werner won on 27 April 1924 in a record time of six hours, 32 minutes for the 432 km (268.45 miles). Lautenschlager came in tenth, Neubauer fifteenth. The new eight-cylinder twin camshaft engines were a fascinating addition to motor racing.

The development of large, supercharged, six-cylinder engines ushered in the era of the grand luxury car, as well as the short-chassis Type K and a renowned pair of touring cars, the Types S and SS. The latter were particularly successful in motor racing; the shorter SSK, built for hillclimbs, challenging specialized Grand Prix racing cars in the unrestricted capacity class. The SSKL of 1931 had a 7.1-litre, six-cylinder overhead-camshaft engine, with a permanently engaged supercharger. Power output was 300 bhp and the car reached a speed of 235 kph (146.03 mph).

In 1926 came the first of a series of successes for Mercedes-Benz in the German Grand Prix. On this occasion they used the 2-litre, eight-cylinder engine. In the same year a significant new racing strategy was introduced, tested for the first time on the Solitude. 'For the first time the drivers were lead through the race as if by invisible threads', said the chronicle. Former Mercedes Grand Prix driver Alfred Neubauer was in fact directing the team using an ingenious system of flags and signal boards.

The Type 8/38 hp, with a 2-litre, six-cylinder engine was launched in 1926 at the same time. This model was of conventional construction, the aim of its designer being reliability, but unfortunately it was characterized by serious shortcomings.

HANS NIBEL

Hans Nibel kept his construction department together after the merger and devoted himself to technical co-ordination, two of the many Benz models being built with the Mercedes star up to 1927. In 1928 he began to rework the Type 8/38 and when he was appointed technical director, succeeding Porsche, at the beginning of 1929 (Porsche having left Mercedes-Benz the previous year), the new model had already been completed – in autumn 1928. This was the Stuttgart 200, which was supplemented by the 260 with a swept volume of 2.6 litres.

Hans Nibel's significant technical innovations set trends even after his death in 1934. He was fully aware of the importance of independent suspension and with regard to the rear axle he referred back to the Benz Tropfenwagen. At Tatra, swing axles had been successful since 1923 and Hans Gustav Röhr had been the German pioneer of this system in 1927. Nibel also set his own standards for springs in the interests of comfort. The first to have had this idea was Wilhelm Maybach, which was reflected in his 1892 patent, while the work of Frenchman Sensaud de Lavaud also influenced Nibel greatly.

At the front, wishbones were used, although a tendency for the wheels to wobble was a known draw-back of this construction. Nibel counteracted this by making the wishbone the operating arm of a hydraulic-piston shock absorber. One advantage of wishbone suspension was that it kept control of the front wheels if a spring broke.

The rear axle was also cleverly designed. The coil springs were paired, one in front of and one behind each swing-axle, giving the necessary support under acceleration or braking. The energy released via the pivot bearing of the supporting rod in which the shafts of the half-axles were turning generated a shearing force transferred via the rubber bearing of the differential encasement to the chassis. The hydraulic piston shock absorber prevented the swinging of the suspension. This principle was applied until 1955, when a new swing-axle arrangement was introduced.

In 1931, during the Great Depression, the compact Type 170, with a 1.7-litre, six-cylinder engine, was launched. This attractive car was available as a limousine with four doors or as a cabriolet with two doors. The chassis works in Sindelfingen, where the 170 was built, had been established in 1915, initially for the wartime construction of Daimler aircraft engines.

A further development of the 170 culminated in the successful 200 series. Hans Nibel improved the SSK to the SSKL and designed a Grand Prix car for the 750 kg Formula of 1934, which was the first of the legendary Silver Arrows. These were also equipped with swing-axles.

The 200 series relied on traditional engine technology with its side valves. Top-class eight-cylinder-engine cars still had rigid axles at this time, but in 1932 Hans Nibel changed all that. The sporty Mannheim 380 S was equipped with rear swing-axles and front wishbones (double-wishbone independent front suspension and coil springs are commonplace today). In 1933, the 380 gained an eight-cylinder engine with overhead valves and a supercharger, setting the style for the famous 500K, 540K and the advanced 'Mighty Mercedes' 700 to follow.

During these years the designs were distinguished by innovations in the smallest details, and the development of racing and record cars surpassed all previous standards. It is also worth mentioning that in 1930 Hans Nibel planned a small car, whose features anticipated the later *Volkswagen* of Ferdinand Porsche, including a rear-mounted flat-four engine with a swept volume of 1.2 litres and 25 bhp. A four-cylinder in-line engine was also considered and a three-cylinder diesel engine with an astonishing power output of 30 bhp reached the prototype stage. In 1933 twelve test cars existed, but unfortunately it proved impossible to overcome vibration problems in any of them.

THE REAR-MOUNTED ENGINE

Moving on in his design ideas, Nibel turned towards streamlining, but he found that he had to compromise when producing a rear-engined car in 1934. This was the Mercedes 130, which remains the smallest car in the history of Daimler-Benz. A poor power/weight ratio impaired its road performance, but it might have been the noise of the air cooling system, not something to help the prestige of the brand name, which led to the installation of the four-cylinder in-line engine behind the axle.

The installation of hydraulic brakes was a very advanced feature, as was the concept of an overdrive, which appeared here for the first time. This was a fourth gear, used at high speeds, designed to reduce wear and save fuel, which was ideal for the new era of the *Autobahnen*; better still, it could be engaged without working the clutch.

For the 2000 km (1243 miles) German Rally, the longest competition in the sporting calendar of the Reich, there were five limousines with 1.5-litre engines. The Roadster was reminiscent of the former Benz-Tropfen sports car. Another Roadster, Type 150V, with front-mounted engine and universal joint proved to be successful as a prototype in motor racing, but there was no hope for the Type 130. After the *succès d'estime* of earlier, the problems of its road performances became insurmountable and the attempt to launch another 'popular' type of car had failed.

In 1934 Max Sailer succeeded Nibel, and became a member of the board of directors in 1935. Born in 1882, he had been one of the great Mercedes team drivers both before and after World War I and he was subsequently appointed director of the development and racing department. His racing triumphs were numerous but he also continued development on the top models, as well as keeping the whole Mercedes-Benz range up to date.

The successor to the four-cylinder 170 emerged in 1936. It was presented as the 170V, which proved a success next to the 170H with its rear-mounted engine. Despite having improved road performance, the 170H was not popular, although it remained available until 1939.

At that time Adler was talking about front wheel drive, but this was not considered by either Sailer or Nibel, so the chairman of the supervisory board acted quickly when Adler's Hans Gustav Röhr became available in 1935. He had paved the way for front wheel drive at the Adler company and together with his engineer

Joseph Dauben he developed a series of models with a 'system engine'. This horizontally opposed unit was fitted to the 130VB (four-cylinder), 190VB (six-cylinder) and 260VB (eight-cylinder). There was, however, no space for overhead valves, something that Röhr considered essential for a new design. Tests were halted after his death in 1937, in favour of work on another project begun by Röhr, the 400V, which was extensively tested in 1938 and was apparently to be put into production. It was a completely new design with V8 engine, overhead valves and rear-wheel drive.

During the 1940s the engine and the integral chassis should have been developed further, but the outbreak of World War II put a stop to that. Daimler-Benz switched to war production, so automobile development work ceased. By 1945, the plants had been destroyed, and when production restarted in 1947 it was with an almost unchanged 170V.

After Fritz Nallinger succeeded Max Sailer in 1942, the 1.7-litre diesel-engined 170D went into production. This model used only 7.5 litres of cheap fuel for every 100 km (62 miles), compared to the 170V which needed 11 litres for the same distance. As a result it caught on well. These first diesel cars were equipped with overhead valves – even the 260D which was built in 1936 for taxi and car rental use.

SAFETY CHASSIS

New design ideas for the various models of the 170 and the first 220 were still based on pre-war concepts, but at the beginning of the 1950s there was a momentous change: the first safety chassis in the world was developed on the basis of a patent granted to Bela Barényi on 23 January 1951.

The sturdy passenger compartment, which featured deformable front and rear sections was revolutionary in chassis design. Barényi created this innovative concept at Daimler-Benz and made further contributions to many other areas of passenger safety. These new ideas were put into practice without delay at the Sindelfingen plant.

For flank protection alone, there were five basic patents, while the roll-over bar was introduced in 1949, and 1951 saw the safety chassis patented, the patent including the *Doppeltrapezform* (double trapeziform), with a guard rail all the way round. In 1958 the safety roof emerged from the design room, in conjunction with the safety door.

A safety steering system was also designed by Bela Barényi and the design has been gradually improved since 1954. The steering wheel hub was replaced by a baffle plate and the steering column could telescope, the outer and inner column being able to collapse as necessary. In 1963, the safety steering wheel was patented, enthusiastic licencees calling it 'ingeniously simple and risk reducing'.

Patents do not last for ever and they will often stimulate new alternatives, but there is always someone who was there at the beginning. Numerous safety standards can be credited to the inventor at Sindelfingen. He also influenced the more general design of motorcars, with the 'pagoda roof line' – flat and yet stiff and suitable for tall doors in low cars, assuring a good field of vision. Barényi had this idea in 1945 but it was first patented in 1960. Deformable rear and front structures were based on a patent from 1941, which was shared by Barényi and Karl Wilfert.

As director of chassis development, Wilfert became the architect of change. He was one of the great experts who contributed to the establishment of the brand name Daimler-Benz from the outset. At the beginning there were a few designers, today there are innumerable people and many famous chief engineers who have left their imprint on development: from Nallinger via Hans Scherenberg and Werner Breitschwerdt to today's board of directors.

CONTINUING INNOVATION

Technological innovations have continued, although these have increasingly been with regard to detail. The outstanding pioneering achievements comprise: use of fuel injection for the first time in mass-produced cars (300SL) in 1954; introduction of systematic crash-tests in 1958; defining all essential safety aspects for the first time in 1967; safety steering in 1967; ABS with analogue technology in 1970; world records with diesel engines in 1976 and 1978 (C111 with a supercharged five-cylinder engine) and the first mass-produced turbo motor car (300SD for the USA) in 1977; and in the production field, dip-priming and improved working conditions with the introduction of a conveyer belt positioned to suit better the physical needs of the workers.

The same year the apprentice department built a car which set a world record for fuel economy driving for 1284 km (797.88 miles) with 1 litre of diesel. In 1980 ABS was introduced for commercial vehicles; in 1981 an experiment was carried out with one hundred methanol vehicles in Berlin; the S-class was equipped with airbags and inertia-reel seat-belts; in 1982, single swing axle, double-wishbone suspension and multi-link independent rear suspension were introduced; in 1983 there was the total encasement of the diesel engine for the first time as well as the setting of world records with the 190 2.3-16; in 1984 the new automotive simulator in Berlin was built; in 1985 came another triumph for the apprentices with a solar-mobile at the Tour de Sol, and in 1986 participation in PROMETHEUS (Programme for European Traffic with Highest Efficiency and Unprecedented Safety). Mercedes have achieved much up to the present; new challenges lie ahead.

INGO SEIFF

Wilhelm Maybach
Gottlieb Daimler's Alter Ego

There are thousands of books about the history of the motor car, and about its pioneers, inventors and pace-setters. These books deal with men who led society into a new era. However, it was the men and women who quietly worked in the shadow of these geniuses that often paved the way and they are rarely mentioned. Quite often they were the more practical in formulating new ideas, which led to all kinds of partnerships, both formal and informal: Berta and Karl Benz, Clara and Henry Ford, Louise and Emile Levassor, Henry M. Leland and his son Wilfred (the founder of Cadillac), Ettore Bugatti and his friend Ernest Fridrich, Ferdinand Porsche and Karl Rabe, Claude Johnson, the 'hyphen' between Rolls and Royce, Enzo Ferrari and Vittorio Jano (during the Alfa-Romeo era) and – the most important team in the history of automobilism – Gottlieb Daimler and Wilhelm Maybach. Without Wilhelm Maybach we would probably never have had a Mercedes car. Before pioneering that legendary car, he had breathed the air of the inspired Daimler during a thirty-five-year association

and he had put the great man's technical inspiration to good use.

The two men had met in Reutlingen in 1865. The thirty-one-year-old Daimler was head of the Maschinenfabrik of the local *Bruderhaus*, where young people were brought up in the Christian faith and trained in the practical application of craftsmanship to many different professions. Daimler was already successful and well established when he met the nineteen-year-old student Wilhelm Maybach, an ambitious technical draughtsman. He immediately noticed the burgeoning talent of the young man and arranged for him to start work at the Maschinenbau Gesellschaft in Karlsruhe where Daimler had been appointed head of the workshop.

This was the start of a partnership which left its mark on an entire technological era. There was, on one hand, the entrepreneur, Gottlieb Daimler who often tended to doubt his own abilities, and, on the other hand, the innovative and confident engineer, Wilhelm Maybach. Paul Siebertz wrote in his book *Gottlieb Daimler zum Ged-*

ächtnis ('In commemoration of Gottlieb Daimler') about the cooperation of the two men: 'What Daimler had in mind was put into a technically practical design on the drawing board by Maybach'. It was a partnership based upon mutual respect, fairness and a sense of decorum.

When the pair met Nikolaus Otto and Eugen Langen in Köln-Deutz in 1872 it was a meeting of titans which resulted in the four most outstanding engine designers and builders of the time agreeing to work together in the Gasmotoren-Fabrik Deutz (now Klöckner-Humboldt-Deutz). In 1876, Otto's stationary four-stroke engine was granted a patent and it became the basis for Daimler's and Maybach's innovative work thereafter.

Daimler and Maybach were especially interested in finding broad applications for the power unit and thus it changed steadily from an upright unit into one suitable for vehicle use and it was then that its potential became unlimited. This process of 'productionization' was one of the greatest achievements of both men.

Following long and depressing set-tos Daimler and Maybach left the Gasmotoren-Fabrik Deutz in 1882, just as Ettore Bugatti was to do thirty years later. Nevertheless, the Cologne-based company had become a springboard to world fame for that headstrong trio.

Wilhelm Maybach performed his role as Gottlieb Daimler's alter ego with admirable consistency and resolution. He had served him, his ideas and his legacy over a period of thirty-five years – and had done so in the best sense of this unfashionable word. L.J.K. Setright, in his book The Designers, draws attention to a monument in Derby which was erected to commemorate Sir Frederic Henry Royce, carrying the simple epigraph: 'Henry Royce, Mechanic'. A 'mechanic' no more and no less, said Setright; this honorary title would also be appropriate for Wilhelm Maybach and perhaps even Henry Ford, the Duesenbergs, Marc Birkigt, Vittorio Jano and the ever-underrated American engineer Henry Martyn Leland (the engineer behind the Oldsmobile, Dodge and Cadillac).

These are the men who really paved the way for the manufacture of motor cars. They believed that they relied not on a marvellous design or on entrepreneurial planning, but rather the attention given to small, yet important technical details which were considered with the most painstaking care. In 1893, Wilhelm Maybach presented his spray carburettor, which in principle solved the problem of effectively mixing fuel with air. Even today, almost every carburettor uses a jet to vaporize fuel. This technological innovation alone should be sufficient to give Maybach a place in the hall of fame of automobile pioneers.

After the death of Daimler on 6 March 1900, Wilhelm Maybach, together with Paul Daimler, laid the foundations for a totally new concept in the construction of motor cars. It was with the era of Mercedes, at the start of the twentieth century that Maybach's genius was most clearly shown.

THE 'SIMPLEX'

The great success of the first Mercedes racer was followed by numerous orders for the car, which was soon adapted to do various jobs. Although Maybach was fascinated by power, other newly founded German motor manufacturers preferred to construct small cars with outputs of around 10 hp; among them Adler, Dixi and NAG. While sticking to his basic principles, Wilhelm Maybach developed further designs, 'whose performance ranged from 8 to 70 hp by improving details and simplifying the operation of the Simplex series. One of these was the 40 hp Mercedes Simplex designed, as a racing car for the Nice Week, from 4 to 11 April 1902, in which it won the 'up-to-1000 kg' class. During the Nice mile race, Degrais reached a record speed of 82.3 kph (51.4 mph) from a standing start, while in the Ostend 1 kilometre race Baron de Caters achieved an average speed of 120.8 kph (75.07 mph), then considered a heady pace for a race even without a standing start.

'The international motor press was particularly surprised by the low weight of only 1000 kg (2205 lb) compared to that of vehicles with similar performance, which generally weighed more than 1500 kg (3308 lb). A major saving was in the engine, whose weight Maybach had been able to reduce to 185 kg (408 lb), in turn bringing the power-to-weight ratio down to 4.6 kg (10 lb) per horsepower, a most impressive result bearing in mind the technology of the time. The Simplex engine was noteworthy for its mechanically operated inlet valves, which ran in T-shaped combustion chambers, a system which found its way on to the high-performance 18/22 hp production engines as well as the large and powerful 60 hp series. Made from 1903 onwards the 60 had overhead inlet valves, whose introduction was not met with universal approval: some engineers predicted cooling problems but Maybach also introduced the honeycomb radiator and established that 7 litres (1.54 gallons) of water was sufficient even when all the engine's performance was utilized. The power of the engine, its quiet running and its great flexibility through-out its speed range were distinct advantages. This came from the mechanical valve operation, which allowed mixture into the four cylinders and exhaust out at precisely determined moments from the newly develo-ped piston carburettor, with its tubular regulator. This regulator adjusted a piston in the carburettor in such a way that an increase in engine speed would reduce the rate of fuel supply. The piston could also be operated from the dash, thereby acting as a throttle.

The axles were initially made of a 'seamless' steel tube, brazed at its ends, but these were soon replaced by I-section forgings. The four-speed gearbox was mounted in a unit with the differential, which drove the rear wheels through countershafts and chains. Maybach was convinced that further development was possible and in 1903 he developed a chainless transmission for the Simplex series. However, faulty materials let him down and this arrangement was only installed by special re-quest.

'When Kaiser Wilhelm II visited the Daimler stand at the Berlin Motor Fair in 1903, and Wilhelm Maybach explained and demonstrated to him the workings of the new Mercedes, the Emperor listened carefully and as he left said: 'Dear Mr Maybach, although your cars are very beautiful, simplex they are not!' Despite this, the Sim-plex series became a major landmark in the history of the automobile industry. It was not long before luxurious Simplex cars were introduced to the Emperor's fleet, and showed all the reliability and elegance that state carriages require'. (From 'Wilhelm Maybach-Leben und Wirken eines grossen Motoren und Autokonstruk-teurs' – Stadtarchiv. Heilbronn, 1979).

NEW CHALLENGE

In the Daimler-Benz book compiled for the hundredth anniversary of the motor car, the following is written about the leading role of the Mercedes: 'At the end of 1902 at the 5th International Automobile and Bicycle Exhibition held at the Grand Palais in Paris, light was shed on the great impact the construction methods of Mercedes cars had had on the development of the motor car. Most of the foreign cars, especially the French cars, changed their look within a year. Almost without exception they had availed themselves of Mercedes-type honeycomb-radiators, gate-type gear shift, accelerator pedal and brakes. Even the most cau-tious motor journalists wrote that the Mercedes cars had established new standards. More enthusiastic colleagues were even of the opinion that the Mercedes construc-tion methods had caused an entire re-evaluation of automobile development.'

Wilhelm Maybach, who was responsible for these epoch-making developments, could be proud of his work. Moreover, by 1907 he was looking for a new challenge. Due to unpleasant clashes with the manage-ment of the Daimler Motor Gesellschaft, he left and accepted Graf Zeppelin's offer of a closer cooperation. Together they established the Luftfahrzeug-Motorenbau GmbH in Friedrichshafen, with Maybach's son Karl as business manager.

Maybach and his son created a sensation there with their light and powerful engines. During the 1920s and '30s Karl also went on to design the high-quality luxury cars which were known as 'the German Rolls-Royce'. Right up to his death on 29 December 1929, however, Wilhelm Maybach had continued apace the develop-ment of engine design, and it is for his technical genius, not his strength as a company man that he is remembered.

Above: Mercedes or Mercedes-Benz Model 24/100/140 bhp Model 630 (1926-1929). The American automobile historian Louis William Steinwedel described this series as the 'founding of a new royal dynasty' – he was referring particularly to the look of the impressive touring cars and the three-pointed star on their radiators.

Technical data: 6 cylinders, 6 240 cc capacity, 100 bhp at 2 800 rpm or 140 bhp at 3 100 rpm with supercharger.

Overleaf: Mercedes-Benz 24/110/160 K 1928-1929. During the 'roaring twenties' this model was one of the best luxury touring cars in the world. Once again Ferdinand Porsche's influence was unmistakable. The 'K' had a 6.3 litre 6 cylinder engine and its most powerful version was capable of 140 bhp or 160 bhp with supercharger (disconnectable roots fan). Maximum speed 145 kph.

Pages 68-69: Mercedes-Benz 18/80 'Nürburg' 460 1930. This model from the popular series is described as a 'Transformation Cabriolet F', with bodywork by the Glaeser company in Dresden. It carries the name 'Nürburg' not because of any brilliant performances at the race track in the Eifel region but because it completed a 20 000 km endurance test at the Nürburgring as part of its road tests.

Technical data: 8 cylinders, capacity 4 622 cc, output 80 bhp at 3 400 rpm, mechanical servo-brakes, maximum speed 100 kph.

Previous page: Mercedes-Benz 500 K 1936. The cars in the 500 K and 540 K ranges were amongst the most elegant ever designed by Daimler-Benz. These two series were meant to replace the legendary S and SS models. They were much more elegant and easier to handle than the mighty models of the twenties and although every bit as powerful as them, they had a much more mannered style.

Above: Mercedes-Benz 370 S, Mannheim, Cabriolet A, 1931. The 'Mannheim' model, built from 1929 to 1934, was seen as a middle-class car and had a variety of bodywork: on offer were 4-seater limousines, Pullman limousines, roadsters and cabriolets. The 370 S shown here cost 13 800 Reichsmarks and was available exclusively as a cabriolet or roadster.

Technical data: 6 cylinders, capacity 3 688 cc, output 78 bhp at 3 200 rpm, maximum speed 120 kph.

Left: Rear light of a Mercedes-Benz 290 B Cabriolet 1936.

Opposite: Mercedes-Benz 500 K 1935.

Opposite and above: 'Blitzen'-Benz ('Lightning') racing car 1909. This monster with its 21 litre capacity spread over only four cylinders was driven by a series of famous drivers including Victor Héméry, Barney Oldfield and Bob Burman around race tracks and on record-breaking drives on both sides of the Atlantic. Victor Héméry set a new world record of 202.69 kph driving a Blitzen-Benz at Brooklands near London, whilst Barney Oldfield, driving the Mannheim bullet, reached a speed of 211.8 kph for the flying mile on the flat sands of Daytona Beach. In 1911 Bob Burman set a new world record of 228.1 kph which stood until 1919.

Technical data: 4 cylinder 21 503 cc engine, bore 185 mm, stroke 200 mm, output 200 bhp at 1 600 rpm, maximum speed (world record) 228.1 kph.

Overleaf: In 1934 Mercedes-Benz built this W 25 Model with its body specially built for record attempts at, amongst other places, the new concrete track in Guyon, Hungary and the Berlin AVUS. Rudolf Caracciola called it the 'Racing Limousine'. This racing and record-breaking car had an output of 370 to 430 bhp depending on the fuel mixture used.

81

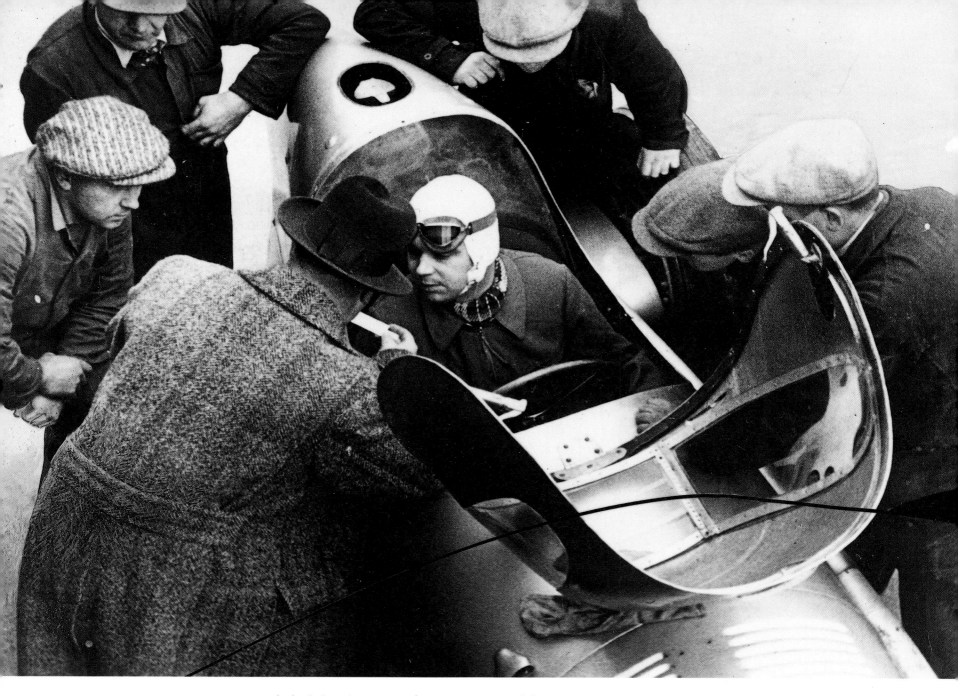

Previous page (top): The legendary Benz Tropfenwagen ('Drop Car') at the Stuttgart Solitude Race, 18 May 1924. At the wheel is Franz Hoerner who finished third with an average speed of 90.3 kph. The bodywork, designed by Edmund Rumpler, seemed futuristic at the time and the 'Drop Car' became the precursor for bodies designed by wind tunnel. The output of its six cylinders (1 997 cc) mounted in the centre of the car, behind the driver, was 80 bhp at 4 500 rpm. For brief periods it could achieve 90 bhp at 5 000 rpm.

Previous page (bottom): 26 October 1936, Rudolf Caracciola is being rolled out to the start on the Frankfurt-Heidelberg motorway for a series of record attempts. He was driving a car based on a 750 kg formula racing vehicle. Its twelve cylinder engine with a capacity of 5 577 cc was, at 300 kg, too heavy for a formula racing car but was well suited to the streamlined chassis. Its output was 616 bhp. The timed results

recorded on 26 October 1936 were: flying kilometre, 364 kph, flying mile, 366.9 kph – both international records in their class. There was even a world record over 10 miles with a flying start with an average of 333.5 kph.

Above: Rudolf Caracciola with chief engineer Alfred Neubauer (back to camera) at the last secret 'war council' before the world record outings of the Mercedes-Benz racing and record-breaking car, also known as the 'Racing Limousine', in 1934. The slip-streaming top above the driver's seat is open.

Opposite: Advertising of 1938.

RUDOLF CARACCIOLA
FÄHRT AUF MERCEDES - BENZ
neue REKORDE!

Bei den am 28. Januar 1938 auf der Reichsautobahn Frankfurt-Darmstadt veranstalteten Rekord-Versuchsfahrten gelang es Rudolf Caracciola, Deutscher Meister und Europa-Meister 1935 und 1937, die bisherigen Rekorde in der Klasse B über den fliegenden Kilometer und die fliegende Meile weit zu überbieten und auf Mercedes-Benz folgende neue Rekorde aufzustellen:

Fliegender Kilometer 432,692 km / Std.
Fliegende Meile 432,360 km / Std.

(Vorbehaltlich der Anerkennung durch die AIACR)

Dabei erreichte der Wagen, der mit EC-Kolben, Bosch-Zündung und Continental Reifen ausgerüstet war, in einer Fahrtrichtung die unerhörte Spitzengeschwindigkeit von 436,893 km/Std., die größte Fahrgeschwindigkeit, die je auf einer Verkehrsstraße erreicht wurde. Ein neuer Beweis für die Beherrschung des Kraftfahrzeugbaues durch

MERCEDES - BENZ

Above: The photo shows the unfinished Mercedes-Benz world record-breaking car with a Daimler-Benz aero-engine DB 603, the T 80 (1939).

Technical data: 12 cylinders, hanging in V formation, output 3 500 bhp at 3 460 rpm, planned speed 650 kph.

Opposite (top): The experimental Mercedes-Benz C 111-IV which Daimler-Benz used to test out aerodynamic limits at high speeds at the beginning of May 1979 on the test track at Nardo in southern Italy, setting five world records in the process. The car was powered by a V8 cylinder Otto engine, turbo-charged by two KKK units, and achieved 500 bhp.

Opposite (bottom): The 'Mercedes-Benz rolling research lab', the C 111-III during world record attempts at the Nardo race track in southern Italy. In this model the three litre turbo diesel engine reached 231 bhp. On 30 April 1978 there was an attempt to break all records over set distances and set times up to 12 hours. It was a success: nine records – from 316.484 kph over 100 kilometres to 314.463 kph over 12 hours – went into the book. Consumption per 100 kilometres: less than 16 litres of diesel fuel!

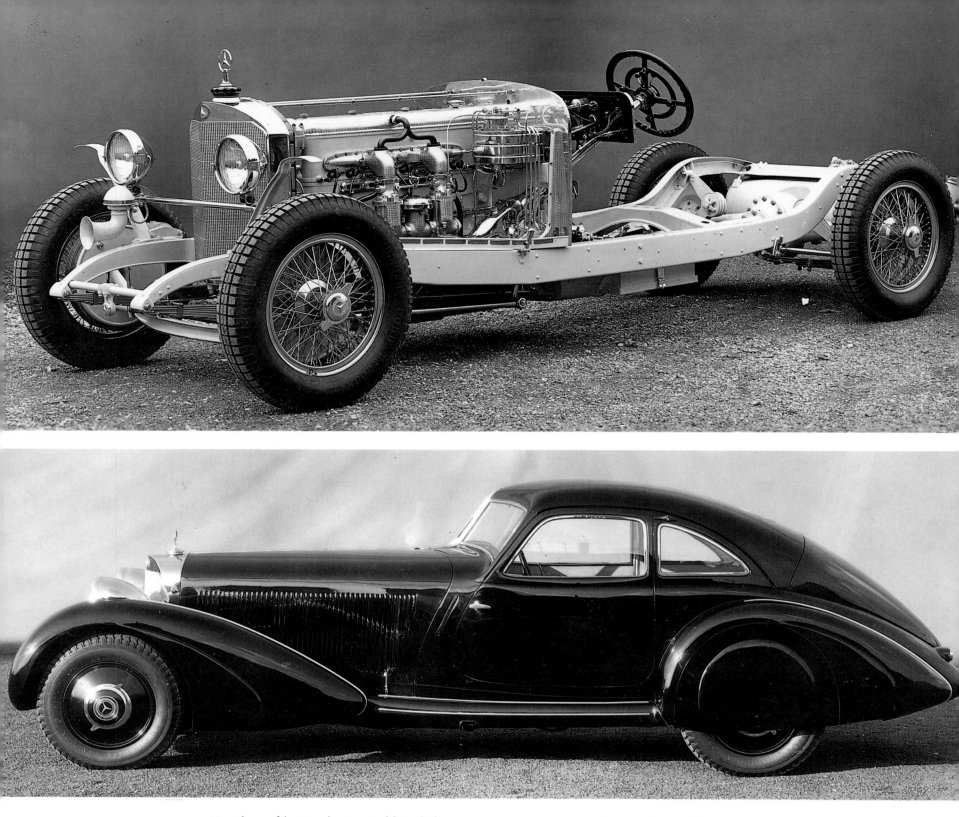

Top: Chassis of the Mercedes-Benz Model SS which, along with variants of it, the S, SSK and SSKL, scored countless successes in races between 1927 and 1933. The output from the seven litre six cylinder engine rose over the years from 140 to 300 bhp. The SS 27/170/225 HP pictured here achieved 170 bhp, and with the supercharger switched on 225 bhp at 3 300 rpm.

Above: 500 K models (1934–36) and 540 K (1936–39) were designed to continue the tradition of the S and SS models. They were more filigreed, more elegant, and a great deal more comfortable. Our photo shows a 500 K Autobahn-Kurier ('Motorway Courier') whose eight cylinder in-line engine with 5 litre cubic capacity reached an output of 160 bhp with the supercharger.

Opposite: 'Nose'-view of a Mercedes-Benz 380 1933. The 380 was available with three types of engine, the M 22 with and without built-in supercharger, and the M 22 K with an integrated supercharger. The 380 inspired the bodywork makers to create a whole series of elegant superstructures from a 2-door tourer to a 2-seater sports roadster.

Technical data: 8 cylinders, capacity 3 820 cc, output: M 22 without supercharger 90 bhp at 3 200 rpm, with supercharger 120 bhp at 3 400 rpm; M 22 K with integrated supercharger off 90 bhp, with supercharger on 140 bhp at 3 600 rpm, maximum speed 130 kph.

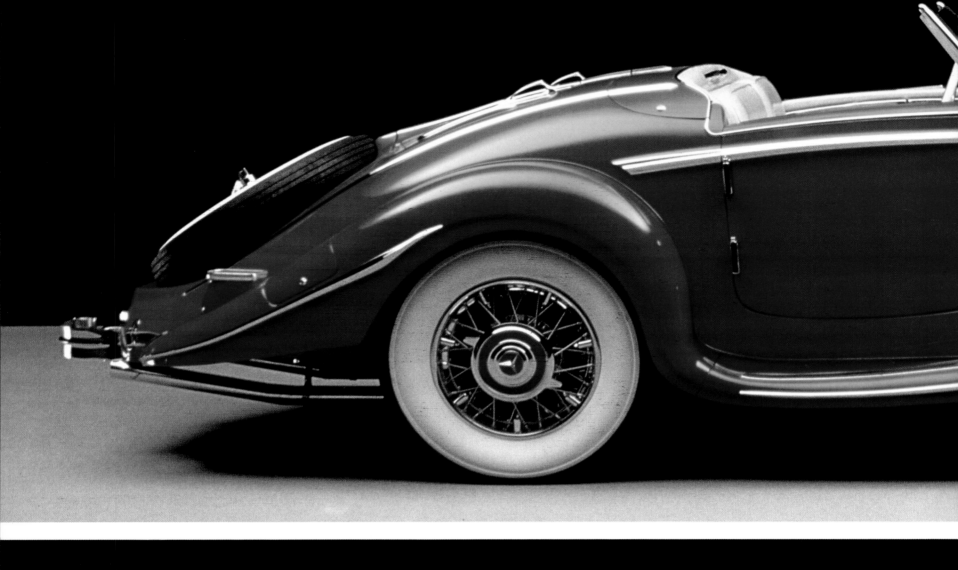
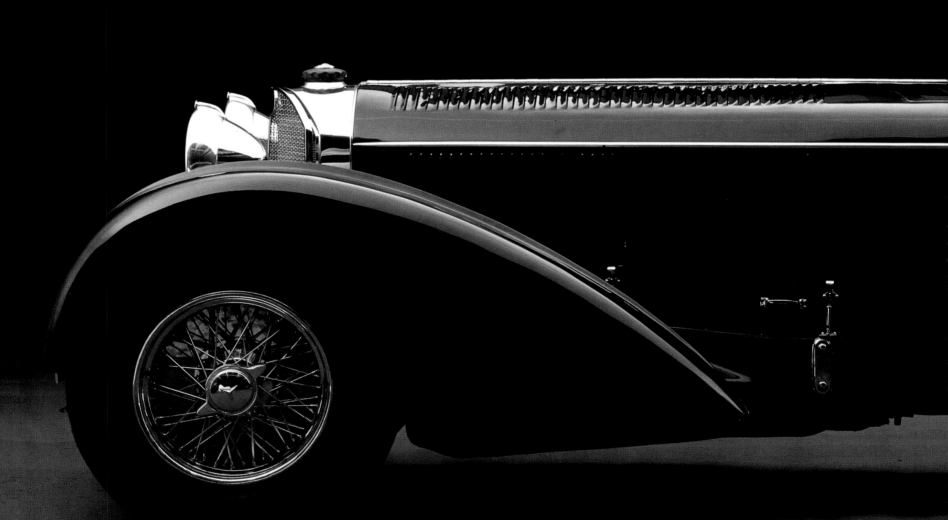

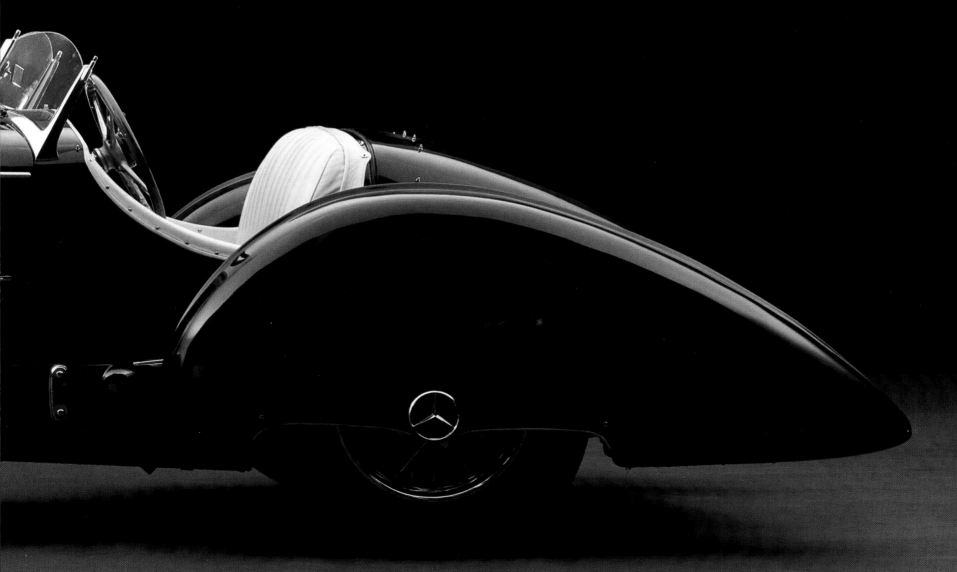

Pages 90-91 (top): Mercedes-Benz Model 500 K Special Roadster 1936. This 500 K is undoubtedly one of the most beautiful cars produced by Daimler-Benz and was in production from 1935 to 1936. Only 25 of these jewels were ever built. Five are still in existence today, two of which are in the possession of Daimler-Benz.

Technical data: see page 72.

Pages 90-91 (bottom): Mercedes-Benz SSK 1930, Graf Trossi. Named after its former owner, the Italian owner-driver Count Trossi. In the thirties Trossi was one of the most successful amateur drivers in Europe and a reliable member of Enzo Ferrari's Scuderia Ferrari, driving an Alfa-Romeo, Trossi also tried his hand at sports car construction.

Technical data: 6 cylinders, capacity 7 068 cc, output 170 bhp at 2 900 rpm, with supercharger 225 bhp at 3 300 rpm, maximum speed 192 kph.

Pages 92-93, previous page and above: Mercedes-Benz S 1928. A masterpiece by the French bodywork designer Jacques Saoutchik.

Technical data: 6 cylinders, capacity 6 788 cc, output 120 bhp at 2 900 rpm, with supercharger on 180 bhp at 3 000 rpm.

Page 97

Opposite: Exhaust side of the bonnet of a Mercedes-Benz SSK 1929.

Opposite: Mercedes-Benz 770, 'Grosser Mercedes',
Pullman Limousine, 1935. A 'Large Mercedes', owned
by the Japanese imperial family, returned to
Untertürkheim in 1971. The dark red car has a
chrysanthemum, the emblem of the Tenno, on the doors.
Along with two other cars of the same model it was part
of the regularly used fleet of cars belonging to the
imperial court.

Technical data: 8 cylinders, capacity 7 655 cc, output
150 bhp at 2 800 rpm, maximum speed (greatly reduced by the
armour plating) 130 kph.

Above: Mercedes-Benz 150, sports roadster, 1935. In
the mid-thirties the trend for streamlining demanded
that the engine unit be positioned in the rear. Foremost
in promoting this design principle were Edmund
Rumpler, Hans Ledwinka, Tatra's chief designer, and
also Ferdinand Porsche. Daimler-Benz wanted to keep
step and created the 130, whose sports version – the 150
– was equipped with a 1.5 litre engine.

Technical data: 4 cylinders, capacity 1 498 cc, 55 bhp at 4 500 rpm,
maximum speed 140 kph.

Overleaf: Coupé Parade. From right to left: 320 N
coupé 1937.

Technical data: 6 cylinders, capacity 3 208 cc, 78 bhp at 4 000 rpm,
maximum speed 130 kph.

300 Sc coupé 1955.

Technical data: 6 cylinders, fuel injection, capacity 3 996 cc, 175 bhp
at 4 300 rpm, maximum speed 180 kph.

280 SE coupé 1969.

Technical data: 6 cylinders, capacity 2 778 cc, 160 bhp at 5 500 rpm,
maximum speed 195 kph.

Opposite: Mercedes-Benz 320, Cabriolet B 1937. A popular travelling car which had a variety of bodywork. The 3.4 litre version – to cope with the growing motorway network – was fitted with the so-called 'ZF-overdrive' which allowed the maximum speed to be the cruising speed.

Technical data: 6 cylinders, 3 208 cc capacity, 78 bhp at 4 000 rpm, maximum speed 130 kph.

Above: Mercedes-Benz 130 1934. Daimler-Benz made a brave venture into the rear-engine territory and presented the 130 with a 4 cylinder in-line engine positioned behind the rear axle. The 130 had four gears with the fourth as a so-called 'speed gear'. But the Stuttgart manufacturers had no luck with the 130 – it was a complete flop.

Technical data: 4 cylinders, 1 308 cc capacity, output 26 bhp at 3 400 rpm, maximum speed 92 kph.

Overleaf (top): Mercedes-Benz 260 D, Pullman Limousine 1936. The 260 D was the world's first ever serially built diesel passenger car. It was the sensation of the Berlin Car Show in 1936. Its bodywork, that of a six-seater Landaulet, was the equivalent of the 200/300 model. According to Daimler-Benz, 2 000 of these cars were produced up to 1940.

Technical data: 4 cylinders, pre-combustion chamber diesel engine, 2 545 cc capacity, output 45 bhp at 3 000 rpm, maximum speed 90 kph.

Overleaf (bottom): The 'cockpit' of a Mercedes-Benz 290 B Cabriolet 1936. The 290 (1933-1937) succeeded the 'Mannheim' but had a considerably smaller engine than its predecessor. Among the variations on the bodywork were again a number of 'cabrio-beauties'.

Technical data: 6 cylinders, 2 867 cc capacity, 60 bhp output (68 bhp after 1935) at 3 200 rpm, maximum speed 108 kph.

INGO SEIFF

Emil Jellinek
and the 'Mercedes' Challenge

The dusty roads of the French Riviera soon became the favourite testing ground of the European car industry which emerged around the turn of the century. This stretch of coastline, called Côte d'Azur after a novel of that name by Stephen Liégeard published in 1888, was the playground of the rich and powerful during the years of the Belle Epoque (1890–1914). And Nice, with its large contingent of British visitors (one area was named the Promenade des Anglais), became its heart.

In fact, British naval officers used to visit the town during the War of the Austrian Succession in the eighteenth century, when it was still part of the Kingdom of Savoy. A Scottish doctor, Tobias Smollett, who had come to Nice in 1763 seeking a cure for his lung condition, praised so highly the balmy air of the Riviera that rich Britons followed in their droves. Unfortunately it was not known then that while the atmospheric conditions of the Côte were beneficial for many ailments, they had an adverse effect on lung sufferers. No matter – the Riviera was established firmly as a tourist

attraction: And another century on, the German philosopher Friedrich Nietzsche was praising the wondrous qualities of the air in Nice and had a square named after him.

Royalty, too, liked to come to Nice. King Leopold II of Belgium, for instance, was able to meet, and one after another, the Swedish King Oscar II, the Czarina Alexandra and Queen Victoria during a stroll along the Promenade. Ludwig I, King of Bavaria, came seeking solace after his unhappy love affair with Lola Montez and threw himself into the town's carnival festivities.

Towards the end of the century, the first motor cars (some still with electric traction) arrived at the Côte d'Azur, joining the horse-drawn carriages. Automobiles became the toys of the adventure-seeking rich. On 31 January 1897, a handful of madcaps organized the world's first hill-climb race from Nice to the mountain village of La Turbie – a distance of some 10.3 miles. The winner was M. Pary at the wheel of a 15-horsepower steam-driven De Dion; his average speed was just under

32 kph (20 mph). He was followed by a second De Dion steamer, driven by the Comte de Chasseloup-Laubat. Third came Lemaitre in a petrol-driven 6 hp Peugeot, 20 minutes behind the winner. The success of the winning car was attributed to the fact that it wore Michelin pneumatic tyres, while the second De Dion still ran on solid rubber. Since the Nice to La Turbie hill-climb had been such a success – with drivers and spectators alike – some of the more enterprising drivers decided to establish the 'Nice speed test'.

On 23 March 1899, the Promenade des Anglais was closed for a race against the clock. The fastest driver was Lemaitre in a 20 hp Peugeot, who covered the 1 mile distance in 95.6 seconds at an average speed of 59.7 kph (37.1 mph). On the following day, Lemaitre also won the Nice–La Turbie hill-climb race, his Peugeot becoming the first petrol car to win such a race.

All of these events were part of the 'Nice Speed Week' which also included long-distance races such as the Nice–Marseilles–Nice. Very much involved in the organization of the Speed Week was Emil Jellinek, today recognized as one of the leading innovators in the history of the car. Forty years of age, Jellinek had made a lot of money from business transactions in North Africa, so he could afford to live on the Riviera, where he soon established a reputation as a *bon viveur* and active car enthusiast.

As early as 1894 he owned a three-wheeled De Dion-Bouton Voiturette, followed by a three-wheeler steam model – the petrol cars on the market at the time were not powerful enough for his liking. In search of ever more potent automobiles, he bought a Benz 'Viktoria', but even this did not satisfy his wish to be the fastest and the best.

Then Jellinek, now forty-three, saw an advertisement for the Daimler Motor Company of Cannstatt in southern Germany. He knew that the very best French engines, such as Panhard & Levassor and Peugeot, were actually manufactured under Daimler licence, so he ordered a Daimler Double Phaeton that generated 6 hp and had a top speed of 25 kph – hardly enough for a man of his ambition. But then he showed his true mettle: instead of changing over to a different manufacturer, he placed an order in 1897 for a car that Daimler

was to build to his very own specification, the main priority being to achieve a speed of 40 kph. To prove that he was serious, he ordered four of them, and Daimler and his colleague Maybach, fascinated by such a challenge and by the detailed specifications that Jellinek produced, agreed to build the cars.

THE PHOENIX

Jellinek admired the increase in capacity that the Cannstatt makers had achieved, but considered their two-cylinder engines outdated. What was needed he said, was something that could keep pace with the products of the more innovative French manufacturers. So Daimler was persuaded to build the 'Phoenix', a four-cylinder model that generated 24 hp – although the figure varies from 23 to 28 hp in contemporary sources. Jellinek entered a Daimler Phoenix in the Nice Speed Week of 1899, but hid his identity behind the name Mercedes, the christian name of his eleven-year-old daughter. There was nothing unusual in using a pseudonym: one of Jellinek's competitors in the race, who called himself Dr Pascal, was in reality Baron de Rothschild.

Jellinek was not very successful in the 1899 race. He was placed reasonably well in the qualifying races, but he was not among the winners in either the speed tests or the Nice–La Turbie hill-climb race. So he went back to the people in Cannstatt: for the 1900 race, he said, he must have a car that would make his opponents tremble. Maybach increased the capacity of the four-cylinder engine to 28 hp – on the starting list, Jellinek was twenty-sixth. The same 5.5-litre four-cylinder engine that was used in the Phoenix squatted under the bonnet, but a new transmission allowed a speed of 80 kph. The speed of Daimler cars had been trebled in just three years.

The publication *Der Motorwagen* described the atmosphere of the 1900 Nice Speed Week: 'A large crowd had assembled. The weather was sunny and there were flower-bedecked cars in great numbers. On the stands distinguished groups of people could be observed, among them the King and Queen of Saxony, the Prince and the Duke of Oldenburg as well as many well known personalities of the motor racing fraternity. Altogether it made a vivid picture which would leave a lasting impression on everybody present. There was a slight contretemps at the start of the Nice–Marseilles race when some of the competitors wanted to drive without silencers in order to decrease the weight of their vehicles. Despite their argument that it was in the public interest to make as much noise as possible, the organizers insisted that no car started without this vital piece of equipment. Not a single famous driver took part in the one-mile race on 31 March; they had either returned to Paris or were content just to watch. That year the race took place not on the road but on the concrete pavement of the Promenade des Anglais.'

Jellinek's dream car proved to be technically misconceived. In a race it was barely manageable. The engine alone weighed 300 kilos and this, together with the huge radiator in front of it, made the vehicle nose-heavy in the extreme. The four-cylinder Benz models, in contrast, were considered tail-heavy.

Emil Jellinek and the Daimler Company had chosen Wilhelm Bauer as their driver in the Nice–La Turbie race on 30 March 1900. Bauer had an excellent reputation as both racing driver and car mechanic. But he was not to survive the day. This is how *Der Motorwagen* (issue VII, 1900) reported the incident: 'There was also an accident during the Nice–La Turbie race which resulted in the death of Wilhelm Bauer, chief mechanic of the Daimler Motor Company. He and his co-driver Braun were in a second Daimler Mercedes. Some hundred metres from the start the track turns and begins to climb. The car was driven at very high speed. In taking a bend Bauer hit a rock wall at one side and banged his head. Braun was only slightly hurt, but Bauer received severe head injuries and died without regaining consciousness.'

MERCEDES JELLINEK

The atmosphere at Daimler was subdued: not only had they suffered their first racing death, but the whole reliability of the Phoenix had fallen under suspicion. Emil Jellinek's reaction to the tragic incident was quite different: now was the time for Wilhelm Maybach and Paul Daimler to design a new racing car, faster than any

of its competitors, and named after his daughter, Mercedes. Jellinek ordered in advance thirty-six Mercedes cars – together worth 550 000 Goldmarks – and showing himself to be a shrewd businessman, he secured the sole Mercedes agency for Austria–Hungary, France, Belgium and the United States.

Daimler agreed to the name Mercedes being used for the cars built in Cannstatt and on 2 April 1900 Jellinek was voted on to the board of Daimler Motoren Gesellschaft (DMG). A new era in the motor industry had begun. Jellinek showed the value of recognizing the desires of customers, some of whom lavished more care and attention on their cars than they did on their spouses – as they still do, ninety years on! He knew all about the 'hidden persuaders' even then: 'A car should have the name of a woman, making it something to love and to cherish . . . , he said.'

Jellinek had little difficulty in convincing Wilhelm Maybach and Paul Daimler (the two closest colleagues of Gottlieb Daimler) of the advertising potential of the Mercedes name. He also convinced them of the need to build a new racing car. The very first Mercedes was a completely new concept: with a long, low, pressed-steel frame; front-mounted, four-cylinder engine with honeycomb radiator; multi-speed gear transmission with gate-type gear control (situated behind the engine and the clutch), and equal size front and rear wheels.

The 1899 Phoenix had generated 24 hp, and had an overall weight of 1800 kilos and a top speed of about 60 kph; this Mercedes, on the other hand, had a 5.9-litre, four-cylinder engine that developed 35 hp, it weighed only 1000 kilos and was capable of 90 kph. What particularly surprised the experts was the favourable power-to-weight ratio of 147 hp/tonne; the new radiator system; the axle construction; the gear unit and the brake system whereby a pedal operated a shoe brake. Two handbrakes were connected to the rear wheels.

'DESIGNER KING'

Wilhelm Maybach's Mercedes left the competition far behind and was now regarded as the acme of car manufacture. He had always striven for the 'highest performance in the smallest space'. Now he had achieved this and, quite justly, at the 1902 Paris Motor Show, he was declared 'designer king'. At speed tests in Nice in 1901, Wilhelm Werner in a Mercedes 35 won the 'Flying Kilometre' race; he also won the Nice–Salon–Nice race and the hill-climb to La Turbie.

These successes encouraged the Cannstatt car makers to increase the capacity of the car they now called Simplex from 40 hp and a swept volume of 6.8 litres to 60 hp and 9.2 litres for the 1903 model. It was with this car that Camille Jenatzy won the Gordon Bennett race. This victory was preceded by a number of very unfortunate events. The Daimler Company had intended to introduce their new 90 hp, 117 kph Mercedes 90 during the Gordon-Bennett race in Ireland, but on 10 June, their hopes turned, quite literally, to ashes. A fire swept through the Cannstatt factory, destroying the cars. Realizing that it would be quite impossible to build new cars in the remaining three weeks, the company bought back from private customers three 60 hp Simplex models that had been built by Maybach in 1901.

Although all its challengers used more powerful engines a Mercedes Simplex, driven by the Belgian Camille Jenatzy, came home first, after 6 hours and 39 minutes. Daimler had made the headlines again.

By 1904, the Mercedes 90s destroyed by the blaze had been rebuilt, so this powerful 12-litre racer took to the circuits. Other car makers, such as Fiat in Italy, Rochet-Schneider in France, Star in Great Britain and Locomobile in the United States, took their lead from the technology developed by Mercedes.

But the 'old' Mercedes 60 was still going from strength to strength: Driven by Vincenzo Florio it came third in the Coppa Florio. Wilhelm Maybach had taken the lifework of his late friend and partner to greater heights. There was now a new motto in Cannstatt: 'The racing car of today is the touring model of tomorrow.'

Jellinek saw all his dreams fulfilled. He drove proudly up and down the Promenade des Anglais in his victorious car, which had been given a new, gleaming white body. He had had the vision and energy to motivate the rather slow and careful Swabian car makers of Cannstatt. He had forced them into action – to the benefit of all. And when Paul Meyan, General Secretary of the French Automobile Club, at the end of another racing week declared emphatically: 'Nous sommes entrée dans l'ère Mercédes' ('we have entered the Mercedes era'), the satisfaction of the Cannstatt company and Emil Jellinek was complete. Mercedes had arrived. The name was patented as a trademark in 1902, and in America the super-rich railway kings such as Frank Gould and the Vanderbilts bought Mercedes cars by the dozen.

Emil Jellinek's star climbed higher and higher. He founded a bank, acquired hotels, bought a large yacht – which he named Mercedes II – became consul general of the Habsburg Empire in 1907 and remained a creative force on the governing board of the Daimler Company. He died in 1918 in Geneva, his last ambition achieved: the authorities had allowed him to change his name to Emil Jellinek-Mercedes.

HANS-OTTO NEUBAUER

The Mighty Mercedes

The German motor industry was seriously affected by World War One. In *A History of Sports Cars*, English motoring journalist G.N. Georgano says: 'The first two years following the Armistice saw very grim conditions in Germany. The shame of defeat, coupled with acute shortages, brought the country nearer to revolution than any other in Western Europe. Strikes were frequent, often accompanied by violence. On at least one occasion, the directors of the Benz company were manhandled by workers as they left their offices. Petrol was strictly rationed, and foreign currency only granted to privileged travellers. Rubber was in such short supply that practically all manufacturers sold their cars without tyres, leaving the buyer to do the best he could to get his vehicle shod. Copper and brass were virtually non-existent, consequently cars possessed a very austere appearance for several years.'

Economic difficulties were not the only obstacle to participating in international car races: Germany and Austria were to be suspended from the French Grand Prix and other important races in France and Belgium until 1924. But when Italy, in an attempt to catch up with the other nations' great automobile manufacturers started promoting for racing the marques Fiat, Alfa Romeo and Maserati, the Germans were filled with renewed enthusiasm for the race track. Ignoring the ban imposed by the victorious powers, on 29 May 1921, a 28/95 hp Mercedes driven by Max Sailer took its place at the start line of the Targa Florio race in Sicily. Sailer's motorcar was a tuned pre-war model. The German driver came second.

Benz registered a sports version of a 10/30 bhp for the first race on Berlin's AVUS. It won. Daimler was also busy producing the world's first supercharged touring car.

From 1922, things started to change at Daimler's racing headquarters mainly due to Paul Daimler's activities. Although Gottlieb Daimler's son was the last member of the Daimler family working at Daimler Motoren Gesellschaft in Untertürkheim, his position was weak.

And when, in 1923, Ferdinand Porsche left Austro-Daimler to work for Daimler Motoren Gesellschaft, Paul left the company embittered and moved to Horch, where he took sole responsibility for the development of an eight-cylinder engine.

At Daimler, Ferdinand Porsche took up Paul Daimler's work on supercharged engines, building on experience gained from aircraft engines made during World War One. Paul had found that supercharging compensated for the drop in engine performance at high altitude. His answer was a Roots blower with two rotors.

At the Berlin Automobile Exhibition in 1921, Mercedes introduced two new mass-produced models, designated 10/25/40 bhp and 10/40/65 bhp. The first number stood for the so-called 'steering hp', the second for the 'effective hp', and the third related to the power from the supercharger. The Roots blower was placed at the front of the engine. It was activated by a multiple disc clutch and a bevel gear, running at three or four times the speed of the crankshaft. When the accelerator pedal was kicked down, the Roots blower was switched on, so it did not run continuously but only when high performance was required.

CONFIDENCE BOOST

The first racing experiments involved a 28/95 bhp sports car, which had been developed before the war. Later, two 1.5-litre cars were entered for the 1922 Targa Florio, but they were unsuccessful. The next stage in the development of the supercharged racing car was the result of Ferdinand Porsche's efforts: in 1923, Mercedes entered three 2-litre supercharged motor cars for Indianapolis. This venture was not blessed with good fortune, but Max Sailer, by coming eighth, and Christian Werner, eleventh, boosted the confidence of the Mercedes team. Both models were raced regularly at home and abroad. Rudolf Caracciola won the mountain race of Münnerstadt, in which he drove a 1.5 litre supercharged car for the first time. Mercedes registered the new 2-litre, supercharged, eight-cylinder car for the Italian Grand Prix in 1924, but the race was clouded by an accident in which Graf Zborowski died. All the other drivers were then taken out of the race.

In 1924, the 15/70/100 bhp was introduced, a supercharged touring car which had a 4-litre engine. This was soon followed by the 24/100/140 bhp, with a 6.3-litre engine and a supercharger. Neither model was designed to be a racing car; they represented the big-powerful touring car and the supercharger gave them extra appeal. Nevertheless, the bigger of the two cars, which in fact had a shorter wheelbase, was also used for racing and, in 1926, formed the basis of the K for (kurz, which means short). This car had a higher compression ratio so its power output rose to 110 bhp and when a supercharger was added, the figure rose to 160 bhp. The K formed the basis of a series of cars that epitomized the sports car of the day.

Their name was Mercedes-Benz, and the marque came about in 1926 when the two companies Benz & Cie and Daimler Motoren Gesellschaft merged. The first products of the combined operation, however, carried just the three-pointed star, which was the Daimler insignia.

By enlarging the cylinder bore of the new Mercedes-Benz had a cylinder capacity of 6789 cc and a power output of 26/120/180 bhp. It was designated 'S', which stood for 'Sport'. The new model made its debut at the Eifel race at the Nürburgring on 19 July 1927, and its driver, Rudolf Caracciola, crossed the finishing line first in the sports-car class, having achieved an average speed of 101.1 kph (62.7 mph). This was the first of a long run of successes, but the S had not been built purely for racing: it was to be sold to the general public as a high performance touring car. A lower centre of gravity was obtained by making the car's chassis smaller. The rear-mounted engine was installed lower in the chassis, which contributed to a lower overall height. Naturally, it found many buyers, even though they had to pay about 30 000 Reichsmark for it. The price alone ensured that this car became a highly exclusive and precious rarity, and only twenty-four were built.

After 1928, a more powerful version of the S was marketed under the designation 26/170/225 hp – 138 were built. The S was available either as a complete car, with a body made by the Daimler-Benz chassis plant at Sindelfingen, or as a chassis for which one had to have a body made by a bodymaker, of which there were quite a few at the time. Although the S had a distinct sporty character, it was often built as four-seater touring car.

'SUPER SPORT'

In 1928, another Mercedes-Benz sports car made its debut at the Nürburgring, an improved version of the S. Its engine had a cylinder capacity of 7068 cc, and its designation was 27/170/225. It also carried an 'SS' tag, which stood for 'Super Sport'. The first three places in the Nürburgring race were taken by Mercedes-Benz SS cars, the winner being Caracciola.

Only 10 days later there was a second premiere: at the Gabelbach Race, Mercedes-Benz introduced the Type SSK (Super Sport Kurz), which was the most uncompromising design yet attempted. Whereas the S/SS had a wheelbase of 3400 mm, the SSK's wheelbase was shortened to 2950 mm. Even the least powerful SSK used the same power unit as the SS and had 27/170/225 hp. The most powerful cars were driven mainly by the Mercedes factory drivers, and had power outputs of 250 and 275 bhp.

The SS was marketed as a four-seater touring car as well as a two-seater sports model. The SSK, however, was built mainly as a two-seater, and was rarely seen as a four-seater. Numerous professional and private drivers owe their reputations and racing successes in Europe and in South America to the SSK: names such as Caracciola, von Brauchitsch and Stuck are all inseparably linked to this type.

All of these cars were the work of Ferdinand Porsche, but in 1928 he resigned from Mercedes-Benz and left Stuttgart, marking the end of the company's 'Porsche period'.

Meanwhile, both the Mercedes-Benz plant and private owners were shortening the chassis of the SS types and turning them into SSKs. These versions either kept the SS engine, or used a more powerful competition engine. This was a common practice among profiteers, since the SSKs were worth much more because of their limited production run. Consequently, a great many of the SSKs in existence today are not original, and experts

are not yet decided about the value of the late conversions.

The SSK was not the last of the successful S-series. At that time there was no uniform racing formula for motor racing, so the 'free formula' was used. In 1930, Mercedes-Benz was still relatively successful, but the S-Types were becoming out-dated. New ideas had to be found for the future, for the new Bugatti Type 51 and the Alfa Romeo 2.3-litre were becoming strong contenders.

In 1931, the worst year of the Great Depression, the Mercedes-Benz 720 SSKL (Super Sport Kurz Leicht) was introduced. German motorsport journalist Paul Simsa describes the economic background into which the introduction of the powerful supercharged car was regarded almost as a provocation: 'Economic crisis, state of emergency, a reduction in civil servant's salaries, an unemployment total of 5½ million. 1931 was one of the very worst years for Germany, and a time of worldwide economic crisis. The fact that Grand Prix races could still be held in those months was only due to the change of regulations to free formula.' The new SSKL has to prove itself, so Rudolf Caracciola drove it in the 1931 Mille Miglia race.

But how was the SSKL developed? The SSK chassis lost 200 kg in weight after being bored through several times. This was typical of Daimler-Benz, and had already been applied to the Benz-*Tropfenwagen*: Porsche's successor, Hans Nibel, was happy to continue the Benz traditions. The engine's swept volume remained unchanged, while the compression ratio was increased to 7:1. The power output of 27/240/300 bhp was quite remarkable, and was aided considerably by the 'Elephant supercharger'.

The SSKL and its genius driver Rudolf Caracciola won not only the Mille Miglia in 1931, but also the AVUS race, the Eifel race at the Nürburgring and the German Grand Prix (also held at the 'Ring). In 1932, an SSKL fitted with a streamlined body won Berlin's AVUS, driven by Manfred von Brauchitsch at an average speed of 194.4 kph (120.5 mph). The SSKL had reached its peak, although variants were raced for some time afterwards. (Regrettably, Mercedes team driver Otto Merz died in an accident when driving a streamlined car, based on the SSKL, during training for the Avus race.)

THE PARIS SALON

Mercedes-Benz was still preoccupied with the supercharger. In 1930, the eight-cylinder 'Mighty Mercedes' had a fabulous supercharger. This car was the biggest, heaviest and most expensive in Mercedes-Benz's vast programme. At the Paris Salon, onlookers crowded around the massive luxury car, which had a 7.7-litre, eight-cylinder engine (in line). Commercial success was not an important consideration in the car's development. Mercedes-Benz was far more interested in finding a competitive counterpart for the gorgeous twelve-cylinder Maybach-Type 'Zeppelin'. The more conservative appearance of the Mighty Mercedes also meant that many heads of state (including the Japanese Emperor) bought it for official purposes.

The next 'Mighty Mercedes', the 380 (1933–4), was built with an exceptionally elegant, filigreed shape, but strangely the car could not find many buyers. It even had a power unit which would suit almost any sporting taste: there was the M22 without supercharger, the MM22 with supercharger and the M22K with an integrated supercharger (the cylinder capacity was 4019 cc, and the power output 90 bhp without the supercharger and 144 bhp with it, at 3600 rpm).

The 500K, introduced in 1934, was an extremely fashionable and elegant car. It was available fitted with a variety of bodies: for example there was the 'normal roadster', the 'special roadster', an open touring car, a convertible, a sports coupé and a limousine.

Its eight-cylinder in-line engine had a cylinder capacity of 5109 cc, and a power output of 100 bhp without supercharger and 170 bhp with supercharger. Technically very sophisticated, the engine had a crankshaft with nine

bearings, the Mercedes-Benz double-carburettor and the Roots blower with two rotors.

The box-shaped frame had independent suspension at the front and a swing axle with an adjusting spring at the rear. The maximum speed was claimed to be 160 kph (99.5 mph), and the driver was advised to fill up with a full 10 litres of oil after 1500 km.

In 1938, just as Hitler's rearmament was in full swing, yet another Mighty Mercedes variant was introduced. It was not designed for ordinary people, but – according to the manufacturer – 'for those who desired a car which was quite outside the ordinary run of things'. Premier Salazar of Portugal and Field Marshall Mannerheim of Finland bought this version, but most of the 88 Type 770s built were bought by the Nazis.

This car had a 7.7 litre, eight-cylinder engine which was equipped with a supercharger, and its power output was 230 bhp at 3200 rpm. There was a special armour-plated version of the car, but its top speed turned out to be drastically reduced: the tyres not being able to withstand more than 80 kph. This car had 40 mm bullet-proof glass all around, electromagnetic locks, a body made out of armour plate 18mm thick and spare wheels on both sides for extra protection. Light-alloy wings reduced the weight a little.

Plans were made for further development of the elegant supercharged cars, but were not realized because of the outbreak of war. The evolution of the supercharger, the standard for which was set by Daimler, Benz and Daimler-Benz, dominated car manufacturing for almost twenty years. The few remaining cars from that time still keep enthusiasts on the jump; they are much-sought-after collectors' pieces, carrying a price tag that reflects their status.

STANISLAW PESCHEL

The Giants
A World Record Chase

The invention of the automobile (the 'self-mover') has taught man a completely new, hitherto unknown, way of moving around. His natural means of mobility, that is walking or running, has been superseded by the automobile. Until then, 'speed' had nothing to do with any technical support (think of the first marathon runner, in 490 BC, who died from exhaustion after completing his run); nor did journeys to faraway places set up any speed records. For example, it took Marco Polo three years to return to Venice from China (1292–5). The car, sporting its fantastic abilities to conquer space and time much faster than it was ever possible for its human creators, soon became a piece of sports equipment itself.

The 'battle against time', the main motto of so many sports, came in at the beginning as a decisive element in motor sport. But if it was the best average speed over long distances that people strove for at first, the absolute speed over short or medium distances soon became an equally important theme of the competitions between marques and nations.

The kilometre, the mile and multiples thereof were recognized as measurements on an international level; the highest speed reached in each case was officially registered, thus creating 'car world records', divided into absolute world records and class records. Yet the first car race ever, which took place in 1894 between Paris and Rouen, had nothing to do with striving for a world record.

No cars with internal-combustion engines took part in the first trials for a world speed record: electric or steam-powered vehicles were the first to fight it out. The first motor speed record was in fact set up by an electric car. On 18 December 1898, in Achères Park, near Paris, the Comte de Chasseloup-Laubat covered 1 kilometre in 57 seconds, driving a Jeantaud and establishing an average speed of 63.157 kph (39.245 mph). The Belgian Camille Jenatzy, also known as the 'Red Devil', was Chasseloup-Laubat's great challenger and on 29 April 1899 on a country road near Achères, he became the first automobile driver in the world to reach the magic 100 kph mark. He too was driving an electric car, known as *La Jamais Contente*.

This record-breaking drive of 1899 may have been a triumph but it also spelt the beginning of the end for electric racing. Its strongest rival, the steam car was showing greater promise and had more opportunities to illustrate its potential. On 13 April 1902, Léon Serpollet made a start by heating up the boiler of his *Oeuf de Pâques* (Easter Egg) and launching the 'Egg' on the Promenade des Anglais in Nice at a speed of 120.8 kph (75.07 mph), but four years later, after a sensational record-breaking run by the Stanley Steamer *Beetle* at Daytona Beach, Florida, steam itself had had its day as a power system for cars.

By the turn of the century, almost every competitive car had an internal-combustion engine and in those days, everybody was familiar with names like Mors, *The Arrow*, Darracq and *Bullet* – to mention just a few of those racers. Mercedes was already among the most successful racing marques and it had not returned empty-handed from those 'battles against the clock'.

The first world record for the German company was achieved in 1901 during the record week in Nice. Lorraine Barrow drove his 35 hp car over 1 mile from a standing start, reaching an average speed of 79.7 kph (49.53 mph). This kind of run, measuring the acceleration of the car over a mile, seems to have proved favourable for Mercedes: a year later, a Frenchman called Degrais stunned his opponents by taking the standing-start world record up to 83.2 kph (51.7 mph). Apart from breaking the record, this was the highest speed ever reached by a petrol-driven car.

ABSOLUTE WORLD RECORD

'Mercedes cars established their good reputation due to their great reliability and robustness during long races, but have shown an equally good performance over shorter distances', reported the *Allgemeine Automobilzeitung* in 1904, after the absolute world record had been established. In Ostend, meanwhile, Baron Pierre de Caters took the flying-kilometre record in his 110 hp

Gobron-Brillié, at a speed of 156.5 kph (97.25 mph).

Right from the start, the Daimler Motor Company knew that raising dust on the racing tracks was a good way to promote their cars. Benz, on the other hand, remained rather reluctant, the founder always having been sceptical about motor sport. His interests reached only as far as events which, today, might be called rallies. Benz cars indeed might have been made for this kind of competition, with their oft-praised reliability.

This low-key approach soon changed after Karl left the company in 1904. Great efforts were made to join the front ranks of the sport: to start with, a French engineer called Barbarou was taken on to supervise racing projects, although after achieving some success he was superseded by Victor Hémery.

While at Benz, it was Hémery's ambition to build and drive the fastest car in the world. He certainly had the right credentials, arriving at Mannheim directly from a good racing stable – that of Messrs Darracq. The road to this goal was embarked upon by building a GP racing car, constructed according to the so-called Ostend formula – that is with a maximum bore of 155 mm, but no restriction on cylinder capacity. This engine already generated more than 150 hp. However, Hémery was not satisfied, going for the 200 kph (124.28 mph) mark, which was at the time thought to be too high for this type of car.

At Daimler's, the world record set in Ostend in 1909 by Jenatzy at 180 kph (111.85 mph) was already coming within reach, but by later that year, Benz could leave all the Mercedes cars standing (and until the two companies merged, in 1926, Daimler never fought back). The management at Benz had that year finally given its go-ahead for a great new racing car. Louis de Groulart, who had already designed the 150 hp engine, returned to his creation, this time increasing the bore to 185 mm, which with only four cylinders gave him a cylinder capacity of 21 500 cc! It could accommodate almost four of the current 560 SE engines. The power output was no less than 200 hp! Before Hémery dared to tackle the 200 kph mark, he took home another world record. At the Brussels automobile race of 1909 he completed the standing-start kilometre in 31.2 seconds, which corresponds to 115.4 kph (71.71 mph). Three weeks later, on 8

November 1909, he was at Brooklands, waiting to thunder down the circuit. There he reached 202.6 kph (125.9 mph) over the kilometre, so at last the Europeans had proved their strength and the American record set up by the 'Beetle', of 205.4 kph (127.64 mph) over one kilometre was set to crumble.

It still survived, however, and Héméry abandoned further trials, knowing very well that more modifications were needed to make the car faster. Another point was highlighted by the correspondent of the *Allgemeine Automobilzeitung*: 'Héméry had gone to the limits of the Brooklands track, although it is the fastest in the world'. He was right and, subsequently, the record seekers had to look for a more suitable venue.

They chose Ormond Beach in Daytona, Florida, where racing drivers had been meeting for a number of years. At low tide, the ocean moves out quite a way, leaving behind a stretch of beach which is firm and level – and still very popular for meetings today, if only at the snail's pace required by law.

BLITZEN BENZ

Hence, the 200 hp monster, known as the *Blitzen Benz*, was transported to the USA at the beginning of 1910. There remained the question of who was to drive the beast, a question which was eventually answered by Ernie Moross who made a quick decision to buy the car and gave Barney Oldfield, with whom he'd worked since 1909, the chance of becoming the fastest man on earth. Moross already possessed a 150 hp Benz, so he knew the marque while Oldfield had previously proven his extraordinary driving skills and it was from this combination of abilities, that Benz was to benefit.

On 16 March 1910, at Daytona, Oldfield put his foot hard down in the *Blitzen* and on his first run reached an average speed of 212 kph (131.74 mph) over a flying mile. This was an absolute world record, to which Barney added two further American records in the course of the following week. The joy back in Germany was immense and even the emperor sent his congratulations by telegram.

Oldfield and Moross knew exactly how to make best use of their newly won fame: like a travelling variety show, they toured the country, staging show races here and there, with Oldfield calling himself the 'Speed King'. But Oldfield was overdoing things, taking part in races which were not sanctioned by the AAA (American Automobile Association); he fell out with the organization to the point where its officials decided to suspend Oldfield and his car from any racing contest.

In the wake of this, the *Blitzen Benz* was purchased by a syndicate in Indianapolis, who re-released it for racing. It was soon mounting a record-chase with Bob Burman at the wheel. In Daytona, he drove at the amazing speed of 228.1 kph (141.74 mph) over the flying mile, setting a world record which remained unbeaten until 1919. The *Blitzen* stayed in America, and won many races, but its record-breaking days were over.

During World War I, motor sport came to a complete halt in Europe, and afterwards, for sport-orientated marques like Benz, Mercedes and, as from 1926, Mercedes-Benz, the post-war period proved a difficult phase. Some hope was raised by initial successes for Mercedes in the Targa Florio in 1922 and 1924, and through considerable progress with the development of supercharging, but inclusion in the world record books was still a long way from being won back.

It was not until 1932 that Mercedes-Benz returned in the record lists again, this time with a famous range of supercharged cars, the SS, SSK and SSKL, which are dealt with in chapter 10. Manfred von Brauchitsch, a private Mercedes driver, owned one of those SSKLs and he decided to take part in a race on Berlin's AVUS circuit.

THE 'CUCUMBER'

He would have made no impression whatsover in that race were it not for the fact that he had met the pioneer of aerodynamics, Baron von Koenig-Fachsenfeld, just a few weeks before. The latter convinced von Brauchitsch that he should have his heavy SSKL's chassis re-designed in order to streamline the car. Koenig-Fachsenfeld put his plan into action within a fortnight and created a car which some cynics called the 'cucumber'. Against all the odds, however, von Brauchitsch won and established a record for his car's class over 200 km by averaging 194.4 kph (120.80 mph).

This triumph also set Manfred von Brauchitsch up very well for the future: the era of the legendary Silver Arrows was about to begin and von Brauchitsch was set to become one of the drivers. Record-breaking, however, was still the domain of Rudolf Caracciola, however – the undisputed star of the Mercedes-Benz racing team.

At that time – 1934 – the new rulers in Berlin were hoping for top performances by German racing drivers to fit neatly into the programme of propaganda which they were developing. Auto Union had already achieved many successes; with their new racing car, Hans Stuck established three speed records in March and five new ones in September 1934. Now it was Daimler-Benz's turn. The company took up the challenge with great ambition.

At the end of 1934, the team travelled to Gyon in Hungary where a new concrete track had recently been built. There, Caracciola managed to set up three new class records (class C; 3.0 to 5.0 litres), as well as a world record over a standing-start mile at 188.6 kph (117.20 mph), achieved in a slightly modified W25.

AUTOBAHN RACES

The only blemish on these achievements was the fact that they had taken place on a foreign track, but Germany had no suitable venue. There was the fast AVUS, but that had a gradient which exceeded the one per cent allowance stipulated by the world record regulations. To solve the problem, the Directorate of Public Motorways was approached in 1935 for permission to use newly finished stretches of the autobahn as venues for record attempts. This permission was granted within two days and a part of the state motorway between Frankfurt-am-Main and Heidelberg was selected for the trials.

The first record runs were made here in March 1936 by Hans Stuck driving an Auto Union and he was able to quickly set up international records in the class B (5.0 to 8.0 litres).

Daimler-Benz looked hard at these successes and decided to put up a car to contest class B. They already

had a suitable engine at hand – a twelve-cylinder unit too powerful for the 750 kg Formula but which seemed to be ideal for record trials. This was slotted into a Grand Prix car chassis, which was then equipped with special bodywork, streamlined through wind tunnel tests. For the first time in the history of racing car construction, even the wheels were almost completely enclosed. Koenig-Fachsenfeld's aerodynamic work was being vigorously applied.

Three weeks prior to Daimler-Benz's record attempts, Alfred Neubauer, the famous Mercedes team manager, was pondering over which existing records could be tackled with the new car. He thought it possible to snatch Alfa Romeo's records over the flying mile and the flying kilometre and hatched similar plans regarding Auto Union's records over 5 km and 5 or 10 miles.

The results which were achieved on 26 October proved him to be right. Rudolf Caracciola drove the flying kilometre at 364.4 kph (226.44 mph) and the flying mile at 366.9 kph (227.98 mph) – both international class records. The existing record over a flying 5 km also fell to Caracciola, despite his car suffering from a faulty gearbox which caused fourth to disengage. The weather could have been much better for the record attempt, too: the wind was so strong and rain so heavy that it proved to be impossible to attack the remaining long distances. The team made up for this on 11 November, however. Alongside two class records for Daimler-Benz came an outright world record over 10 miles with a flying start; the average speed was 333.5 kph (207.23 mph). Daimler-Benz's preparation for the 1937 record week, which was to take place in October on the motorway between Frankfurt and Darmstadt, was extraordinarily meticulous. The twelve-cylinder power unit already tested in 1936 was now able to generate a massive 736 bhp, which made it the most powerful engine to have been built for any of the company's road vehicles. Special attention now had to be paid to the shape of the body and in order to achieve a favourable drag coefficient for the car, detailed work was carried out on a quarter-scale model and the aerodynamics were checked in the wind tunnel. The final result was a drag coefficient of only 0.18 for the full-size car.

116

WIND TUNNEL TESTS

Despite all these efforts, the car took no records. At speeds of around 400 kph (248 mph), its front end tended to lift off the road, so the attempt was quickly suspended. Back at the workshop, engineers worked full-time on finding a solution to the problem. The cure turned out to be modification of the nose by closing the air-cooling intakes and effecting other changes suggested by further wind tunnel tests.

The danger of a lift-off was thus eliminated and the drag coefficient further reduced at the same time. This, however, left the problem of cooling the engine, which was overcome by simply running the hot water through a container filled with half a cubic metre of ice. Given that the record runs were held over short distances, this was a perfect solution.

On 27 January 1938, Caracciola arrived in Frankfurt, accompanied by Neubauer and von Brauchitsch who was to act as reserve driver, and they found themselves amidst an ordered chaos of participants. Auto Union were there, too, Bernd Rosemeyer wanting to ensure that he kept his record. The track had been sealed off and telephone wires laid; in essence, everything was in place. Only the weather proved to be an obstacle – with ice on the road, the air of optimism started to deteriorate, but in the afternoon the competitors received new hope from the weathermen at Frankfurt airport, who predicted that conditions would be favourable on the following day.

Neubauer rushed to the telephone, ordering the Stuttgart factory to transport the recörd car to Frankfurt immediately. It arrived at 7 am the following day.

At 8.20 am, Caracciola went to the start line and half an hour later he held two records, records which were to stand until 1964. He achieved 432.7 kph (268.88 mph) over the kilometre and 432.4 kph (268.69 mph) over the mile – and these remain today the highest speeds ever achieved on an ordinary road.

For Caracciola, however, this was a day of triumph and grief, for Bernd Rosemeyer died in his attempt to retake the record for Auto Union.

It was not until February 1939 that Caracciola again entered the cockpit of a record-breaker, this time on the motorway near Dessau, which is now in East Germany. For this attempt he used an impressive 3-litre racer trimmed down to a slippery shape and he set up four international class D records (2 to 3 litres).

UNFULFILLED AMBITION

The German team managers and their drivers still had one unfulfilled ambition at the back of their minds. The *Blitzen Benz* had held the absolute land speed record since 1911, so this mark constituted a particularly attractive target. The first person to take up the challenge was the Auto Union driver Hans Stuck, who had an unquenchable desire to become the fastest man in the world. But where do you get an engine capable of developing at least 2500 bhp?

An idea came from the fact that this figure was the same as the power given by the Rolls-Royce aero engine which shot Sir Malcolm Campbell's *Bluebird* across Bonneville salt flats at an average speed of 484 kph (300.76 mph). Daimler-Benz did have an aero engine, the DB 601, with the kind of power which would suit Stuck's purpose, but his first task was to find an engineer to design the car. He was able to talk Ferdinand Porsche into doing the job for him, because Porsche had great faith in Stuck as a driver. More good news came from the German Department of Aviation, who agreed – no doubt for reasons of prestige – to provide two of the required Daimler-Benz aero engines. But who was to build the 'bullet on wheels'? Auto Union turned down the offer, so Stuck approached Daimler-Benz. After initial hesitation in the boardroom, clearance was given and Stuck was accepted as the driver, even though he had raced Grand Prix cars for Auto Union!

THE T80

A concept was soon outlined. This would be an extremely light car: instead of the usual 4–6 tonnes, the T 80 – as the car was named in house – should only weigh 2.8 tonnes. In order to transfer the enormous power of the engine onto the road without any loss, a layout with two rear axles was chosen, and to avoid wheel-spin when changing gears, an early form of hydraulic torque converter was introduced in place of the clutch. Another novelty was a system whereby the speed of the driven rear wheels was controlled by the freewheeling front wheels: if the driven wheels were to spin, sensors would reduce the engine's torque – an early form of traction control. The designed top speed was 550 kph (341.77 mph).

Construction of the T 80 began in 1937, but where should the car be tested? Bonneville salt flats (USA) were first considered as a possible venue, but this idea soon had to be dropped because of the deteriorating political climate and the fact that national officials remained adamant that a German world record had to be set up on German soil. This prompted the construction of a race track near Dessau, but this turned out to be too short and undulating to be of real use. Nevertheless, officials still stuck to the idea of racing the T 80 there.

Meanwhile, the record had fallen to American George Eyston, at 575 kph (357.31 mph), a performance that slightly worried the German side. Porsche put in a request for more horsepower – there was talk about 3000 – which did not present a problem for Daimler-Benz; the DB 601 had, by now, become the powerful DB 603, capable of meeting such high demands. The body-work was also modified to make the car capable of reaching 600 kph (372.84 mph). By adding another three zeros to the top speed we would arrive at the cost Daimler-Benz incurred in developing this project, but the investment did not pay off.

Shortly before completion of the T 80, World War II broke out, and the project was terminated, so the car never had a chance to flex its muscles in anger. Today it is a permanent exhibit in the Daimler-Benz museum at Stuttgart.

At the end of the war, the Daimler-Benz works was devastated; roughly eighty per cent had been destroyed by allied bombing raids. The then chairman of the board, Wilhelm Haspel, depressingly summed up the situation by saying: 'at that point in time, the company had practically ceased to exist'. In view of the urgent need to rebuild normal production nobody thought of motor sport – not even of world championships.

THE C 111 RECORD-BREAKER

Reconstruction of the works was not far short of miraculous and it gave rise to a third era of competition for the company, lasting from 1952 until 1955 and relating to the great successes of pre-war years. Yet after the organization's farewell to racing in 1955, it was to be a further 21 years before Daimler-Benz sent another racing car onto the tracks. It was a long-standing test model, known as the C 111. Engineers at Daimler-Benz had already tested a number of different versions of the Wankel rotary-piston engine in this car, but the energy crisis of 1973, together with basic concept-related doubts, had led to the end of that particular Wankel test series (see *The C 111*). The C 111 only returned to the fore when Daimler-Benz engineers were looking for a vehicle in which the outstanding performance potential of the diesel engine could be demonstrated.

Diesel engines for motor cars have a great tradition at Daimler-Benz and when it was planned in 1975 to turbocharge the five-cylinder diesel car engines which had been launched the previous year, the C 111 provided a spectacular test bed for the unit. The turbo-diesel C 111 went to record trials on the 12.6 km track in Nardo, southern Italy, on 12 June 1976, and by the end of this session, which was run entirely by members of the Daimler-Benz test department, sixteen records for this type of car, as well as three absolute world records, covering distances of 5000 miles, 1000 km and 1000 miles, had fallen. Interestingly, these world records had up to that point been achieved with cars powered by Otto engines – and this version of the C 111 was not even designed as a racing car! After those 64 hours, the diesel engine could shed its lame-duck image and take pride in attributes such as speed and reliability.

It is clear that, for the first time, Daimler-Benz went to the race track not to hunt for records but to prove the worth of their production models. The experience gained in these record runs could now easily be integrated into the production of the five-cylinder engine.

As soon as the records were safely home, the Daimler-Benz engineers embarked on a new project. They knew that the potential of the new engine had not yet been fully exploited, so they chose to insert the power plant into a car purpose-built for racing. That was the idea behind the C 111-III, a truly remarkable car with an aerodynamic drag coefficient of only around 0.195. A one-fifth scale model was made and tested in the wind tunnel, before the full-size body took shape. This was mounted on the already proven chassis of the car's predecessor and the engine – this time generating 230 bhp – was installed. The result was astonishing indeed. The car could achieve 325 kph (201.96 mph) with a diesel consumption of 17.5 mpg.

On 30 April 1978, at midnight, a new record run began – again at Nardo – in an attempt to break all existing records for up to 12 hours duration. Drivers for this series were journalist Paul Frère, Mercedes-Benz Switzerland's PR-man, Rico Steinemann, and Guido Moch, manager of the company's Stuttgart test track. Like the hands on a watch, the car made its rounds hour after hour. However, shortly before the 12 hours were over, the run had to be suspended due to a faulty tyre. For the team of drivers, which now included Dr Liebold, the project leader, this meant racing for another 12 hours in 2½-hour segments.

This time, success was complete: altogether, nine world records were set. Daimler-Benz documents state clearly and simply: 'the records have been broken. Proof has been obtained. Experience has been gained. The production series will benefit from this.'

The performance peak of the 3-litre engine had been reached, but there were other reasons which made it seem sensible to get the C 111 back on to the road. During the trials that followed, the influence of aerodynamic design changes and the fitting of spoilers was examined – at speeds of more than 400 kph (248.56 mph). Furthermore, tests using the latest plastic materials were carried out and special attention was given to research on tyres.

For these tests, the C 111-IV was given a petrol engine of the original 4.5-litre type, but with two superchargers to increase its effective swept volume to 4.8 litres. Its eight cylinders developed no less than 500 bhp at 6200 rpm.

Trials took place on 5 May 1979 – again at Nardo – and resulted in five absolute world records. The following were reached from a standing start:

320.6 kph for 10 kilometres
335.4 kph for 10 miles
375.6 kph for 100 kilometres
367.3 kph for 100 miles

Besides that, Dr Liebold who drove to take all these records, emphatically improved on the outright closed-circuit record of 355.9 kph, set by the American Mark Donohue, by reaching the breathtaking speed of 403.978 kph (251.032 mph).

This brought the C 111 era to a close. It had proved an extremely valuable period from which a wealth of data and facts had been gathered. This series of tests had been in many respects far ahead of its time. Arising out of this, all that was applicable to ordinary road vehicles was adopted on the Daimler-Benz production lines.

A 50 000 KILOMETRE TEST

The summer of 1983 saw another Daimler-Benz test team at the Nardo test track, accompanied by three Mercedes 190 E 2.3–16 production cars. This was the sporting variant of the 190 series that had been introduced already, and the trial was intended to prove, in the most spectacular fashion possible, the model's reliability. The test agenda called for a *tour de force*, for the vehicles were to be driven the equivalent of more than once around the circumference of the earth – 50 000 kilometres – at full speed.

The distance was achieved in exactly 201 hours, 39 minutes and 43 seconds, with two of the cars showing no technical problems whatsoever. Even the third car broke only its distributor rotor arm – a minor part – which led to a three-hour long enforced break. Since regulations state that no new parts may be used during a record-breaking run, two rotor arms were sawn apart and a replacement unit glued together from their parts. After this bit of ingenuity, it was full steam ahead, this incident providing the only excitement for the mechanics – if you do not count the tension during the 240 pit stops for supplies. The results were something to be proud of:

Average speeds

World records:

247.5 kph	25 000 km
247.7 kph	25 000 miles
247.9 kph	50 000 km

International class records:

247.0 kph	1000 km
246.9 kph	1000 miles
246.9 kph	5000 km
246.7 kph	5000 miles
246.8 kph	10 000 km
246.8 kph	10 000 miles
246.7 kph	6 hours
246.6 kph	12 hours
246.7 kph	24 hours

You could not have wished for better proof that the 2.3–16 was ready for production; it has formed part of Daimler-Benz's product range since the summer of 1984 (albeit now enlarged to 2.5 litres). Meanwhile, with the help of the French tuning company 'Snobeck Racing Service', the car has developed into a piece of sporting equipment with a remarkable success rate.

Thus we come to the end of a brief history of record-breaking by Daimler-Benz. We have learnt about the significance of striving for records and how this has changed throughout the years. If the first record-breakers were struggling to reach a set goal, a certain amount of nationalist thinking came in during the period between the two wars. In both eras, though, the setting up of records was down to individuals and their cars, specially prepared for that purpose. Today, record attempts are a matter of teams of drivers and it is not just the figures reached which constitute success. Much more important is the sum total of experience gained and the influence it will have on the development of production cars.

Above: Prince Heinrich of Prussia, brother of Germany's Kaiser Wilhelm II, was an automobile pioneer. He not only instituted the Prince Heinrich rallies, generally acknowledged as the start of rallying as a sport, but also originated the idea of windscreen-wipers. Here Prince Heinrich is at the wheel of a Benz-Tourer at the Herkomer Rally in 1906.

Above and opposite (bottom): The French Grand Prix is still called the 'Grand Prix of Grand Prix' today, and on 4 July 1914 in Lyon it ended in a triple triumph for Mercedes. After 20 laps, a total of 752.6 km, Christian Lautenschlager came in first in a time of 7:08:18 followed by the Frenchman Louis Wagner and Otto Salzer, both driving Mercedes. The victorious Mercedes team had a 4.5 litre four cylinder ohc engine which achieved 115 bhp.

Otto Salzer is shown above, while opposite Louis Wagner works in the pits with his co-driving mechanic.

Opposite (top): A Mercedes Racer which was similar to the '1914' winning car was sold under mysterious circumstances for $6 000 to the American racing driver Ralph de Palma who in 1915 – whilst Germany was already at war – won the Indianapolis 500 in it.

Overleaf: Mercedes appeared for the first time after the war, at the 1922 Targa Florio, with an 'army of technicians' as a contemporary source put it. Seven cars from Untertürkheim rolled out for the start, amongst them the Italian, Count Guilio Masetti in his private pre-war 'Lyon' Mercedes. Masetti (our photo) won with an average speed of 63.09 kph.

122

Ralph De Palma, Winner - 1915

Above: Rudolf Caracciola driving through the village of Capelle, near Pescara, in his W 154 on his way to winning the 1938 Coppa Acerbo (Italy).

Opposite (top): Hermann Lang in the pits for refuelling and a wheel change during the 1937 German Grand Prix. Rudolph Caracciola won the race.

Opposite (bottom): Engine of Type W 165 (1939), the first V8 engine of Daimler-Benz.

Technical data: The small 8 cylinders of the W 165 'Tripolis' had a capacity of 1 492 cc, 254 bhp output at 8 000 rpm, maximum speed 273 kph.

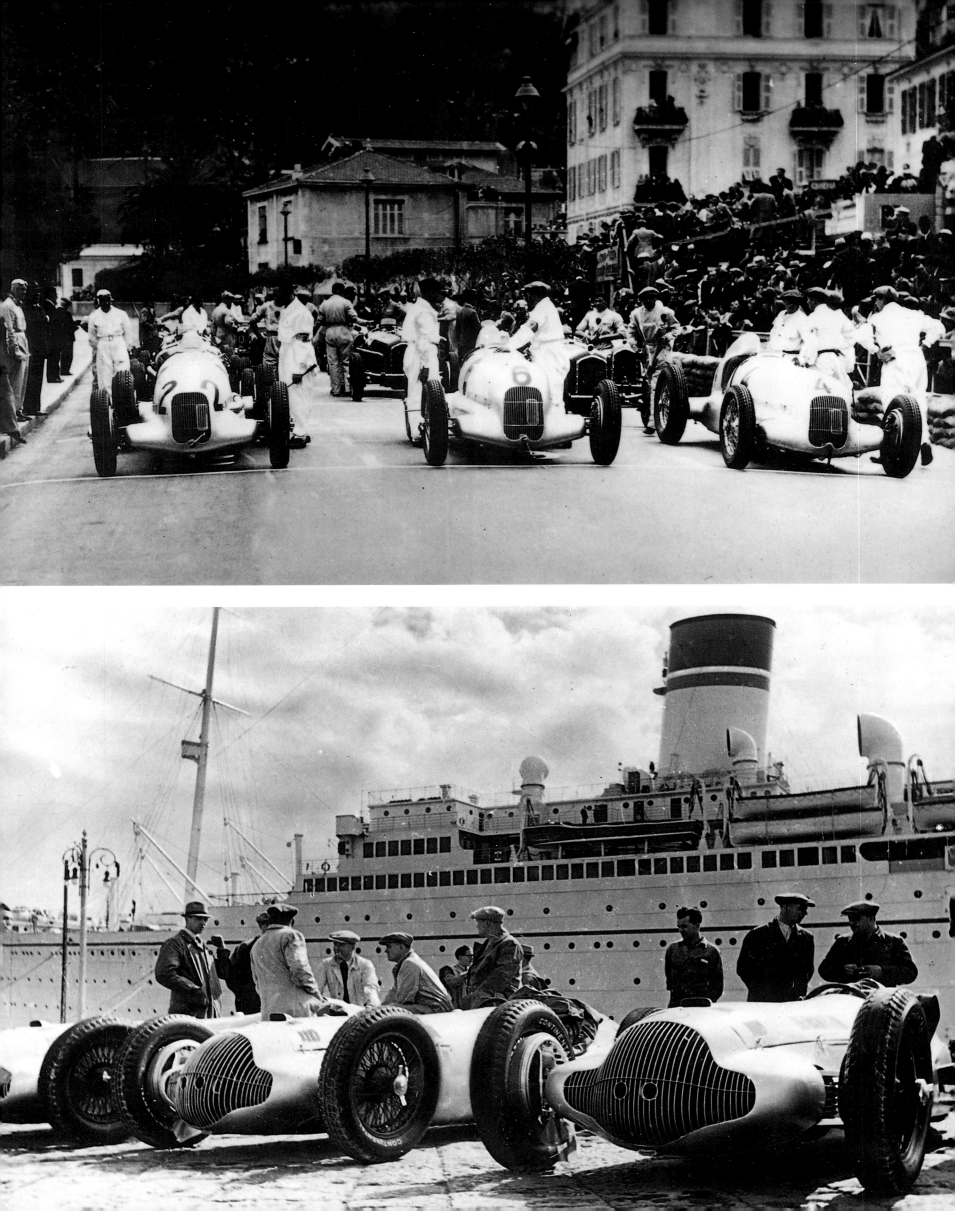

Opposite (top): Rudolf Caracciola became European champion in 1935 driving a Mercedes during the second year of the 750 kg formula. However, at the Monaco Grand Prix which Mercedes-Benz entered for the first time with its Silver Arrow, it was Luigi Fagioli who came first in his Mercedes-Benz with an average speed of 93.6 kph, which, at the time, was a new track record. The picture shows the start of the race.

Opposite (bottom): Races have been held since 1925 at the Mellaha track in the blazing heat of Tripoli (Libya). Between 1935 and 1939 Mercedes-Benz Silver Arrows won every race: in 1935 with Rudolf Caracciola (with an average speed of 198 kph); 1936 Hermann Lang (216.3 kph); 1937 Hermann Lang (212.5 kph); 1938 Hermann Lang (205.1 kph); and in 1939 with Hermann Lang in the 1.5 litre voiturette class (Mercedes-Benz W 165), with an average speed of 197.72 kph. The picture shows the Silver Arrows shortly before being loaded for Tripoli.

Above: Mercedes-Benz Formula Racing Car W 125 1937. Hermann Lang, one of the most successful drivers of the Silberpfeile ('Silver Arrow'), at an 'oldtimer' race at the old Nürburgring. The W 125 was the last representative of the 750 kg formula generation – one of the all-time great supercharged cars. In the one and only year it was in service it put Mercedes-Benz drivers on to the winner's rostrum no less than 27 times.

Technical data: 8 cylinders, 5 663 cc capacity, 646 bhp output at 5 800 rpm, maximum speed 330 kph.

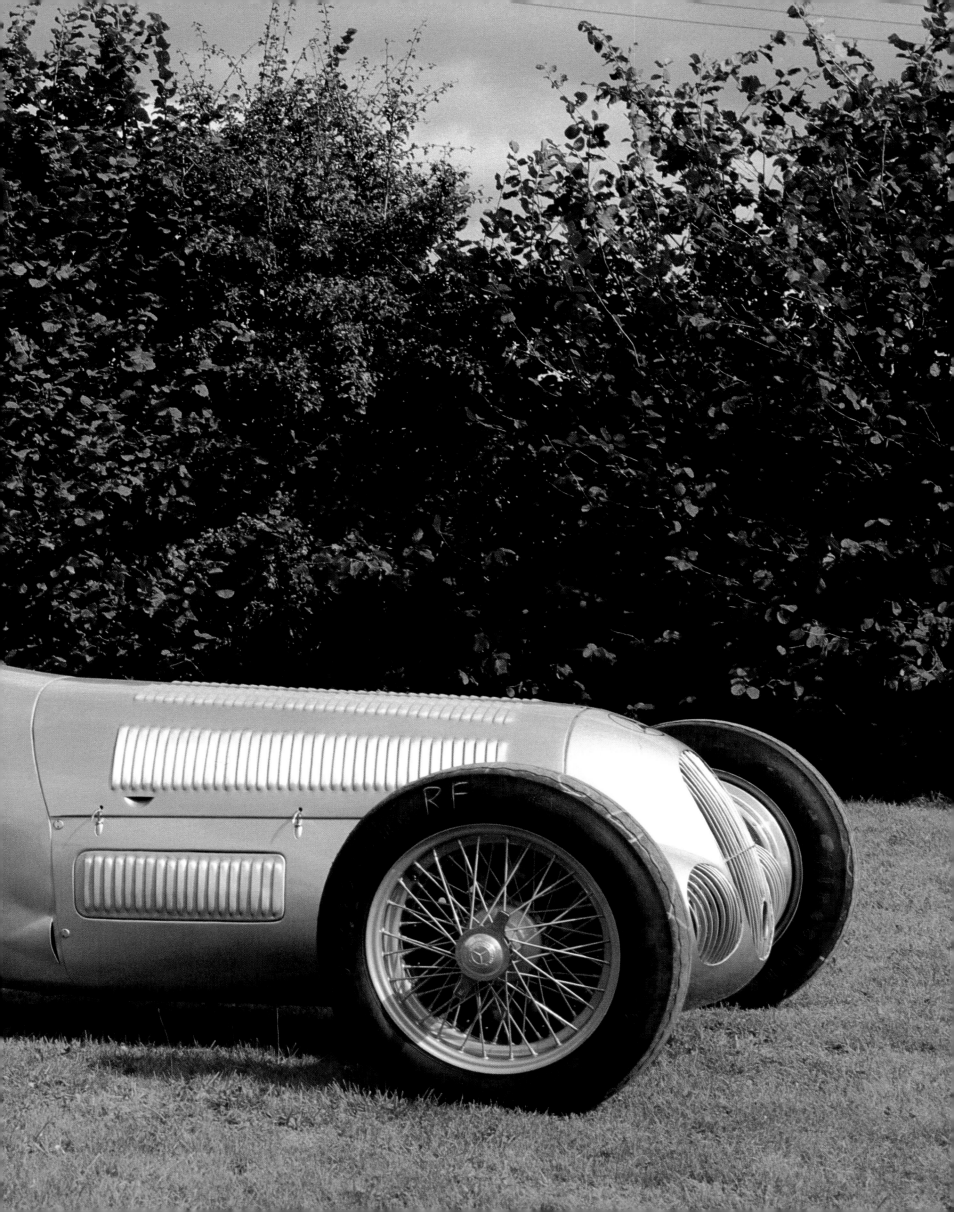

Pages 130-131: Mercedes-Benz Formula Racing Car W 154 1939 at a post-war 'oldtimer' race at the Nürburgring. The new racing formula introduced in 1938 limited the capacity of supercharged engines to 3 litres. The racer developed to match this, the W 154 being based on many years' experience with the W 25 and W 125 – both Silver Arrows accustomed to winning. Mercedes-Benz won six important international races in 1939 with the W 154, including the German Grand Prix at the Nürburgring (Caracciola).

Technical data: 12 cylinders, 2 962 cc capacity, 485 bhp output at 7 800 rpm, maximum speed 315 kph.

Pages 132-133: The W 125 1937, the crowning glory of the 750 kg formula. The car was said to be the most powerful and most impressive Grand Prix car ever to race on the courses of the world. It was not until 30 years later that its power potential was surpassed, by the 3 litre Formula 1 car of 1966 to 1969.

Previous page: The 'cockpit' and the left front wheel of a Mercedes-Benz Formula racing car W 154 1939.

Above: Hermann Lang in a W 154 at a 1986 'oldtimer' race at the Nürburgring, bringing back memories of the glorious pre-war successes of the Silver Arrows.

INGO SEIFF

95 Years of Racing

Seven years after launching the first Benz and Daimler motor cars, the editor of the Paris newspaper *Petit Journal* thought it time to test the horseless carriages for reliability. In the midst of the festive Christmas season, he announced to his readers: Our newspaper has decided to further this new and revolutionary form of horseless transportation. With this in mind our paper is offering a competiton . . . '.

The trip was to cover the route Paris–Rouen and to take place on 22 July 1894. The list of entries included 102 vehicles, many of which still existed only on paper and had not passed the design stage. They claimed to have the most extraordinary constructions: there were the 'gravitation-cars', the 'pneumatic-cars' and the 'lever-cars'. After a strict selection procedure only twenty-one vehicles were accepted.

On the morning of 22 July 1894, they gathered at the Boulevard Maillot in Paris for the 126 km (78.30-mile) Reliability Trial. The Trial was not just for fame and glory, but a prize of 5000 francs for the winning car,

which also had to be the fastest and 'least dangerous' car, as well as being 'easy to handle' and 'not too expensive to run'. The time limit for completing the 126 km was 12 hours.

It is worth noting that only petrol and steam-driven vehicles took part in the race. At intervals of 30 seconds the cars began the race to Rouen, breaking for lunch in Nantes. The enormous steamer of the Comte de Dion had taken the lead immediately in Paris, and was the first to reach Rouen. The steamer took only 5 hours and 35 minutes to complete the distance, but the Comte was not in luck. His vehicle did not meet the competition's other requirements: it was neither easy to handle nor to manoeuvre; it weighed 2 tons and required 800 litres of water, and apart from the driver it also had to carry a stoker. The protest placed by the drivers of petrol-driven vehicles was accepted and the De Dion steamer was downgraded to second place. A Panhard & Levassor and a Peugeot, both powered by Daimler engines, were declared joint winners.

This could be called the first joint venture in the history of the automobile. Altogether there had been five Panhards and five Peugeots, under the auspices of Gottlieb Daimler and his son Paul, in the race from Paris. A new carburettor developed by Wilhelm Maybach had helped to give the winning French cars more power. Although Karl Benz was not at all convinced about the value of these Reliability Trials, he had made available the Benz Viktoria to his French agent Emile Roger. It took fourteenth place.

Although the main aim of these Reliability Trials was to cross the finishing line, the success of Daimler and Benz's petrol-driven cars created a sensation in France. The specialist magazine *Le Génie Civil* wrote 'The Paris–Rouen Trial has attracted the interest of the general public to vehicles powered by combustion engines like a beat on a kettle-drum. If the motor car is properly and sensibly used, it will transform our entire transport system and our mobility.'

The world's first real motor race, which took place on 11–13 June 1895 and covered a distance of 1200 km (746 miles), electrified motor-sport enthusiasts. The gruelling race began at the Place d'Armes in Versailles, passing through the valley of Chevreuse via Limours, Etampes, Orléans and Tours and then on the Route Nationale 10 to Bordeaux and back to Paris. Emile Levassor entered his two-seater, powered by a new Daimler engine. This was a two-cylinder, in-line engine that was even more powerful than and lighter than the previous V2 engine. It weighed only 80 kg (176.4 lb) and with a cylinder capacity of 2400 cc it produced 4 bhp at 800 rpm.

The rules stated that the distance had to be driven 'in one stretch' and 'as quickly as possible'. Levassor's car, using the new Daimler engine, had a pedal-operated friction clutch and a gearbox which he described thus '*C'est brutal, mais ça marche!*' (Crude, but it works!). Emile Levassor was the first to reach Paris on 13 June 1895, after driving for 48 hours and 47 minutes and maintaining an average speed of 24 kph (14.9 mph). Although he won the race, since his car was only a two-seater and the race was for four-seaters, he was downgraded to third place, and the two Peugeots that had reached Paris 6 and 9 hours later, were awarded first and second place. Mean-

while, Daimler could point triumphantly to the fact that it had supplied extremely reliable power units to the Frenchmen Levassor and Peugeot. Despite his 'defeat' Levassor was very pleased; he had wanted to prove that already, in 1895, motor vehicles powered by combustion engines were capable of withstanding the strain of such a trial.

Another Peugeot, *L'Eclair*, took part in the race piloted by the brothers André and Edouard Michelin. During the long-distance race they tested pneumatic tyres for the first time. They had fifty punctures, including twenty-two resulting from worn inner tubes, and abandoned the race after 90 hours. Emile Levassor, who usually had a sixth sense for everything innovative, himself did not see any future for air-filled tyres . . . .

'CITY RACES'

These first motor-sport competitions could not have taken place had it not been for the Daimler engines.

The long-distance Paris–Bordeaux-Paris race in 1895 heralded the beginning of a series of 'city races'. Chroniclers refer to thirty-five races held between 1895 and 1903. The most important of these started in Paris – the Paris–Marseille–Paris race, in which a Panhard & Levassor using a four-cylinder engine and having a power output of 8 bhp competed for the first time in 1896. Unfortunately, the racing pioneer Emile Levassor had a terrible accident, which resulted in his death a year later. Gottlieb Daimler had now lost his most important and influential business partner.

Other important city races were the Paris–Amsterdam–Paris (1898), Paris–Bordeaux (1899), Paris–Toulouse–Paris (1900), Paris–Berlin (1901) and Paris–Vienna (1902). Frequently, the winning motor cars were powered by Daimler engines, and in the 1899 Paris–Bordeaux race, the first five home had Daimler engines.

The roots of motor racing were really established during this decade, aided particularly by the organizing ability of the French who ushered in the new sport. In 1896, they set up the Automobile Club de France (ACF).

Benz did not think much of motor racing, even though his cars, which had a reputation for reliability, would have had a good chance. His French agent, Emile Roger, took part in the Paris–Rouen Reliability Trial in 1894 and the American Oscar Mueller came second in the first American motor race in 1895. The Chicago–Evaston–Chicago race, organized by the *Chicago Times Herald*, covered a distance of 54 miles. Only two cars reached the finishing line, a Benz and a vehicle designed by Frank Duryea. Six cars registered for the race, including two electro-cars.

In 1897, two Benz motor cars participated in the Marseille–Nice–La Turbie race, but to no avail. Meanwhile, other brand names had considerably improved the reliability of their cars. Fritz Held, who entered his 12 bhp Benz racing model, was successful in the German race Berlin–Leipzig. But after this event, news about Benz's racing successes died down.

At the turn of the century, Emil Jellinek struggling for a more powerful Daimler racing car was successful. The arrival of the first Mercedes car signposted a new era in the development of the car and motor racing.

The turbulent development of motor racing had a significant effect on automobile manufacturers who had to design more competitive engines every year. Instead of looking for ways to obtain maximum performance, they concerned themselves mainly with the design of larger, and therefore more powerful engines. By contrast, Maybach, in the Daimler tradition, pursued the concept of maximum power in the minimum space.

JAMES GORDON BENNETT

It was not just the Mercedes that changed the course of motor racing, but also the American publisher (*New York Herald*) James Gordon Bennett, who lived in Paris. It was he who finally ended the long-running dispute among racing drivers: which nation could build the best and fastest cars.

Above all, Gordon Bennett wanted racing drivers – often extravagant individuals – and manufacturers to become accustomed to regulations. So he decided that future international racing events should be held on a more professional and sporting basis. He announced a competition in which national teams, comprising three cars, would compete against one another. The legendary Gordon Bennett agreed to draw up the rules in association with the Automobile Club de France (ACF) and the race was announced internationally. Each country could register up to three cars; which were to have an empty weight of between 400 and 1000 kg (881.84 and 2204.6 lb); at least two drivers were to sit next to each other and to have an average weight of 60 kg (132.28 lb) – otherwise additional weights had to be added to compensate for any difference; all the cars' components had to be produced in the country of origin; the distance of the race was to be drawn between 550 km and a maximum of 650 km (341 and 404 miles); and the club or the country that won was to organize the next race for the following year. The Gordon Bennett races, having their own formula and being excellently organized, were the first serious motor-sport events in the recent history of the car.

The third Gordon Bennett race in 1902 was won by the English driver Selwyn Francis Edge in a Napier, so Great Britain had to organize the event in 1903. For safety reasons a closed circuit was chosen for the first time, near Dublin in Ireland. This was the first big motor racing event held in the British Isles, and was only possible after a special act of Parliament permitted the race to take place on public roads.

Each participating nation was gripped by enthusiasm and a competitive urge to win. France wanted to repeat its 1901 success and to regain the cup, while Great Britain intended to win with a Napier as it had the previous year. Mercedes, however were favourites.

Then a devastating fire in the assembly hall between 9 and 10 June 1903 destroyed the Cannstatt Daimler works and all the 90 hp Mercedes that were to take part in the race. Daimler had to act quickly. The American Gray Dinsmore, who lived in Paris, made his 60 hp Mercedes touring car available, as did Maybach, though his car had to be fitted with a temporary racing chassis. A third touring car was requisitioned from the Riviera.

The 1000 kg (2205 lb) weight restriction meant some quick modifications had to be carried out, but the Germans' efforts were rewarded. The Belgian driver Camille Jenatzy won the race in a 60 hp Mercedes. He was 11 minutes ahead of de Knyff's Panhard, and maintained an average speed of 89.18 kph (55.38 mph).

This was the first significant Mercedes victory, but the marque soon clocked up further wins, and the American millionaire W.K. Vanderbilt, in a 90 hp Mercedes, set seven American records. The highest average speed was 148.5 kph (92.28 mph). In 1906, a 40 hp Mercedes driven by Fritz Erle, won the Heidelberg–Königsstuhl mountain race. One year later, Erle won the third Herkomer race in a Benz. (The Herkomer races consisted of reliability trials initiated by a German professor of art). These races marked the beginning of motor rallies.

FRENCH GRAND PRIX

At this time, Mercedes was far more successful than its opponent, Benz. The third Grand Prix of the ACF in 1908 in Dieppe, especially, was a great triumph for Mercedes. The first GP had been won in 1906 by the Hungarian driver Franz Szizs, driving a Renault, and the second GP by Felice Nazzaro, who won in a Fiat. Mercedes had spared no efforts in preparing itself for the 1908 GP, as a victory at the French Grand Prix was then considered to be the pinnacle of motor racing. The circuit was a dusty, stony, dirt track, 77 km (47.85 miles) long. Christian Lautenschlager won in a 135 bhp Mercedes, which produced a maximum of 1600 rpm and had a swept volume of 12.8 litres, distributed over four cylinders each the size of a milk churn. During the gruelling race he maintained an average speed of 111.1 kph (69.04 mph).

But 1908 also brought a sensational victory for Benz, when Victor Héméry won the 438-mile race from St Petersburg to Moscow driven on indescribably muddy roads. In the French GP, Lautenschlager had won ahead of Héméry, who had had a puncture and also suffered an eye injury from an airborne stone, while the Prinz Heinrich race, initiated by the eldest brother of the German Kaiser and held in the same year, was won by Erle in a 50 bhp Benz. At the Florida meeting in 1909, the Americans David Bruce-Brown and George Roberts established three world speed records in a 150 bhp Benz. The top average speed was 184.0 kph (114.34 mph).

At the end of 1909 a Benz 'monster' appeared, creating a great stir. This was the 'Blitzen-Benz', a four-cylinder, 200 bhp engine which had a cylinder capacity of 21 904 cc. One year later, the American champion Barney Oldfield, who drove around America with a motor-car circus, set an American record for the standing mile: his Blitzen-Benz taking just 40.5 seconds (see The 'Silver Arrows'). At the US GP, on a 668 km (415.10 mile) track in the Savannah, two 150 bhp Benzes were successful. Bruce-Brown and Héméry took first and second place respectively.

BROOKLANDS AND INDIANAPOLIS

Meanwhile, racing tracks were now being purpose-built, and this opened up new avenues for the sport. In 1907, the Brooklands track in South-West London was opened, and two years later came the 'brick-oval' of Indianapolis. The Brooklands circuit became a test and development centre for racing and touring cars. In 1909, Victor Héméry set a number of new world records for the standing start and flying-start half-mile and mile, covering the half-mile in 205.8 kph (127.88 mph), and the kilometre in 207.7 kph (129.06 mph), the latter being a new world land speed record. Mercedes triumphed again in 1915, when Ralph de Palma won the fifth 500-mile race in Indianapolis. He was in fact very lucky to get his car to Indianapolis before the outbreak of World War I in Europe.

Before the war, innumerable races had been held each year, but one stood out: the ACF GP at Lyon in 1914, where Mercedes took the first three places. While this victory was a triumph for Germany, it was a national catastrophy for France.

Even in 1916, when Great Britain and Germany were fighting the battle of the Skagerrak, Palma was driving his Mercedes in races around the US, winning in Kansas City and Omaha, but losing in Chicago.

Only a year after World War One had ended, international motor racing was set in train again. The 500-mile race in Indianapolis was won in 1919 by Howard Wilcox driving a Peugeot. In the same year, a young driver appeared in an Italian CMN, at the Targa Florio. His name was Enzo Ferrari and he was to become the most legendary figure in international motor racing.

In 1921, Daimler took up racing again for the first time since the war. Max Sailer took second place in the Targa Florio, driving his six-cylinder 7250 cc Mercedes which developed 95 hp. Italian drivers Ferdinand Minoia and Count Masetti were also successful that year. They won the Italian Alpine Cup and the Italian GP in Brescia respectively in their Mercedes, a car which had, in fact, been built before the war.

The early twenties saw more innovative engine design and the arrival of the supercharger. This 'respiration system', based on the superchargers that had been used in aircraft engines during World War One, increased the performance of the engine. The onset of the supercharger era was speeded up by the new Grand Prix formula that operated between 1922 and 1925 and restricted swept volumes to 2 litres.

Mercedes and Fiat became the forerunners in the construction of supercharged engines. In 1922, Mercedes successfully presented its range of four-cylinder engines which had swept volumes from 1.5 to 2 litres. Paul Daimler was responsible for these. When Dr Ferdinand Porsche joined the Daimler Motoren GmbH as head engineer in 1923, he devoted himself to perfecting this engine concept.

At the Targa Florio in 1922, Mercedes was represented by seven cars from three different series. They entered two pre-war 4.5-litre engines for Lautenschlager and Salzer, plus Masetti's privately owned example, blown 28/95s for Sailer and Christian Werner, and a pair of new 1.5-litre supercharged four-cylinder machines for Scheef and Minoia. The latter had dohc engines said to generate 80 bhp at the limit, but their chassis design was indifferent, and they came only twentieth in the race and third in their class. As for the others, Masetti won outright at 63.09 kph (39.2 mph), Sailer was sixth, Werner eighth and Lautenschlager tenth. The regulations of the new GP formula made it relatively straightforward for the engineers. Apart from the limited cylinder capacity, racing cars had to be designed as two-seaters, and had to weigh not less than 650 kg (1432.99 lb).

In 1923, Daimler sent three supercharged four-cylinder Mercedes to Indianapolis. The 2-litre cars had a power output of 120 bhp – a quite remarkable 60 bhp per litre. It became apparent in the 'Indy' however that the American racing car designers had learnt even more. The Millers, Duesenbergs and Chevrolets dominated the scene while the sixteen-valve Mercedes floundered. Max Sailer and Christian Werner finished eighth and eleventh respectively.

One year later, in 1924, Ferdinand Porsche entered three supercharged Mercedes for the Targa Florio; the drivers were Alfred Neubauer (who later became the famous Mercedes-Benz racing team leader), Christian Werner and the old champion Christian Lautenschlager. Under the auspices of Porsche, Christian Werner won the Targa Florio race on 27 April 1924, in a record time: he covered a distance of 432 km (268.45 miles) in a time of 6:32:37 hours, and at an average speed of 66 kph (41.02 mph). Neubauer came fifth and Lautenschlager tenth. Stuttgart was jubilant, and the 'Technische Hochschule' awarded a doctorate *honoris causa* to Ferdinand Porsche. But despite this success, the supercharged 2-litre car was still not considered satisfactory.

THE BENZ 'TROPFENWAGEN'

Although Mercedes was more involved in racing activities than Benz during the early twenties, a very unusual Benz racing car emerged and was entered for the Monza GP in 1923 driven by Ferdinand Minoia. It took fourth place. This was the streamlined Benz *Tropfenwagen*, constructed to the design of Edmund Rumpler in Mannheim in 1922. The power output of the six-cylinder suction engine had been increased to 90 bhp. The car was particularly interesting because of its dohc engine, mounted between the cockpit and the rear axle – the first mid-engined layout so far in the history of the car. Furthermore, the Benz had an unusual streamlined drop shape, and used a rear swing axle – all other cars at that time used rigid axles. The mid-engined concept was not taken up by Auto Union until one decade later.

The '20s were the era of the supercharger. Although there were set-backs, engineers were convinced that the future of racing lay with this type of engine. Ferdinand

Porsche decided to enter the supercharged eight-cylinder Mercedes at the Italian GP in 1924. The 2-litre engine had a power output of 170 bhp and it could spin to 7000 rpm – then considered to be very high. The car's handling, however, was extremely tricky, and the chassis did not meet the requirements of the fast Monza track, resulting in the withdrawal of all four Mercedes.

This misfortune was overshadowed by the tragic death of the Mercedes driver Count Louis Zborowski, whose car crashed into a tree. He had become well known for his various 'Chitty-Chitty-Bang-Bangs'. The Chitty-Chitty-Bang-Bangs were built at Higham, his home near Canterbury in Kent, for the express purpose of taking part in the fastest Brooklands handicap races and for long-distance touring. The recipe of Count Zborowski was to install World War One aviation engines in high-geared, pre-war chain-drive chassis. The car called Chitty I appeared in 1921.

After Mercedes' failure at Monza in 1924, the eight-cylinder car was not entered for any more GP races. It was, however, converted into a two-seater and was successful in many sports-car races. At the sports car GP of Germany, held at the AVUS in 1926, the young Rudolf Caracciola finished first in a supercharged eight-cylinder. The supercharged four-cylinder engines were also very successful.

THE 'S'

In 1926, the German motor-car industry took on a new complexion: Daimler and Benz merged, and they built a radical, large six-cylinder engine. In 1927 Ferdinand Porsche designed the Type 26/120/180 bhp which was also called the 'S'. Its engine had an overhead camshaft, operated via a vertical shaft. This supercharged sports car was based on a touring car, and between 1927 and 1931 four variants were developed.

Although only 300 or so S-series cars were built (146 of the S, 112 of the SS, thirty-three of the SSK and five or six of the SSKL), they were remarkably successful in international motor-racing. In 1927 Rudolf Caracciola, in his four-seater, won the opening race at the Nürburgring, and Otto Merz came first in his S at the German

GP, at the same venue. During the subsequent year Caracciola and Werner won the German GP in the SS; in 1929, Caracciola won the Tourist Trophy in Belfast driving an SS; in 1930, he won the Irish GP and in 1931, the German GP, both times in an SSK. That was the year the SSKL was introduced, and Caracciola, assisted by Sebastian, immediately won the Mille Miglia. 'Carratch', as he was called affectionately by his fans, also won the Eifel race in 1931, the German GP and the AVUS race. At the Spa 24-hour race in 1931, Prince Djordzadze and G. Zehender won in the SSK. They dominated mountain racing, winning also the European mountain championship, and achieving records at the Mont Ventoux and the British Shelsley Walsh mountain race. And at the wheel of the streamlined SSKL, Manfred von Brauchitsch won the AVUS race in 1932. In so doing, however, they concealed the fact that the weight of the SSKL was too great for the car to be really competitive any longer.

In *The History of the World's Racing Cars*, the authors Richard Hough and Michael Frostick introduce the era 1931–3 with the heading: *Fascist Conquest – Nazi Challenge*. This was because the dictators Benito Mussolini (in power since 1925 in Italy) and Adolf Hitler considered motor racing an ideal medium through which to arouse national enthusiasm and convert it into national prestige. Law and order was not only restricting citizens' democratic freedom, but also regulating Formula one. There are some Italian automobile historians who believe that Alfa Romeo's return to GP racing was also as a result of Mussolini's efforts. The creation of Alfa-Romeo's Type 8C and Type A had, to a certain degree, become a political issue.

When Hitler came to power in 1933, the new 750-kg formula was already in preparation and was to become popular from 1934 until 1937. The 'Silver Arrows' made by Mercedes-Benz and the 'Silver Fishes' from Auto Union, ushered in a new era in GP racing. From the outset, the Mercedes-Benz cars were more reliable than those of Auto Union and fascinated motor-racing fans all over the world. The two-volume edition of *100 Jahre Daimler-Benz* describes the arrival of the Silver Arrows: 'The new cars with the Mercedes star changed the very scene at racing tracks. Even the British magazine *Motor*, known for its cool understatement, could not conceal its enthusiasm: "The aerodynamic chassis, the dreadful noise from the exhaust and the roar of the supercharger, as well as the impressive acceleration came as a great surprise to the entire world." Daimler-Benz's approach to taking part in motor-racing had changed and was new. Motor-racing had become a science. Strategy and tactics were as important for a victory as the technical potential of a racing car, and the ability of the driver. The wheel change and re-fuelling during the race had been practised until both jobs could be done by three mechanics in 30 seconds, provided that the drivers could stop their cars exactly at the marked place and switch off the engine. Although they still had the most difficult part to play, the lonely drivers had become just the final link in a chain. "Racing successes", said head engineer Nallinger, "consist of ninety-five per cent preparation and five per cent luck."'

THE 'SILVER ARROWS' RETURN

After World War II, the Daimler-Benz plant in Stuttgart-Untertürkheim lay in ruins. No-one thought the Silver Arrows would compete again, although the old racing team, headed by Alfred Neubauer, did not completely abandon hope. The most successful pre-war champion, Rudolf Caracciola, who survived the war in Lugano, was still suffering from the effects of racing accidents, but his passion for motor-racing took hold again in 1946, and he was registered for the 1946 Indianapolis race. What car should he use? Alfred Neubauer wrote in his memoirs, *Männer, Frauen und Motoren* ('Men, Women and Engines'), that two Voiturettes (1.5-litre 'Tripolis') had been taken into Switzerland before the war, to protect them from bombs, fire and the Allies. They had hardly been put into storage at Daimler-Benz's Zürich subsidiary when the Swiss authorities confiscated them.

Caracciola remembered these two cars when he made his Indianapolis plans. Together with his mechanic, Walz, he began the 'reactivation' of the Silver Arrows, and one morning the citizens of Zürich were awoken by the high-pitched noise of the roaring supercharger. The Silver Arrows were running again and ready for 'Indy'.

However, the Allied Control Commission, which administered confiscated German property, opposed the plan. One year after the war, Great Britain vetoed the return of the Silver Arrows to Indianapolis. They had no real objection to Caracciola, but a Mercedes entry was simply too much. The American Joel Thorne lent Caracciola his 'Thorne Special' to drive, but the post-war debut of the German driver ended in disaster. During training he had a serious accident, and not until 1952 did he regain enough confidence to take part in the Mille Miglia, where he came fourth.

Despite the efforts of the British, the first years of the post-war period did see a Silver Arrow at Indianapolis. In 1947, via a secret and circuitous route, a 3-litre Type W 154-M 163 racing car, built in 1939, reached the circuit and rolled to the start, driven by Duke Nalon. The private American driver fought his way through to fourth place, when engine failure forced him to abandon the race. The same thing happened one year later to Chet Miller in the same car.

In 1950, Alfred Neubauer was appointed head of the new motor-racing department. Of the situation at that time, he said: 'In Unterturkheim there were still two old, tame Mercedes racing cars of the 3-litre formula, built in 1939. These cars were quite rattly, and it would not be possible to build up a racing department around them. In a Berlin scrapyard another two cars of the same type were discovered. It cost us a new Mercedes 170V. An "old for new" deal was agreed. Of the four old cars we fixed up two models for racing and one for training.'

THE ARGENTINIAN GRAND PRIX

Daimler-Benz wanted to take three Silver Arrows to the Argentinian Grand Prix in 1951. The drivers selected were Hermann Lang, Rudolf Caracciola and Manfred von Brauchitsch, but the latter's political escapades lost him his place in the team, and former service engineer, Karl Kling, stepped in. In the end, 'Carratch', too, had to be replaced, due to illness. Thus, Juan Manuel Fangio was lured away from Alfa Romeo. The pre-war cars from Unterturkheim suffered from the fact that they lacked the latest technological developments: twice, José Gonzales won at Argentina in a Ferrari, joining the international league of top drivers. The aged Silver Arrows twice took second and third place, and afterwards the cars, their heyday over, were ready for the museum.

Mercedes-Benz returned seriously to international competitions in 1952. The 300SL sports car, whose six-cylinder engine had been derived from the limousine, competed on the most important tracks in the world.

Two years later, the Daimler-Benz board of directors decided that the team should participate in a new GP formula for 2.5-litre un-supercharged engines or supercharged 0.75-litre engines, of unlimited weight. The minimum distance for the Grand Prix was set at 500 km (310.7 miles) or three hours. The Argentine driver Juan Manuel Fangio, who became world-famous for his skills, won the world championship in 1954 and 1955 in the eight-cylinder, un-supercharged-engined W196 from Stuttgart.

In 1955, the Untertürkheim engineers came up with a model that left the competition standing. It was the 300SLR racing car, directly derived from the W196. The new car bore some of the technical characteristics of the formula racing cars, but on account of its swept volume of 3 litres and its eight-cylinder engine it belonged to the family of free-formula sports cars.

Daimler-Benz's withdrawal from active motor racing in 1955 was a blow to many enthusiasts, but the company did not abandon racing altogether. After having retreated from formula racing, it entered touring and sports cars for international long-distance races and reliability trials. Such rallies had for many years been overshadowed by the Grand Prix races but, while speed is not the most important thing, they are valid tests of endurance for drivers and cars alike.

From 1955, Daimler-Benz was greatly involved in international rally sport. The Mercedes-Benz vehicles were derived from production cars and were modified only according to the regulations. Mercedes teams were present at all the most hazardous and prestigious rallies: in 1956, Schock/Moll won the European championship of touring cars; coming second in Monte Carlo in a Type 220, winning the Acropolis in a 300SL, winning at Sestrière and coming tenth at Geneva in a 300SL. In 1957, the marque notched up victories in sixty rallies and

long-distance reliability trials, including a win by Andrés-Portolés in a 300SL at the fifth Rally Around Spain, victory at the 1694 km (1052.65 miles) Caracas–Cumana–Caracas race, and triumph for Paul O'Shea in the American Sports Car Championship in the same car.

During the '60s, the company entered the 220SE, the 300SE and the 230SL at rallies as well as at touring car races. In 1977, the 280SE was used for the 30 000 km (18 642 miles) London–Sydney Marathon in which Mercedes gained a double victory. In 1979, Daimler-Benz entered the 450SLC for various championship-rallies.

The marque's motor-sport activities today continue with the 190E 2.5-16 which competes in Group A of the German touring car championship and is proving a great success for the company. In this car, the four-valve concept, developed for racing-car engines, has been developed to today's technical standards. A mass-produced car had been created that has the type of performance reserved for racing cars a decade ago. Five teams participated officially at the German touring championship with the assistance of the company. While Johnny Cecotto (4) and Dany Snobeck (2) achieved six individual victories in eleven competitions, and Roland Asch of the BMK-team was runner-up, Daimler-Benz presented its 'bigger brother', the Mercedes-Benz 190 E 2.5–16, as early as August 1988. This was by no means the end of the development. Mercedes-Benz AG wanted to be particulary competitive in the challenging German touring car championship, and so the evolution of the Mercedes-Benz 190 E 2.5–16 followed naturally. Larger wheels, modified front and rear spoilers, mudguards and the enlargement of the wheel track as well as the lower bodywork underline the differences with the previous model. By comparison with the standard 190 E 2.5–16 the absorption is more tightly defined. The shortstroke powerplant has great potential. For the racing model the Mercedes-technicians believe that they can achieve an output of 315–320 hp (so far they have reached nearly 300 hp) and a more favourable flow of the torque.

Nevertheless, no German model takes part in Formula One racing: a thorn in the side for many German motor sport enthusiasts. Will the successful participation of the Sauber-Mercedes in the sports car world championship (Group C) be enough to compensate for this? Formula One fans can be glad however, that Mercedes-Benz AG have intensified the successful collaboration with the design and construction teams of Peter Sauber in Hinwil near Zürich. At each event two Sauber-Mercedes C9s started the competition for the sports-prototype world championship in 1989.

After the 5-litre, V8-engined Sauber-Mercedes C9 from Untertürkheim had become one of the most successful group C sportscars of 1988, the head of the team, Peter Sauber, set his sights even higher. Results from 1988 were already impressive: winner at the 'Super-cup' with Jeans-Louis Schlesser, runner-up in the sports-prototype championship, five victories in ten starts for Jean-Louis Schlesser, Mauro Baldi and Jochen Mass.

The power plant of the Sauber-Mercedes C9 is the familiar V8-engine of the S-class with a KKK-double turbosupercharger (M117 – two valves, 515 kW/700bhp) which was replaced at the beginning of the 1989 season by a performance-optimised 32 valve powerplant (M119 – four valves with an exhaust turbosupercharger). According to the regulations governing group C, such a powerplant is admissible until the end of 1990: but from 1991 onwards only un-supercharged engines to a maximum of 3.5 litres will be permitted (as a counterpart to the Formula One). At the moment Mercedes-Benz is developing a power plant exclusively for the sports racing car of the 1990s.

This long-term planning might just be an indication that Mercedes-Benz intends to become number one in the sport again. Group C is destined to one day outstrip Formula One, not only in technical terms, but also in its popularity.

INGO SEIFF

Karl Kling
The Story of a Grand Prix Driver

For a young German motor sport enthusiast, it has always been desirable to undertake an apprenticeship with Daimler in order to become a permanent employee. In 1927, when he was 16 years old, Karl Kling was accepted as an apprentice motor mechanic at the Daimler Benz branch in Giessen, thus realizing his dreams.

1927 was a remarkable year. Charles A. Lindbergh flew across the North Atlantic from west to east in 33.4 hours; the Nürburgring was opened to the public and a Mercedes-Benz Type S, driven by Rudolf Caracciola, won the opening race. In the USA the last of the 15 070 033 Model T Fords, produced since 1908, left the production line. It was no surprise then that towards the end of the 'Roaring Twenties', Kling, now 17 and burning with ambition, achieved his first motor racing triumph on a 250 cc Zündapp motor cycle. In 1934 he qualified as a master mechanic and in the same year he purchased a small car, already prepared for motor sport, in which he successfully participated in several touring events.

A new and important period of Karl Kling's life began when, in 1936, at the age of 26, he joined Daimler-Benz AG in Untertürkheim as a service inspector. From 1938 he was a conscientious member of the 'works' racing team, undertaking exhausting reliability trials. Today, these are known as rallies, but the old competitions did not have the flair of today's international events. The trials were named Ostpreussen-Fahrt [East Prussian race], Italienische Alpenfahrt [Italian Alpine race], Drei-Tage-Harz Fahrt [three-day Harz mountain tour] and so on and they made remarkably stiff demands on the cars which took them on.

When the Tour of Poland was held in 1938, Kling found both bad and good luck. Carrying the headline 'Karl Kling: Blessing in Disguise', the late edition of the *Berliner Illustrierte Nachtausgabe* ['Night Edition'] on 28 June 1938 reported from Warsaw: 'The third phase of the Poland race, starting in Warsaw, passing via Lublin to Lemberg, and then onto Zakopane, a total distance of 841 km (522.6 miles) ended in disappointment for the

German team. Kling, one of the three team-drivers, crashed and was forced to drop out. The accident occurred at night on the road approximately half-way between Warsaw and Lemberg. Kling had lost precious time repairing a faulty alternator and had been eager to regain this. On a straight stretch of road, with Kling driving at full speed, a level-crossing without warning lights suddenly emerged directly in front of his car. It was too late to brake and Kling could only attempt to lessen the impact by steering his car into a sandpit. The car overturned, but the passengers were unharmed, as if protected by some guardian angel.'

For such reliability trials, cars known as 200V (cross-country two-seater, with 54 bhp, four-cylinder, 2007 cc engine) and 230SV (cross-country two-seater, with 68 bhp, six-cylinder, 2289 cc engine) were used. At the time these were considered advanced, having the fuel tank placed on top of the back axle to improve weight distribution. The chassis were – like today – made of an alloy even lighter than the aluminium ones. The engines had side valves and a fixed-venturi carburettor. The 230 (W153) was first exhibited at the Berlin Automobile Fair in 1939, having been produced towards, the end of 1938, but World War II prevented its complete development, although it remained an important design concept until the 1950s, influencing thinking in the 170S and 220, according to German motoring journalist Werner Oswald.

GRAND PRIX TEST

The outbreak of World War Two interrupted the Silver Arrows era, and this interruption in turn drastically affected Karl Kling's racing career. Towards the end of 1939, with races at Monza planned, he and his colleague Hans von Rauch, were due to be tested for their suitability as Grand Prix drivers. A test car with a two-stage-supercharged 3-litre, twelve-cylinder engine was on the drawing board, but the outbreak of the war put paid to these plans.

Nearly eighty per cent of the Daimler-Benz plants in Sindelfingen and Unterturkheim were devastated in World War II, and a full year after the war ended had still not been rebuilt, yet Karl Kling, with great energy and indestructible optimism, was one of the first to revive motor racing. With an old but superbly restored sports car, a BMW 328, and despite brake problems, he easily took second place in the first post-war race.

Kling's great chance came in 1948, however, when engineer and former German motor cycle champion Ernst Loof presented him with his Veritas racing and sports cars. Before the war, he had worked in the competition departments of Imperia, Auto Union and BMW and his Veritas models were based on the BMW 328, a successful pre-war sports car, which had won the limited Mille Miglia in 1940, driven by the man who was later to become head of the Porsche racing team, Huschke von Hanstein.

Karl Kling raced with a 2-litre Veritas sports car, which left all the other competitors in his wake on the fast Hockenheim circuit, a win that was repeated four weeks later during the Tour of Bavaria. By the end of the 1948 season, Kling had won every event he entered and became German 2-litre sports car champion. During the next two years he again managed to hold on to this title, obtaining maximum points whilst doing so.

In 1950, Kling moved into Formula Two, driving a Veritas-Meteor, but an accident prevented him from achieving his customary mastery in the first race. However, he did win, at the Solitude circuit near Stuttgart, one of the most beautiful and difficult of German tracks. And on the Grenzlandring, north-west of Cologne, he won the fastest race of 1950 at an average speed of 203.8 kph.

All these events served to confirm Kling's talent and experience, so it was quite natural that for 1951 he should be re-signed by the Mercedes-Benz team. The Allgemeine Deutsche Automobil-Club (ADAC) agreed to his idea of organizing a 6-hour touring-car race on the Nürburgring. Karl Kling reminisces: 'After the war, the Nürburgring was still in quite good condition. Only the stretch near the start/finish-line had been slightly damaged, having served as an aircraft runway during the war, and that could be repaired easily. For this event I was originally registered with an Opel Kapitän. My friend Toni Ulmen had offered me a 2.5-litre car. I got to know Toni during my time with Veritas and we agreed to a hand-shake contract, which, in those days, was quite normal among sportsmen. I had already driven a few laps in the Opel Diplomat and proved to be faster than Toni. Other competitors included a Mercedes-Benz team, with a 170S driven by Rudolf Caracciola and Hermann Lang, two successful pre-war Grand Prix drivers. Top drivers these may have been, but the team was starting all over again with a simple 170S.

'During practice, Toni and I were undoubtedly faster than the Mercedes-Benz drivers. It is true that the 2.5-litre Opel engine had overhead valves and was more powerful than the side-valve engine of the 170S, but the handling of the Opel was not as good as that of the Mercedes-Benz. The fact that I was recording fast lap times in the Opel was observed by Rudolf Uhlenhaut, at that time director of the development department at Daimler-Benz, who then asked me to drive the 170S for a change. There was nothing I wanted to do more; I needed no extra incentive to put up a better time than the famous works drivers, who enjoyed celebrity status.'

As it happens, Karl Kling's arrangement with Opel did not work out. Still being an employee of Daimler-Benz, he was 'delegated' to drive the 170S, because Uhlenhaut had reported to Stuttgart that the Opel would definitely win the race if driven by Kling. 'Driving a Mercedes-Benz again, I took every possible risk; going uphill at the Nürburgring, Toni Ulmen came closer in his Opel, while I was faster downhill, on the stretch between Hatzenbach and Breitscheid. Finally, I won the race and proved again that I should be recognized as a racing driver.'

NÜRBURGRING TESTS

When in 1951 Daimler-Benz decided to take part in two races in Argentina, using 3-litre cars from 1939 (see 'The Silver Arrows'), tests were held on the Nürburgring in order to select the drivers for these races. Alongside the long-experienced Grand Prix drivers, like Rudolf Caracciola and Hermann Lang, there was also Karl Kling. He well remembers those test-sessions, which were of great importance to him: 'Until then the Veritas-Meteor was the fastest car I had piloted, but now I had to control

420 bhp at the 'Ring'. Immediately, I was faster than Caracciola and Hermann Lang. I do not really want to say that at that time Caracciola was no longer regarded as a top driver, he just did not reach a reasonable time and he therefore decided to withdraw.

It is well known that our start in Argentina was a fiasco. We had insufficient information about the track; and the petrol quality was simply a nightmare, not to mention the extreme heat . . . . I managed to take fourth place despite a burnt piston.'

Participation in two non-championship races, particularly ones a world away in remote Argentina, did not help Daimler-Benz to return to the international competition scene, as they had quietly planned so long before. What was needed was manpower to launch a comeback in the usual Daimler-Benz style. After the war only 6000 employees, including engineers, administrators, sales staff and factory workers, went back to work at Daimler-Benz. The company was, however, optimistic and dedicated itself to regaining international standing and reputation, with the result that by 1952 about 29 000 people worked in modern D-B manufacturing plants, erected on top of the war-time ruins.

This impressive reconstruction also ensured a new base for sporting activities. Although the racing formula which ended in 1953, made it difficult to change the status quo, Mercedes no longer wanted to be ignored by the rest of the motor racing world, as indicated by the saying 'Quantity stands for itself, but class requires constant proof of efficiency'. In 1952, real success came with the legendary Mercedes 300SL sports car (see The Dream Car). This model was a further development of the previous 300 and 300S, and its basic design features maintained the characteristics of the touring cars.

THE CARRERA PANAMERICANA

Driving one of these, Karl Kling competed very successfully. He won the Berne Grand Prix in 1952, at an average speed of 145.2 kph (90.2 mph) and came second during the Grand Jubilee Prix for sport cars, held at the Nürburgring. Partnered by Hans Klenk, he also came second during the Mille Miglia, at an average speed of 128 kph

(79.4 mph), and won the legendary Carrera Panamericana in Mexico at an average speed of 165.01 kph (102.5 mph). This mammoth race covered a distance of no less than 3371 km (2023 miles).

Looking back to those successes, Karl Kling remembered: 'Street racing, like the Mille Miglia or the Panamericana suited me very well, in contrast to Juan-Manuel Fangio, who did not like the Mille Miglia at all, because he preferred to drive on tracks that he could practice on. I found it easy to memorize a course, even if it covered hundreds of miles. I toured the route of the Mille Miglia about twenty times and after that I was able to drive at full racing speed without a "prayer-book". For the Carrera Panamericana, only one practice drive was possible, which was certainly not enough to get to know this dangerous track properly; about ten runs would have been needed. Since I have quite a good memory for unusual and dangerous sections, I could come to the start of the Carrera without being too nervous.

During the Mille Miglia in 1952, I managed only second place, together with my co-driver, Hans Klenk, right behind the Ferrari driven by Bracco and Rolfo. We had fallen into second place as a result of previous dramatic events. I was leading until Siena, when we had to make a tyre-change and we were thwarted by the screws on the Rudge hub; it was as if they had been welded together. It took us 20 minutes to loosen the screws with a sledgehammer. Nevertheless, after a wild chase we caught up to take second place, separated by only 2 minutes from the triumphant Ferrari.

To win the Carrera Panamericana was an ambition of many top drivers. It did not require a superhuman effort as is sometimes claimed, but it was certainly much more exhausting than most other events. The race was well organized and covered a large track section of the Panamericana, which runs from Alaska to the southern tip of Argentina.

The roads were generally good, except in little villages where we had to deal with pot-holes. Of course we collided with wild or straying animals. I was involved in a spectacular accident with a vulture. The giant bird smashed into our windscreen, which burst into a thousand smithereens. We continued with a kind of grille, which gave our 300SL a military feel.'

'The Daimler-Benz competition cars used were not specially prepared. The supply of spare parts and depots along the track was far from today's standards. Radios did not exist and there were only two depots along the stretch to Mexico City.

Before the start, the Mercedes-Benz drivers had to make a decision about money. Team Chief Alfred Neubauer requested an agreement; either start commission plus expenses or the prize money. I had little trouble convincing my friend Hermann Lang, to accept the more risky remuneration. The Carrera Panamericana was then the richest race in the world. The winner received 90 000 DM, which was a great deal of money for me in those days. I shared about half of it with the Mercedes-Benz crew.'

Altogether, 1952 proved a glamorous year for Karl Kling. He was made German 'Sportsman of the year' in 1952 and was awarded the highest decoration for a German sportsman, the 'silver laurel', which was presented to him by the President of the Federal Republic of Germany, Professor Heuss.

There were no major racing activities for Mercedes in 1953, so Karl Kling, with official blessing, was invited to represent Porsche and Alfa Romeo as a guest driver. Kling remembers the races with the Alfa Romeo *Disco Volante* (Flying Saucer) with rather mixed feelings. 'The car was easy to drive and could have been successful, if only it had been strong enough to meet the demands of a gruelling race. Leading the Mille Miglia near Lago di Bosena, the back axle of my *Disco Volante* cracked. It was also in the *Disco Volante* that I suffered the worst accident of my life. During practice for the 6-hour race on the Nürburgring in 1953, I smashed into a concrete bridge near Breitscheid. I had not fastened my seat belt and I suffered serious internal injuries, including a fractured breastbone. I was hospitalized in Adenau for six days and was so close to death that I was given the last rites . . . .'

NEW GRAND PRIX FORMULA

It was natural that Karl Kling should join the works team which was formed for the new Grand Prix formula of 1954. The W196 was powered by a short-stroke, eight-cylinder, in line engine with a swept volume of 2.5 litres and direct fuel injection. In the French Grand Prix at Reims, Karl Kling came second behind Fangio, also driving one of the new W196s in their debut race. Kling then took fourth in Spain and fifth in Germany. Not only was he a very fast driver, but he also had to strive against handicaps.

'At home, I naturally wanted to do my best in front of the 300 000 spectators who had travelled to the hills of the Eifel. For final practice, the regulations demanded that the actual race car be used. My car arrived on Saturday, almost at the end of the practice session, so there was only time left to do half a lap. Consequently, I had to start from the back of the grid, which was bad luck in an event like this, on a track which I like and in front of hundreds of thousands of Germans. I knew every single inch of the 'Ring'. With a test-car I even beat Fangio, but that did not count now.

'I started the race like a thing possessed. I was ruthless as never before. The hunt was on from the start and I followed the leader, Fangio, for a long time; I even managed to overtake him, but I already had a fuel problem. I had been losing petrol, so I had to stop at the pits. Normally, we drove non-stop, without changing tyres or refuelling.

'After leaving Fangio behind, a rear suspension link broke on my car, so that it was hanging down on the road. I stopped at the pits and tied the whole thing together with a piece of wire, then carried on with the rear axle twisted to take fourth place.

'The trouble with the fuel was due to a ridiculous problem. The weld joint on the bottom of the tank had broken, causing a leak, then dripping fuel was being swirled up by the radiator fins and drum brakes right onto my back. I was soaked in fuel and the stuff burnt horribly on my skin. This, in conjunction with the broken rear axle which the car had sustained, did not really contribute to an enjoyable race.

'The situation turned out to be no better in the Italian Grand Prix at Monza, in which a universal joint broke. Finally, though, I was compensated for all the previous mishaps, when I won the Berlin Grand Prix on the AVUS track.'

THE 300 SLR

The 300SLR, introduced in 1955, like the W196, was a fascinating car to drive. Its engine was adapted from the W196s, but it had a swept volume of 3 litres and was constructed in light alloy. The advantage of the 300SLR over the W196 was its extra torque and a 310 bhp power output.

It was in 1955 that Daimler-Benz made its greatest motor racing effort. Three types of sports and racing-car were used during the season – the 300SL, the 300SLR and the W196, with Karl Kling retained as a driver. He won the Swedish Grand Prix with a 300SL at an average speed of 143.9 kph (89.4 mph). In the 2.5-litre Grand Prix formula, he came third in England, driving a W196, while in the Tourist Trophy and the Targa Florio, driving a 300SLR, he took second place.

Daimler-Benz withdrew from racing at the end of 1955 and Karl Kling took over as manager of the motor racing department (the factory still supported private efforts), organizing among other things the touring-car race of 1968. By that time he had succeeded the legendary racing team manager Alfred Neubauer. Kling remembers: 'He was pragmatic by nature and enjoyed being in charge, but also paid great respect to people who stood up for their own opinions. We had a great relationship.'

Despite his new occupation and status Karl Kling could not resist the challenge of two further motor sport events. In 1959, together with the now-deceased TV journalist Rainer Günzler, he won his class in the African Rally covering a distance of 8727 miles [14 063 km] in a 190D, and he won again in 1961, driving a 220E. He also took a class win in the Rally Algiers-Central Africa-Algiers, over a distance of 11 500 km (7141 miles).

Karl Kling retired in 1970, but he still has his opinions as to what characterizes a top-class racing driver. 'First there's the absolute determination to win, and a recognition of one's own limitations, as well as being intrepid. Going into a race preoccupied by worries of possible accidents, or even death, is completely hopeless. If you think like that you should not even consider motor racing. I say again, fear is the enemy of a driver.'

INGO SEIFF

The 'Silver Arrows'

It was in 1932, when the Great Depression was at its height and thirty million people were out of work worldwide, that the Alliance Internationale of the Automobile Club Reconnus (AIACR) announced a new 750 kg racing formula to run from 1934 until 1937, which was to put an end to the era of the so-called 'free formula'.

In the same year, Alfa Romeo introduced its new secret weapon: the eight-cylinder P3, also known as the Tipo B. This initially had a cylinder capacity of 2654 cc and developed 215 bhp at 5600 rpm, but two years later the engine was bored out to 2905 cc, to give a power output of 255 bhp at 5400 rpm. The straight-eight consisted of two four-cylinder blocks, each of which was supercharged by a Roots blower.

This was the year of this powerful Italian racing car, particularly since Daimler-Benz had withdrawn from motor racing at the end of 1931. The Depression had left its mark on the Stuttgart works and left the German team driver Rudolf Caracciola unemployed. So he signed for Alfa Romeo and began the 1932 season driving the Type Monza, later moving on to the P3, the model in which Tazio Nuvolari won the Italian Grand Prix at Monza on 5 June 1932.

The fact that the works P3 competed against an Alfa Romeo Monza from the Scuderia Ferrari indicates how varied motor racing had become in that year. At the end of the season, however, the Alfa Romeo factory ran out of money and withdrew its P3, so there was only Enzo Ferrari from Modena to uphold Alfa Romeo's reputation with his Scuderia. In 1932, Ettore Bugatti, whose racing cars were always elegant, from his base in romantic Molsheim in the Alsace introduced his supercharged Type 51, with a 2.3-litre eight-cylinder engine, to the circuits. And he followed this soon after with his Type 54, whose 4.9-litre engine was also used in the Type 50 and the four-wheel-drive Type 53. The following year, 1933, provided the last indulgence for the free formula, before 1934 ushered in a new motor racing era in the shape of the 750 kg formula.

In 1933 Bugatti, Maserati and Alfa Romeo won all the big races, Bugatti doing especially well. Achille Varzi triumphed over Nuvolari (Alfa Romeo) in Monaco and Tripoli and also won the Berlin AVUS race. Alfa Romeo won with the P3 at the Czechoslovakian GP at Brno and the Spanish GP in San Sebastian. Louis Chiron taking first place in both races.

When the so-called 'free formula' (1931–3) had come to an end, there was a change in the direction of development within motor racing. As Swiss motor journalist Adriane Cimarosti recalls:

'From the mid 1920s until the introduction of the 750 kg formula, Italian, British, French and American engineers had concentrated their efforts mainly on increasing performance by using superchargers, whilst totally neglecting the chassis.' This was to change.

THE NEW 750KG FORMULA

The end of the free formula left racing stables and wealthy private racing drivers with mixed feelings; on that one hand, they had enjoyed the relaxed regulations which had allowed engineers to tinker; on the other hand, however, it put a welcome stop to the ever increasing lust for speed and over-powerful engines. This was achieved by the introduction of a weight restriction. The regulations for the 750 kg Formula fixed among other things, a maximum weight of 750 kg (1654 pounds) not including fuel, oil, water and tyres, a maximum width of the chassis of 85 cm (34 inches), free choice of fuel: and a maximum race distance of 500 km (311 miles).

In fact, there was a gap of almost two years between the announcement of the new formula and the first competition featuring the newly designed racing cars. The previously successful companies Alfa Romeo, Bugatti and Maserati therefore had enough time to prepare for the new regulations. At any rate, their cars were well within the weight limit and could easily be adapted to the new measurements. For example, the Alfa Romeo P3 had a weight of only 700 kg (1543 pounds).

What could be expected from German racing stables, especially from Mercedes-Benz? Due to the worldwide economic recession, the Stuttgart-based company had finally decided to withdraw from racing in 1932 and their ace driver, Rudolf Caracciola, had gone to Alfa Romeo. A great change in German motor racing was brought about by the rise to power of the Nazis in 1933. Hitler soon realized that the success of German racing cars would be good for international prestige, so the German government sponsored the work of Auto Union (headed by Dr Ferdinand Porsche) and of Daimler-Benz (headed by Hans Nibel, who died in November 1934). The government finances available, in addition to bonus payments for any competition won, covered only a small proportion of the actual expenditure of the companies, however. Each stable was granted annually 225 000 Reichsmark and bonuses of RM20 000, RM10 000 and RM5000 were paid for the first three places. This was a mere drop in the ocean, as Daimler-Benz apparently spent RM4 000 000 on its team each year.

THE W25

The first Mercedes-Benz built according to the new regulations was the supercharged, eight-cylinder W25 with a swept volume of 3.36 litres. The first model, the W25A, produced a power output of 345 bhp at 5888 rpm and could manage 300 kph (186 mph). The W25 had independent suspension at the front with horizontal coil springs and wishbones, and, at the back, swing-axles with a leaf transverse spring. Although the Daimler-Benz design office had access to many of the findings relating to the rejected SSKL, the concept was completely new.

The W25 was an immediate success. On 3 June 1934, at the twelfth International Eifel race, Manfred von Brauchitsch won with the first 750 kg formula car from the Stuttgart workshop to compete. Hans Stuck with an Auto Union, followed in second place (the sixteen-cylinder Type A 'P'-car, designed by Ferdinand Porsche, had a swept volume of 4.36 litres, giving 295 bhp).

Prior to this victory on the gruelling Nürburgring, known as the 'green hell' circuit, there had been several days of dramatic racing. Rudolf Caracciola had returned to the Mercedes-Benz team, but was still suffering from

LIÉGE · ROME · LIÉGE 1956

PAR ZAGREB

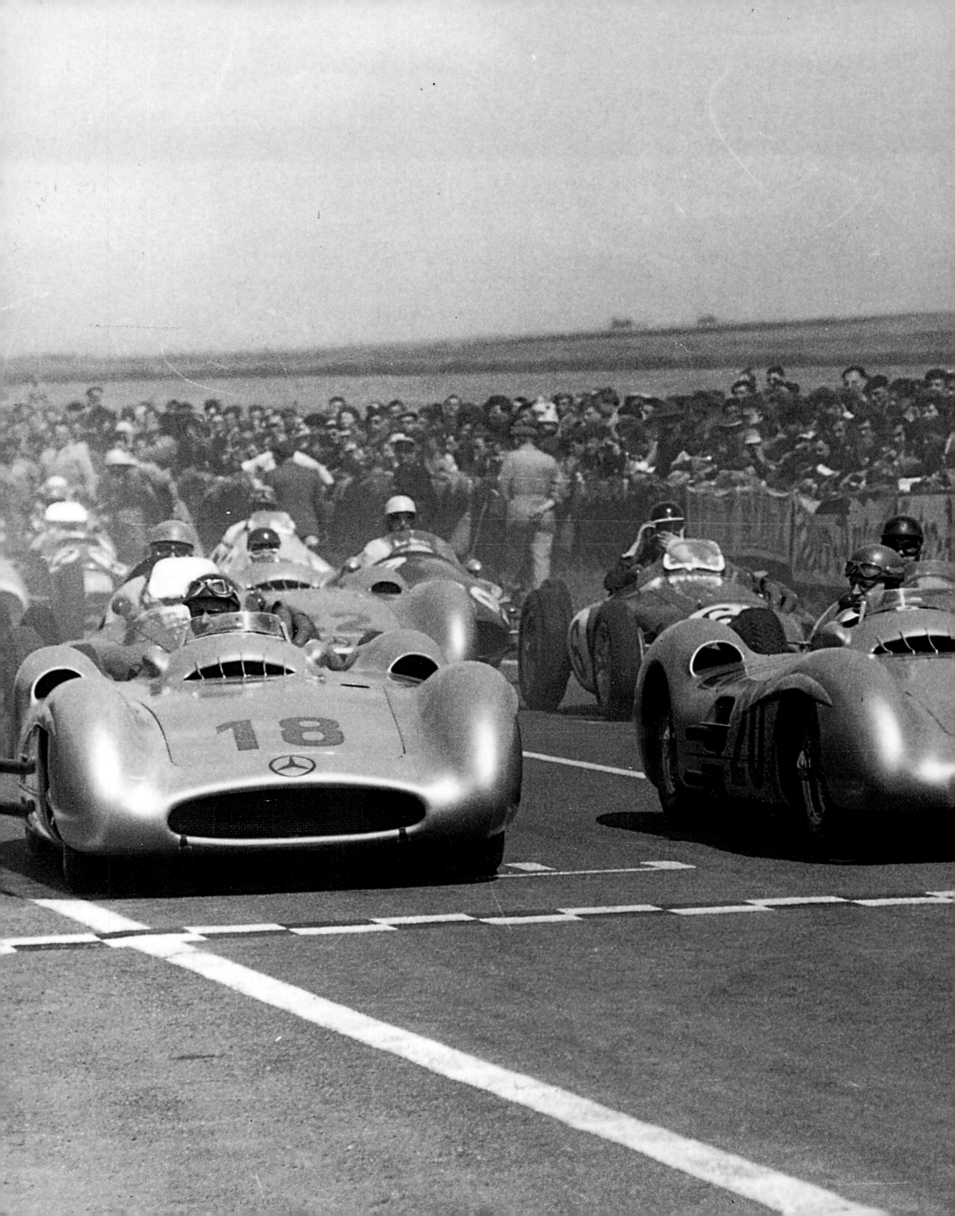

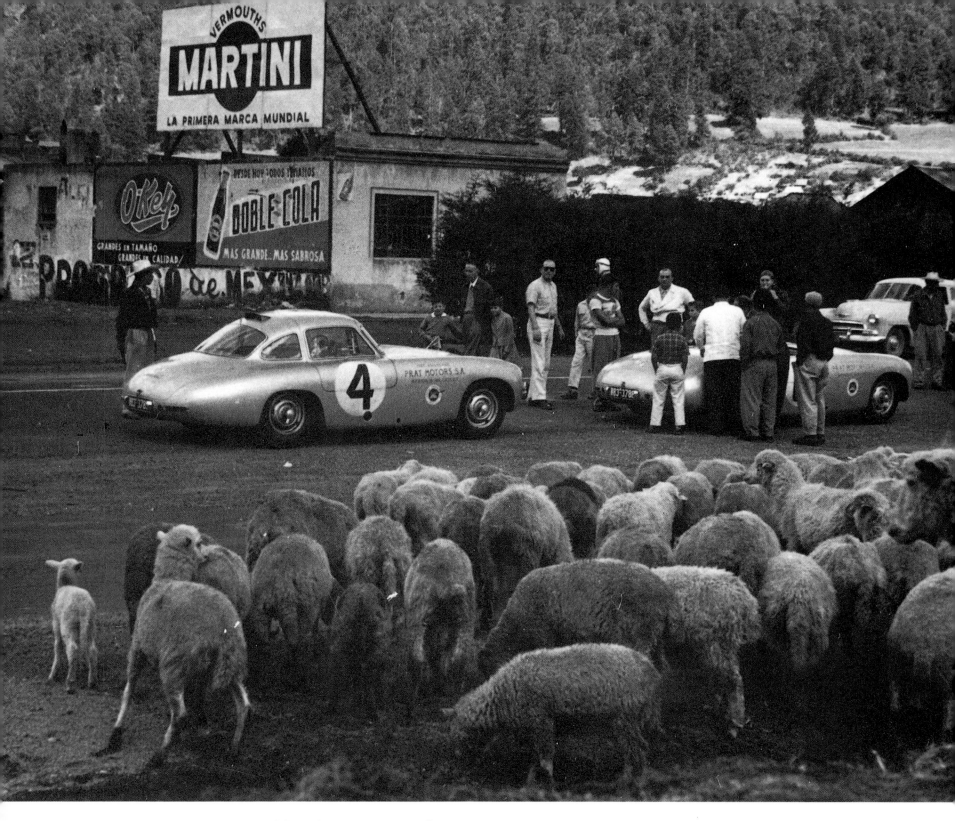

Page 153: *A 300SL on the track during the Liège-Rome-Liège Rally, 1956, also known as the 'Marathon de la Route'. It was held for the last time in 1964 and was considered the crown of rallying achievement by drivers and manufacturers. The organizers were so convinced of the mercilessness of their brutal endurance test that they allowed any modification to participating cars without compunction. In 1955 and 1956 Olivier Gendebien and Willy Mairesse respectively won in their Mercedes-Benz 300SL.*

Previous page: *In 1954 Mercedes-Benz returned to Grand Prix racing (formula 2.5 litre). Their debut was at the French Grand Prix in Reims on 4 July 1954 with three W 196s. Juan Manuel Fangio won ahead of Karl Kling whilst the young Hans Herrmann withdrew early. The picture shows Fangio (No. 18) next to Kling (No. 20) at the start. Next to them is a Maserati.*

Above: *The Carrera Panamericana, run over 3 369 km of Mexican roads, was considered by rallying experts to be one of the greatest challenges of all due to its blend of the harsh and the fascinatingly exotic as this picture from 1952 shows: a herd of sheep crowding around two 300SLs. The race was won by Karl Kling (with his co-driver Hans Klenk) in a 300SL at an average 165.5 kph.*

Opposite: *The legendary Mercedes-Benz team leader, Alfred Neubauer, discusses tactics with his driver Karl Kling during practice for the 1954 British Grand Prix. On the day of the race the Silver Arrows had to concede defeat, their streamlined bodies not being suited to the airfield course at Silverstone.*

Opposite (top): Start of the British Grand Prix, on 16 July 1955 at Aintree. Two Mercedes-Benz W 196s appeared on the front row: Stirling Moss (No. 12) and Juan Manuel Fangio (No. 10). Moss won, world champion Fangio was second and Karl Kling third.

Opposite (bottom): The up-and-coming Stirling Moss had already caught the eye of Mercedes-Benz team leader Alfred Neubauer in 1954 as he steered his Maserati 250F over the winning line in a number of important races. Neubauer placed the talented Briton under contract and he took to the Silver Arrow immediately. In 1955 he won the British Grand Prix at Aintree and the Targa Florio in a 300 SLR (with Peter Collins), the Mille Miglia (with Dennis Jenkinson), the Tourist Trophy (with John Fitch). The picture shows Moss at Aintree.

Above: Stirling Moss with his co-driver John Fitch (to his left) after winning the Tourist Trophy in 1955.

Overleaf (top): During practice for the 1952 24-Hour Le Mans Mercedes-Benz confounded the experts with a so-called 'air-brake', mounted on the roof of a 300SL, which could be produced from the rear of the car as needed. The provocative effect which it had on the opposition was probably Alfred Neubauer's intention. Due to problems with mounting it was not used during the race.

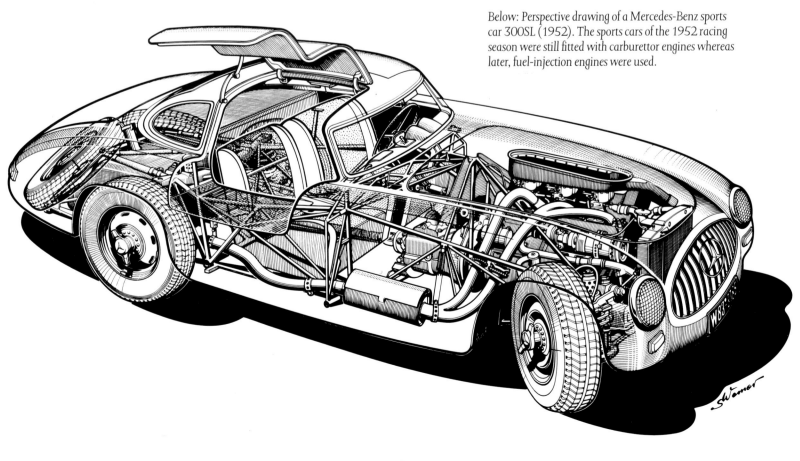

Below: Perspective drawing of a Mercedes-Benz sports car 300SL (1952). The sports cars of the 1952 racing season were still fitted with carburettor engines whereas later, fuel-injection engines were used.

Page 161: Mercedes-Benz 300 SLR 1955. A total of 10 free-formula 300 SLRs were built including two special coupés and an unfinished one. The cars were not for sale. All the experience gained from the W 196 Formula Racing Car was applied to the 300 SLR. This made it the most successful racing sports car of the 1955 season, which was also Daimler-Benz's last for decades.

Technical data: 8 cylinder fuel injection engine, 2 981 cc capacity, 310 bhp output at 7 400 rpm, maximum speed 300 kph.

Pages 162-163: Two 300 SLRs, including (left) a special coupé.

Pages 164-165: The 'Gull Wing' doors of a 300 SL.

Previous page: This SLR special coupé was not used for racing but was primarily driven by Rudolf Uhlenhaut, for many years the director of research at Daimler-Benz, as a fast touring car.

Above: Stirling Moss in a 300 SLR at an 'oldtimer' race at the Nürburgring. Along with Manuel Fangio, he was Mercedes-Benz's top driver in 1955.

Opposite (top): The eight cylinder in-line engine of the 300 SLR with the M 196.I standardization.

Opposite (bottom): Only with difficulty could the two spare wheels be crammed into each of the 'boots' of the four 300 SLRs at the Mille Miglia, 1955. They had to vie for space with the 265 litre fuel tank. Stirling Moss and his co-driver Dennis Jenkinson covered the distance of more than 1 585 km to win the race in a record time of 10 hours and 17 minutes, at an average speed of 156.3 kph.

Overleaf: 300 SLR.

Opposite: Mercedes-Benz W 196 1954/1955. This type designation was actually only carried by 'thoroughbred' Formula 1 racing cars with 2.5 litre engines. The W 196, whose 'insides' are shown here (the oil tank and in front of that the petrol tank), had a 3 litre engine from the 300 SLR under its bonnet which can be seen by its 'hunchback' (bump). This was to create space for the leads of the fuel injection pumps. This combination, chassis of the W 196 and engine of the 300 SLR, was used, for example, at the free formula GP in Buenos Aires in 1955.

Above: The same W 196 at an 'oldtimer' race at the new Nürburgring.

Overleaf: A 'Sauber'-Mercedes-Benz V8 in the first race of the Sports Prototype World Championship 1989 at the Suzuka race course in Japan. The Swiss engineer, Peter Sauber, is preparing the Mercedes-Benz C 9 for an attempt at the world championship. The engine unit of the Sauber-Mercedes, the familiar V8 engine from the S class, with KKK dual-turbo-charge (M117-dual-valve, around 700 bhp) was replaced at the start of the 1989 season with an optimalized engine with 32 valves (M119-quad-valve with turbo-charge exhaust). Output around 720 bhp, with a top speed of well over 300 kph.

Page 176 (top): A Mercedes-Benz E 2.3-16 (Group A Rally version) during competition at the International German Rally Championship, 1988.

Page 176 (bottom): Mercedes-Benz took part in the German Touring-Car Championship with several 190 E 2.5-16 'Evolution' cars. Output in the racing version was around 315-320 bhp.

severe injuries sustained in an accident at the Monaco GP in 1933 and was not fit to take part in the first race on the Nürburgring. A further disaster was to occur the day before the race. The legendary head of the Mercedes-Benz racing team, Alfred Neubauer, remembers in his book *Männer, Frauen and Motoren*: 'The night before the race the cars are weighed and found to be too heavy! Only 750 kg (1654 lb) is admissible for the new formula, excluding fuel, cooling water, oil and tyres. However, when the mechanics push the first car on to the scales, it shows 751 kg (1656 lb). What now? The race is tomorrow. It is impossible to remove major parts. Everything was calculated exactly to the gram. "Think of one of your famous tricks," says Brauchitsch, "otherwise we are in a fix!" "In a fix?" I say, and have an idea. Of course, the paint, that is the solution. Throughout the entire night, mechanics scrape the beautiful white paint off our racing cars. And when they are put on to the scales again in the morning, they weigh 750 kg (1654 lb) precisely.'

SILVER SKIN

The shiny silver skin of the W25 had been revealed, a fascinating sight; this is how the legendary silvery look of the Mercedes-Benz racers was created – the 'Silver Arrows' had been born! More triumphs lay ahead: Luigi Fagioli was the winner at the Coppa Acerbo in Pescara and in the Spanish Grand Prix, while Rudolf Caracciola, with Fagioli, won first place in the Italian Grand Prix.

In 1935 the former racer Max Sailer took over the racing department and the improved W25 set out for its unprecedented series of victories: Monaco GP (Fagioli), Tripoli GP (Caracciola), Berlin AVUS races (Fagioli), Eifel races (Caracciola), French GP (Caracciola), Barcelona GP (Fagioli), Belgium GP (Caracciola), Swiss GP (Caracciola) and Spanish GP (Caracciola). Rudolf Caracciola became European champion and, in 1935, German champion. Some motor racing historians look on 1936 as a year of misfortune for the Stuttgart Silver Arrows. Attempts at putting in more powerful engines for the W25 had not paid off convincingly, while at Auto Union a young driver had caused a sensation and become a national hero, an inspiration to the whole German nation, by

driving Porsche's rear-engined cars with great bravura; his name was Bernd Rosemeyer. Caracciola had to be content with two victories in Tunis and Monaco and Daimler-Benz felt so perplexed that they did not even consider taking part in some Grand Prix.

In 1937, the last year of the 750 kg formula, Mercedes-Benz racers scaled new summits. Hermann Lang won the Tripoli Grand Prix with a W125, a victory described by a British motor racing journalist as 'the apotheosis of the 750 kg formula'. In fact, the new Silver Arrow demonstrated that the creators of the 750 kg formula had made a mistake: it had been their intention to limit performance by the introduction of a weight limit but in reality they had paved the way for a previously unheard-of performance explosion. The W125 developed 646 bhp at 5800 rpm, and its eight-cylinder supercharged engine had a cylinder capacity of 5660 cc. Its maximum speed was 330 kph (205 mph), and with higher gearing nearly 370 kph (230 mph).

During that season a fascinating rivalry developed between two sets of German Silver Arrows, Auto Union also having presented its C type in silver finish. This car had a 6.33 litre, 545 bhp engine and although the drivers from Zwickau (now in East Germany) could not repeat their impressive series of victories of the previous year, Bernd Rosemeyer won the Eifel races, the race at Pescara, the Donington GP and the Vanderbilt Cup in the USA, while Rudi Hasse won the Belgian GP and Ernst von Delius the Grosvenor GP in South Africa.

The Mercedes-Benz team made a great leap forward in 1937. 'In addition to a superior engine in which the supercharger blew in fuel mixture rather than air (constant-vacuum carburettor instead of fixed-venturi unit), the car had a completely new chassis with light but rigid oval tubes in which a new rear axle proved to be a real success. Instead of swing axles with a leaf spring a rigid axle was used. The final drive was transmitted by half-shafts from a four-speed transaxle unit in a true De Dion configuration. The W125 became the basis for the W154 of the 3-litre formula of 1938 and 1939' (Paul Simsa in *Auto, Motor und Sport*). The list of Mercedes-Benz Silver Arrows victories for 1937 was impressive: Tripoli GP, 524 km (326 miles), winner Lang, average speed 216.3 kph (134.4 mph), new track record; Berlin AVUS race, 290.3 km (180.4 miles), winner Lang, average speed 261.7 kph (162.6 mph), new track record (this was the fastest average speed reached at a race anywhere in the world until 1959); German GP, 501.8 km (311.8 miles), winner Caracciola, average speed 133.2 kph (82 mph), new track record, von Brauchitsch took the second place; Swiss GP, 364 km (457 miles), winner Caracciola, average speed 158.6 kph (98.6 mph), second place Lang and third place von Brauchitsch; Italian GP 360.9 km (224.4 miles), average speed 131.3 kph (81.6 mph), new track and lap record, Lang took second place; Brno GP in Czechoslovakia, 437.1 km (271.6 miles), winner Caracciola, average speed 138.4 kph (86 mph), new track and lap record, von Brauchitsch in second place.

The Grand Prix season of 1938 was overshadowed by political tensions in Europe, Neville Chamberlain meeting Hitler in Germany to placate the Geman dictator and to try to preserve peace. Technically speaking it was also an eventful year. Nylon was invented and the TransIranian Railway, running from the Caspian Sea via Teheran to the Persian Gulf, was opened after eleven years of construction. The German physicist, Hahn, together with Straßmann, achieved nuclear fission in uranium by bombarding it with neutrons, and Malcolm Campbell set a new world water-speed record of 130 mph.

EVER-INTENSIFYING QUEST

As the ever-intensifying quest for greater performance in the 750 kg formula appeared to have got out of control, the new regulations for 1938–40 planned a reduction of the swept volume to 3 litres with supercharger or 4.5 litres without. In the past, the main objective had been to obtain maximum performance within the weight limit, but the new formula called for maximum performance with a limited swept volume. Mercedes-Benz continued to use a supercharged engine and the team showed that its engineers were able to deal with this new technological challenge.

The W154 had been developed for the 3-litre formula and was based on the proven W125 chassis. 'In 1936 the original swing-axle design was developed into a De Dion rear end. Different from the eight-cylinder-engined earlier cars, the W154 had an angled V12 engine and its propeller shaft ran down the left-hand side, which allowed for a lower cockpit. After numerous detailed improvements, a very beautiful high-performance car had evolved, which was lower to the ground. The performance was increased during 1938 from 425 bhp to 476 bhp and the W154 could reach maximum speed of more than 300 kph (186 mph)' (Paul Simsa in *Auto, Motor und Sport*).

TRAGIC DEATH

During the 1938 season the W154 won six out of eight races, the German team of Caracciola, Lang and von Brauchitsch having been joined by the young British driver Richard Seaman. Team chief, Alfred Neubauer, had spotted him on several occasions, confidently driving Maseratis, Delages, Aston Martins and ERAs around Europe's racing circuits. In 1938, he won the German Grand Prix at the Nürburgring with a W154 but met his tragic death in 1939 during the Belgian Grand Prix at Spa. He was leading with thirteen laps to go when he lost control on a stretch of wet track and crashed into a tree. He died in hospital shortly after the accident and his body was taken back to Putney, London, where he was buried. Among the many wreaths was one from Adolf Hitler.

The 3-litre, V12-engined Auto Unions were again in direct competition with the W154. The *pièce de résistance* of the Zwickau racing stable was the Italian champion, Tazio Nuvolari. Ferdinand Porsche had left them to devote himself entirely to the development of the Volkswagen, but Nuvolari immediately won the Italian GP and Donington GP.

For 1939, the chassis of the W154 was used again, but the Silver Arrows from Untertürkheim were given new, elegant and highly distinctive bodywork and the V12 engine was refined. With the W154-M 163 specification, this Silver Arrow was the crowning glory of an ingenious series of racing cars. The earlier parallel Roots blowers were replaced by a two-stage supercharger, so that two blowers of different dimensions worked in succession. The oil was pumped around by no fewer than nine pumps and the engine produced 483 bhp at 7800 rpm, and an amazing performance of 161 bhp per litre.

In 1939, the Mercedes Silver Arrows were the most successful cars in Grand Prix racing. Hermann Lang won the Grands Prix of Pau, Belgium and Switzerland and the Eifel races, too. Caracciola won the German GP and Hermann Lang became European champion.

The last GP before World War II was organized under very sombre circumstances. The drivers élite had gathered at the beginning of September in the Yugoslav capital for the Belgrade Grand Prix. On 1 September 1939, Hitler's troops had invaded Poland and by the time the race began on 3 September, Great Britain had declared war on the Third Reich. Tazio Nuvolari was the winner of this 'war GP' with Auto Union, while Manfred von Brauchitsch came second with a Mercedes-Benz W154.

It is also worth mentioning an oddity in the regulations which aimed to put an end to the German Silver Arrows at the end of the 1930s. This was the *voiturettes category*, for 1.5-litre engines, which was dominated by Alfa Romeo and Maserati. Since the Italians did not stand a chance against the powerful GP racing cars of the Third Reich, they announced in determined style that only racing cars of a lesser swept volume could enter the 1939 races, hoping that the German engineers would run into difficulties.

Adriano Cimarosti describes how Daimler-Benz met this challenge: 'Between September 1938 and April 1939 the sensational type W165 was created, whose chassis was planned to be similar to that of the "large car": the front wheels were given coil springs and parallel wishbones, while at the rear there was a De Dion axle and suspension by torsion bars. The blown 1.5-litre engine with four camshafts was the first V8 (a 90-degree unit) from Daimler-Benz. The single stage supercharged engine had two carburettors and gave 256 bhp at 8000 rpm, which represented a new peak value of 170 bhp per litre. The Alfa Romeo which dominated the *voiturettes* category had a power output of just 200 bhp. The W165 made its debut on 7 May 1939 at the Tripoli Grand Prix, where Hermann Lang and Rudolf Caracciola came first

and second, respectively.

Even if the Italian interference did not end the winning ways of the Mercedes-Benz Silver Arrows, the *voiturettes* category had a great impact on Grand Prix racing after World War II. When the FIA (Fédération Internationale de l'Automobile) decided to take up Formula One racing, there were no new designs in existence. All that remained from the pre-World War II era for example were (supercharged) 1.5-litre cars of the ERA, Alta, Alfa Romeo 158 and Maserati 4CL type. These formed the basis of the re-birth of formula motor racing in 1947.

At first Mercedes-Benz played no part in this new beginning in Europe; it was not until 1952 that Daimler-Benz returned officially to motor racing.

RETURN TO THE TRACK

The official return of the team to international motor racing revitalized the entire sport, the 300SL paving the way with countless victories in races and rallies. Daimler-Benz's decision to construct a new Grand Prix car dates back to 1952 and the 300SL which raced in that year, can be seen as the inspiration for this. The new GP car, designated the W196, made use of 300SL elements such as the spaceframe chassis and the canted engine, which produced 280 bhp at 8500 rpm. The eight-cylinder in-line engine, with a swept volume of 2.5 litres, had direct fuel injection, and desmodromic valve gear – without springs. Depending on the type of circuit, the W196 was also used with a streamlined body and covered wheels, in which form it could reach a speed of 275 kph.

The dry weight of the streamlined model was 680 kg and with open wheels this fell to 640 kg. The race formula introduced for 1954 stipulated either a 2.5-litre normally aspirated engine or one of 750 cc with a supercharger. There was no weight limit and the minimum race duration was set at 500 kilometres or 3 hours, with a change of drivers permitted.

The reasons for Daimler-Benz's return to the Grand Prix scene were twofold. The first was straightforward company policy and the second was one of nostalgia, as

1954 was the sixtieth birthday of international motor sport and the participation of Mercedes-Benz in motor racing. The first race for the new Silver Arrows, at Reims on 4 July 1954, was of great significance, as it took place forty years to the day after the French GP of 1914, which ended with a 1-2-3 for Mercedes and was the last great race before World War I. The W196 did not participate right from the beginning of the 1954 season, the races in Argentina and Belgium both being won by Manuel Fangio with a Maserati. Subsequently, he transferred to the Mercedes-Benz team and drove the W196 to a trouble-free victory in the French GP at Reims, crossing the finishing line 0.2 seconds ahead of his teammate Karl Kling. Also worth mentioning is that only six of the twenty-two cars reached the finishing line.

There was also some disappointment. In the British GP at Silverstone, the streamlined body proved to be a great disadvantage, greatly impeding the field of vision of the driver. Fangio had to let Froilan Gonzales and Mike Hawthorn in their Ferraris and Onofre Marimon in a Maserati pass him. However, at the Nürburgring, the Italian GP and the Swiss GP, Fangio won again and finished the season as world champion. In addition to his victories with Mercedes-Benz he counted two wins with Maserati, reaching a total of forty-two points.

In 1955, Fangio faced competition from the young Stirling Moss, who had left Maserati to become his teammate, alongside second driver Karl Kling, Hans Herrmann and, later, Piero Taruffi. The W196 was slightly modified for the new season, the engine now producing 280 bhp at 8700 rpm. The engineers at Daimler-Benz developed three different chassis: the standard wheelbase was 2350 mm (92.5 in), as in 1954, but there was also a medium-sized version at 2210 mm (87 in) and an even shorter variant at 2150 mm (84.6 in). In 1955, the Silver Arrows were unbeatable. The series of victories had begun with the European GP at the Nürburgring on 1 August 1954 and the team won twelve out of fifteen races in 1954 and 1955.

While the competition was paralysed by the continuing rise of the Mercedes star, new racers were being developed by the German company. The 300SLR was technically similar to formula racing cars, but was a free-formula sports car, with its eight-cylinder fuel-injected, 3-litre engine (based on the W196 unit). The successful 300SL 3-litre sports car of 1952 had been developed from the touring car, but international competition demanded the development of a purpose-built sports-racer, in this case designated the 300SLR (S = super; L = leicht – light; R = rennen – race;). Its engine produced 300 bhp at 7500 rpm and it had a maximum speed of 290 kph (180 mph).

Now Daimler-Benz had two types of racing car, covering the broad spectrum of competition. Even the 300SL touring car managed to 'clean-up' successfully in its category.

In 1955, Daimler-Benz managed to gain the highest awards in all three racing categories: the European touring car championship fell to Werner Engel (300SL); Juan-Manuel Fangio became world champion for the second time in the 2.5-litre Grand Prix formula; Mercedes-Benz took the manufacturers' world sports car championship with the 300SLR.

The 1955 Grand Prix season proved to be a Mercedes-Benz festival. The Silver Arrows won the GPs of Argentina (Fangio), Belgium (Fangio), the Netherlands (Fangio), Britain (Moss), and Italy (Fangio). The 300SLRs were triumphant in the Mille Miglia (Moss/Jenkinson), the International Eifel races (Fangio), the Swedish Sports Car GP (Fangio), the Tourist Trophy (Moss/Fitch) and the Targa Florio (Moss/Collins).

The fact that Daimler-Benz abandoned their interest in Grand Prix racing at the end of the 1955 season came as a great shock to many motor sport enthusiasts at home and abroad. It was not until 1988 that the factory returned to the tracks, in the World Sports Car Championship; and for 1989 the famous silver livery of the cars was reinstated.

INGO SEIFF

The C111
Variations on a Theme

Since the earliest times, man has striven to produce movement by mechanical means, thus sparing human energy. It was found possible to increase muscle power by using levers, but human input it seemed was indispensable – that appliances and machines did not run by themselves was believed to be a fundamental natural law.

Eugen Diesel wrote the following in an essay on the prehistory of the diesel engine: 'Mankind has applied itself since the times of Aristotle and Archimedes to the problem of creating physical and above all mechanical means for generating power and movement " by itself" . . . . But the absolute practical requirement of generating mechanical power by means of the water wheels of mills, as occurred in the British coal mines of the eighteenth century, apparently did not occur in ancient times or in the middle ages . . . . Philosophy played a decisive role in the search for perpetual motion, for the 'by itself', for mechanical power. Yes, philosophy was midwife to the birth of our engines in the following way: at the beginning of the thirteenth century, constructors and inventors heard from the speculative theologians that Aristotle had 1600 years previously pointed out the mystery of god's power, which keeps the stars in perpetual rotation without the application of any other power. The rotating heaven with all its stars appeared to be a *perpetuum mobile*, forever in motion "by itself" . . . '.

The idea of the *perpetuum mobile* haunted men for many centuries. Leonardo da Vinci, an inventor of genius, poked fun at these fantasists. He came up with the law of conservation of energy, and soon he too was obsessed by the idea of building a motion machine, an energy source, realising that it had to be done with the help of heat. He doodled designs for steam appliances – bellows, fire machines and cannons – but, lacking in tools and materials as well as practical experience, he could not build the machines.

However, his intuition was correct, as the Dutch physicist, mathematician and astronomer Christiaan Huygens (1629–95) proved when he built his exploding powder machine. He made no use of available natural forces, but gunpowder instead. In 1673, the Dutchman generated reduced pressure in a cylinder by exploding gunpowder, so that a piston was driven by external air pressure into the cylinder, thus performing mechanical work. It was a successful experiment, but unfortunately it could not be converted into a reliable, repeating machine.

Huygens' assistant, Denis Papin (1647–1712), continued the work of his mentor. In 1690, he constructed a simple atmospheric steam engine which, instead of gunpowder, used steam to create a vacuum. It then condensed as water in the cylinder. This Papin engine was impractical, but anticipated the basic elements of the highly effective atmospheric steam engine.

James Watt's double-action steam engine came seventy years later, sparking off the furious mechanization of the industrial revolution in Britain. Now man had at his disposal a 'power and motion engine', which was truly capable of producing superhuman energy. It was not long before the arrival of the 'automotive' steam truck (1771) of the French engineer Nicolas Joseph Cugno (1725–1804), and more than 100 years later, in 1873, Amédée Bollée put an end to experiments with steam, when he produced his steam omnibuses.

THE GAS ENGINE

Meanwhile, the development of gas engines continued apace, speeded by the discovery of lighting gas. In 1860, the Belgian Jean Joseph Etienne Lenoir (1822–1900) built a gas engine, which was refined and improved by Nikolaus August Otto, a German salesman from Cologne (1832–1891). He wanted to convert it to burn liquid fuels, such as spirits, so it would not be dependent on lighting gas, which could only be obtained in certain areas. A patent application of 1861 shows that even then he visualized an engine 'for the locomotion of passengers along country roads'.

In *Vom Dampfwagen zum Auto* ('From steam carriage to Automobile'), Erik Eckermann writes: 'The Otto four-stroke engine of 1876 ended the 200-year-long search for a suitable engine for use in trade and small businesses, and ten years later in automobiles as well.' But Otto got entangled in the undergrowth of patent law, and did not succeed in protecting the four-stroke process. His patent application, through which he had hoped to be confirmed as the spiritual father of the four-stroke engine, was not upheld, for the French engineer Beau de Rochas had exactly explained the four-stroke process in 1861, but had not been canny enough to gauge its monumental significance.

But Nikolaus Otto is generally considered the inventor of the four-stroke process, which has kept the vehicles of the world in motion for more than 100 years, by suction, compression, combustion and emission. Steam power fell by the wayside, on account of its low efficiency and the great weight of steam-powered vehicles.

The supremacy of the four-stroke engine has not been shaken to this day; there have been only two serious alternatives – the gas turbine engine and the Wankel engine, and the latter brings us to our subject of discussion.

Many technicians were dissatisfied with the brute force with which the piston, via a connecting rod, turns the crank – 'a monster of the physical world', said Paul Simsa in *Auto, Motor und Sport* – and they attempted to find a more elegant way to provide energy in the cylinder. The rotating piston engine, invented by the brilliant German Felix Wankel (d. 1988) created a new concept in motoring that radically reduced the number of moving engine parts.

THE WANKEL ENGINE

In the German newspaper, *Die Welt*, Heinz Horrmann wrote: 'The advantage of the rotary engine is that the same effect is obtained with a simple rotation of the piston as is obtained in the customary stroke engine only with a complicated mode of operation and expensive technology. The Wankel engine has no pistons pumping up and down, no valves, springs, levers or cams. It is a four-stroke engine that runs through all four strokes with a single rotation of the rotary piston. The piston is in the shape of a triangle which rotates in the oval interior of a water-cooled housing. Three expanding and contracting spaces are cleared in the process, in which the four-stroke process of suction, compression, combustion and emission takes place. The exchange of gases is controlled by the slits in the piston itself. The Wankel engine delivers drive power with every revolution, whereas the piston engine only delivers drive power with every other revolution. There are further advantages: low weight, low space requirements and a significantly smaller number of moving parts.'

By 1930, Wankel had a pretty clear idea of how to make the piston in the engine rotate, rather than thump up and down. Overall, he worked on his rotary engine for about 25 years, and his catchphrase was 'So ein langsamer Mensch wie ich', ('a slowcoach such as myself'). His archives are filled with filing cabinets and boxes of notes in which his 'predecessors' are all noted down. In every industrial state there are at least 6000 patents relating to the rotary engine – the engine is indeed an inventor's nightmare.

In the early 1930s, a research contract was drafted for him at Daimler-Benz, requiring only his signature – but it was never signed. Wankel remembered: 'The General Director of Daimler, Wilhelm Kissel, came striding into the room, and said mockingly: "These endless inventions are the bane of our life. We never get round to production!"' Wankel remembers his furious reply: 'If a certain Gottlieb Daimler had not made any inventions, you would not have a car factory today, but a cabhorse-hire service.' General Director Kissel was impressed, and counselled patience. But Wankel went instead straight to BMW, who had hired him to test seals, rotating slides and rotating piston engines.

The NSU Spider was the first production car to use a Wankel rotary engine. Daimler-Benz had long completed tests on the Wankel engine, at first with the two- and three-rotor versions, which were carried out in 1960. Subsequently, the Wankel unit was tested in all appropriate vehicles, from cars of the W110 class (rear-finned cars) right down to a W107 coupé.

Daimler-Benz really got cracking on the Wankel engine from 1969 to 1973, when experiments were carried out using three- and four-rotor engines in the C111, a test lab on wheels. Why did they start? In his book *Mercedes-Benz C111 – eine Fahrzeugstudie* ('Mercedes-

Benz C111 – a study of a car') Belgian motoring journalist Paul Frère reminisces that during the '60s he had a conversation with the then director of passenger vehicle development, Rudolf Uhlenhaut. The vexed question of why Daimler-Benz didn't figure in formula one racing was raised, and Uhlenhaut replied: 'We don't need it and we don't have the time for it – and because racing car technology has changed so much in recent years, we don't even know whether we could do it any better than the others.'

Everyone else, all over the world, had contracted Wankel fever. Every car company of quality had bought a licence. And Daimler-Benz, too, as we have seen, was exploring this new aspect of motor technology. 'It provided a good opportunity,' said Paul Frère, 'to construct a fast car of moderate engine size, incorporating the latest discoveries in automotive and synthetic materials technology, as well as new in-house solutions. Those were grounds enough to justify the production of the C111.'

In a communication from the development section of Daimler-Benz, Stuttgart (E. Enke and E. Loeffler) we read: 'Significant characteristics of this vehicle are its mid-engine construction, installation of a three- or four-rotor Wankel engine, high-powered performance, favourable weight distribution under all driving conditions and a low centre of gravity, exact rear-axle steering, fuel tanks in the door sill and a body constructed of synthetic materials.'

A vehicle was to be built for the three- and four-rotor engines that had been developed at Daimler-Benz, so that this powerful drive apparatus could be tested on the road. At the same time, more advanced synthetic materials were to be tested both for the body and for new steering elements. The immense engine power available led to great expectations of its top speed. To make the fullest possible use of this power, the following conditions had to be met:

The vehicle had to be light, and satisfy the needs of the most discriminating driver.

The centre of gravity above the driving surface had to be very low.

Low air resistance was required, ie a low front surface area and favourable air drag.

The aerodynamic stability had to be great, ie there could not be great lift of descending force on the axes at high speeds. And if the front axle should lift, even at very high speeds, it had to be guaranteed that the car would be pressed back onto the driving surface by the air forces.

The centre of gravity along the length of the car had to be such that, on the one hand, very high lifting forces could be transferred to the road without the wheels slipping, and on the other, the car could drive through curves at extremely high speeds without any axles swinging out of the direction of travel. That meant a centre of gravity approximately in the centre of the car, which should not change even when the fuel tank was emptied.

It had to have an optimally adjusted undercarriage and axle construction with exact wheel steering.

The tyres had to be able to cope with the speeds expected from the car.

The driver had to be made as comfortable as possible to minimise driving fatigue.

The gestation period had to be short.

In its three-rotor embodiment, the engine had a chamber capacity of 600 cc, comparable to a swept volume of 3.6 litres, and 280 bhp at 7000 rpm. In its four-rotor embodiment, it had the same chamber capacity, comparable to a swept volume of 4.8 litres, and 350 bhp at 6500 rpm. The maximum torque was 30 mkg (216 lb ft) and 40 mkg (289 lb ft) respectively. The four-rotor engine weighed 180 kg (396 lb) with starter, dynamo and air filter, giving a power to weight ratio, 1960 bhp/tonne. The engine had direct injection for each three- or four-piston chamber, and transistor ignition with one surface gap plug per rotor.

A 1970 Daimler-Benz press release said: 'Daimler-Benz caused astonishment and speculation with the exhibition of the C111 test vehicle at the International Automobile Exhibition in Frankfurt in 1969. A step into the future had been taken, and the Wankel engine and the composite chassis had been unified into a single concept.

In spite of its elegant, aerodynamic shape and the impressive test drive results, it is perfectly clear that the C111 is a test vehicle which is being developed into a pinnacle of technology and style beneath the eyes of the public. It gives everyone interested in cars an insight into Daimler-Benz's research and development. Meanwhile, half a year has passed. New results have been obtained in aerodynamics, stability, synthetic material processing, and not least the rotary engine, which are to be presented at the Geneva motor show, in a further development of the C111. With its four-rotor Wankel engine with an eccentric shaft on five bearings, whose chamber capacity corresponds to the swept volume of a 4.8-litre piston engine, the maximum torque increased from 30 mkg (216 lb ft) to 40 mkg (289 lb ft) between 4000 and 6500 rpm, and the power increased from 280 to 350 bhp (DIN). Thanks to its excellent power-to-weight ratio of 278 bhp/tonne, the Geneva C111 accelerates from rest to 100 kph (62 mph) in 4.8 seconds.

The car body of glassfibre-reinforced synthetic material with an integrated roll-over hoop, which is bonded and riveted to the base-frame assembly in order to increase rigidity, was refined. All windows were enlarged and the sightlines diagonally backwards were improved by reshaping the bonnet. The air inlet at the front of the car was made more effective and the outlet on the top front was adjusted in size and shape to the quantity of air required to improve its cooling properties.

The headlamp flashers are now in the cool air inlet, and large round rear lights guarantee improved visibility. The new one-blade windscreen wiper has a considerably increased wiping area. Out of operation, the wiper is lowered and not visible. By a few functional changes to the car body, aerodynamic properties were improved and air resistance decreased by eight per cent.

The high torque of the engine made it necessary to replace the single-dry-plate clutch with a double-plate clutch. The petrol tanks located in the side covering consist of soft aluminium with synthetic foam material. The fuel injection (now with a four-piston injection pump), transistor ignition and car body did not require any changes.

The design of the "C111 test lab" as a two-seater sports car with a medium-sized engine allows extremely high demands to be made on the car body and assemblies. Further intensive work on the C111 is intended to answer many open technical questions.'

THE WANKEL POWERED C111

The initiation of the first C111 (which still had a temporary sheet-aluminium body) took place on 1 April 1969 on Daimler-Benz's track in Stuttgart-Unterturkheim. Records show that the adjustment of the undercarriage in fact presented more problems than the 'new' engine. The combination of rear diagonal full floating axle with broad racing tyres, which had little flexibility under lateral forces, was not really suited to a car of that kind. The result, according to Paul Frère, was 'unsatisfactory performance on the straight, and excessive load-transfer during fast cornering . . . In order to be able to combine acceptable comfort with satisfactory roadholding, even under the most demanding conditions, a rear axle with wishbones and oversteer, in the manner of a modern Grand-Prix car, was built, in which the constructor had a free hand in changing tracking and toe-in . . . .' The first five vehicles in the programme, provided with synthetic bodies, already had rear axles with wishbones.

In test drives of the first car on 15 July 1969 on the Hockenheim racetrack, this axle proved optimal. In subsequent extended test drives on A-roads, motorways and the Hockenheim and Nürburgring tracks, the main concerns were testing the tyres and conceiving a new gearbox, in which an electric switch locked the first and reverse gear levels, to avoid gearchanging errors. The single-plate clutch first installed was replaced by a twin-plate clutch which, on account of its lower level of pressure, allowed less transmission.

The speed of the C111 when fitted with a three-rotor Wankel engine was very impressive: top was 270 kph (167 mph) and it accelerated from 0 to 100 kph (62 mph) in 5 seconds. The engine's flexibility was not so good, however, and these days one would consider its overtaking skills on the motorway pretty poor. Paul Frère wrote: 'Particularly on the motorway, one had the feeling in overtaking that the speed of the operation did not match the external appearance of the vehicle. This changed radically with the installation of the four-rotor engine.'

Sure enough, the four-rotor engine brought greatly improved flexibility, mainly because of the thirty-three per cent increase in torque (and also because the 40 mkg 289 lb ft torque was now delivered between 4000 and 5500 rpm, a speed of about 1500 rpm less).

After wind-tunnel testing the body was further refined, and the quality of the interior and sound and heat insulation were improved. The test car, now called C111-II, had been transformed into a veritable high-speed machine.

END OF A LOVE AFFAIR

According to factory reports, its top speed was more than 300 kph (186 mph) (as measured by Dr Hans Liebold, the project leader) and it could reach 100 kph (62 mph) from zero in 4.8 seconds. In March 1970, the C111-II was the star of the Geneva car salon. Many people thought the car would make a worthy successor unforgotten 300SL. Blank cheques accompanied by orders for C111-IIs arrived at Unterturkheim from all over the world.

But the head of Daimler-Benz finally decided against serial production, possibly doubting the dependability and longevity of the Wankel engine. Further improvements were made, but just as the Wankel engine reached optimum reliability and longevity, the 1973 oil crisis put a stop to the advance of this revolutionary powerhouse. Paul Frère: 'Meanwhile, the laws relating to exhaust emission had been sharpened in so many countries that the Wankel engine no longer seemed of relevance to the Stuttgart development engineers.'

The inventor, Felix Wankel, who died aged 87 in 1988, gave precise expression to his feelings on the failure of his engine in Germany in an interview in the

March 1986 issue of *Manager* magazine in 1986: 'For Felix Wankel, two people above all were responsible – Harald Quandt and Friedrich Karl Flick, at the time the two largest shareholders of BMW and Daimler-Benz respectively.

'In both companies, a decision in favour of the engine was on the verge of being taken. But the change-over of the assembly lines from reciprocating-piston engines to rotary engines, which would have cost huge amounts of money (certainly 1 billion marks), would have been too expensive for the dividend-hungry main shareholders' – That is how Wankel sees it, and he gives an account of events from the period as evidence.

'The engine itself, with comparably few parts and of very simple construction, had long been cheaper to manufacture than reciprocating-piston engines. Some-one who backed up that claim was the head of engine construction at Daimler-Benz, Wolf-Dieter Bensinger, who died in 1974.

'In a visit at the beginning of the '70s, Bensinger, a great supporter of the rotary engine, got very worked up and told Wankel: 'We have calculated exactly the cost of the new engine with reference to the machines that the machine builders have made. If it were only ten or twenty per cent cheaper than the present one, we wouldn't have mentioned it to you. But it will be forty per cent cheaper, and we can produce at double the present rate with the same team and the same number of machines.'

Prof. Hans Scherenberg, previously member of the managing board and head of the R & D department of Daimler-Benz, does not agree with that argument however: 'The Wankel project did not founder against the opposition of Messrs Flick and Quandt – they never argued with us technicians. On the contrary, when we started developing the V8 engine, I was called to the Flick company to give a speech which touched on the subject of the Wankel engine. I made it clear that we had to start without delay on manufacturing the neccessary equipment for the parallel construction of the Wankel engine.

On this occasion I expressed the belief that I considered the construction of the V8 engine indispensable, for we were not at all certain at the time whether the Wankel engine would win the day. Flick assented without argument to this "parallel development" (as did the Quandt company). The major shareholders took the risk of letting us build manufacturing equipment for two completely different motoring concepts.'

TECHNICAL DIFFICULTIES

'Today we know that the Wankel engine at Daimler-Benz foundered solely on technical difficulties. Against positive characteristics such as quiet running and favourable speeds of rotation, one had to balance considerable disadvantages: higher fuel consumption, problems with the purification of exhaust gases and with the seals. There were also difficulties involved in the installation of Wankel assemblies in the engine rooms: the universal joint housing had to be higher, for, in the Wankel engine, drive runs from the middle of the engine to the rear wheels, so it has to be placed higher than is the case with the reciprocating-piston engine shaft.

'Furthermore, it had become clear by then that there was still considerable development potential in the reciprocating-piston engine, not to mention advantages it had over the rotary engine, such as a more compact combustion chamber, better fuel consumption and, with regard to valve action, better control and more variants. A further disadvantage of the Wankel engine was its incompatibility with the diesel principle.

'Mercedes-Benz's four-cylinder diesel engines were always closely tied to the corresponding Otto engines, both in terms of their design and their development. A combination of a similar nature would have been impossible for the diesel-Wankel. Individual development, meanwhile would have been very much more expensive. Taking into account also the effects of the oil crisis of 1973, one can understand the company's decision to bid farewell, not without regret, to the Wankel engine.

'It was not just Daimler-Benz that had doubts about the Wankel engine: of the original twenty-eight companies that took out licences (among them Rolls-Royce and General Motors) – turning Wankel into a millionaire – twenty-seven dropped the idea.

Only the Japanese firm Mazda remained loyal to the

Wankel concept. To date it has sold more than two million cars fitted with the rotary engine, among them the successful RX-7 sports car, but it's significant too that the company has an extensive programme for the development of ultra-modern reciprocating engines – a clear vote in favour of the Otto concept developed more than 100 years ago.'

In the last years of his life, Wankel found contentment. Two years before his death, he said that the German automobile industry had made its peace with him. He was referring to the contract made in 1985 between himself and Daimler-Benz: the Stuttgart company taking over his research institute in Lindau on the Bodensee, in order to secure the future of his life's work beyond his death.

Prof Hans Scherenberg has his own view: 'I have a great deal of respect for Felix Wankel. He is the only person to have developed a conceivable alternative to the Otto engine for driving an automobile that became ready for series production (NSU, Mazda, Fichtel &

Sachs). The gas turbine has still not reached that degree of development.'

The C111 test vehicle had a fascinating rebirth in 1976, though without the Wankel engine. The 190 bhp C111-IID and the 230 bhp CIII-III 3-litre, used a five-cylinder diesel engine, which featured an exhaust gas turbocharger and boost inter-cooling. The successful diesel-class world record attempts carried out in it on the Italian racing track of Nardo are discussed in detail on pages 118–119.

The main goal of these record attempts was to break the (unofficial) speed record on a circuit. Since 1975, it had stood at 355.854 kph (221.123 mph), set by the American racing driver Mark Donohue in a Porsche 917/30 which had more than 1000 bhp. The C111, now a C111-IV, was given its third engine variant – the 450SE's 4.8-litre, eight-cylinder Otto engine which had two exhaust gas turbochargers and 500 bhp. And, on 5 May 1979, the Daimler-Benz test engineer, Dr Hans Liebold circuited the Nardo course at 403.978 kph (250.47 mph).

HANS-KARL LANGE

Hitting the Heights
Comparing the 560 SE (1988) and the 300 SEL 6.3 (1968)

'It is only possible to distinguish its exterior appearance from that of other 300SEL models by the 6.3 badge on the right-hand corner of the boot lid, and by its different lighting units. This sentence is of significance only because in the time that it takes you to read it, the 300SEL 6.3 accelerates from 0 to 100 kph.'

That is an extract from the Daimler-Benz brochure of 1968, when the top model made its debut. The 6.3 was, and remains, a quite extraordinary car. Its acceleration and sheer power often bettered the performance of exotic sports cars. And yet this very quick 250 bhp machine came from the production line of a manufacturer whose 200D model series had begun with a sluggish 55 bhp. In 1968 there suddenly appeared a yawning gap of 3.5 litres and 80 bhp between the previous 300SEL and the new 6.3-litre model.

Twenty years later, in spite of its 279 bhp, the 560SE/SEL is no more than the top model of a production series. By contrast, introducing the 6.3 seemed like madness for a company famous for shunning excess.

It was a true marriage of giants that brought the Mercedes-Benz 300SEL 6.3 to the Geneva show. Until then, the standard-bearer was the 300SEL: Its 2.8-litre injection engine delivered 170 bhp and had its work cut out in pulling the 3564 lb and 16 feet long air-suspended limousine. With the harsh, metallic noise it produced the 300 sounded almost like a sports car at high engine speeds. That did not quite suit the SEL's image as a fast, comfortable car, and, in comparison, BMW's six-cylinder engines were noticeably smoother and quieter not having to lug such huge weights around . . . something had to be done.

Luckily, there was a large – a very large – V8 in Stuttgart's arsenal, the M100. It displaced a colossal 6332 cc, and its maximum power output was 250 bhp. Since 1963, this engine had powered the 600, Mercedes' top model which, at 56 500 DM (twice as much as a 300SEL) was exclusively aimed at captains of industry, the film business and politicians. To cram this super engine into the 300SEL seemed almost frivolous. In retrospect the 300SEL 6.3 still seems like a project that could only have been conceived and executed by a few committed car enthusiasts; and that's probably just the way it was.

Rudolf Uhlenhaut, director of passenger car development at Stuttgart-Untertürkheim, frequently used to call the 6.3 an *Auto zum Brausen*, literally a car for kicking up storms. And Uhlenhaut was good at storming: in the Silver Arrow years he had no difficulty in equalling the times reached by Fangio and Moss, while Erich Waxenberger, director of test-driving was also renowned as a fast driver, being able to complete the Stuttgart-Munich run (200 km/125 miles) in about an hour in a 300SL. It was Waxenberger who decided to run the 300SEL 6.3 in saloon car races between 1969 and 1971. Another man who was just as important was Joachim Zahn, later to become president of Daimler-Benz AG; it was he who, when all was said and done, succeeded in selling the idea of the 6.3 to the management.

And it was a success right down the line. The cast-iron V8 produced a massive torque of 370 lb ft at only 2800 rpm and the maximum power of 250 bhp was achieved at only 4000 rpm. Despite its automatic gearbox, the 1.9-ton car sprinted to 100 kph in 6.5 to 7.6 seconds – depending on factory specifications and test results. The top speed of between 220 and 225 kph (136–139 mph) matched that of the Porsche 911S with a 170 bhp, 2-litre engine, which was definitely second-best in acceleration. Meanwhile, among contemporary limousines only two of the élite could hold their ground. The elegant Maserati Quattroporte was driven by a 'small' 4.7-litre V8, which with four overhead camshafts and four Weber twin-choke downdraught carburettors produced about 290 bhp. Maserati's own figures spoke of a top speed of 230 kph (143 mph) with acceleration to 100 kph (62 mph) in 7.5 seconds. By contrast, it was a tuned 5.4-litre Chevrolet Corvette V8, whose 355 bhp provided similar performance, thumping beneath the bonnet of the impressive Iso-Rivolta Fidia.

The 300SEL 6.3 also looked good in the company of four-seater Gran-Turismo coupés: The Iso-Rivolta GT ran at just over 230 kph (143 mph), a Ferrari 365GT 2+2 managed 240 kph (149 mph) and the Maserati Indy 4200 was just a length faster. Unlike these hand-finished

exotic creatures, the 6.3-litre Mercedes appeared as an unassuming standard saloon, with automatic gearbox, air-suspension, and a long wheelbase. In 1968 the price of almost 40 000 DM was a high one, but all the same, no fewer than 6256 found buyers by the summer of 1972, among them Formula One drivers such as John Surtees and François Cevert. The 6.3-litre V8 turned the sober 600 into a true driver's car and its characteristic understatement could be increased by removing the tell-tale '6.3' from its rear. And as countless drivers of the smaller engined S-Class limousines had their 2.5-litre and 2.8-litre S and SE models kitted out with the double windscreen wipers from the 6.3, the profile of the company's most powerful car on the roads was lowered yet further.

THE 'SMOKE BOMB'

The understated power of the quickest Mercedes of its day was made even more potent by tuners AMG. In standard form, the 6.3-litre engine was unstressed at only 40 bhp per litre. In the cramped engine bay packed out with the drive unit and sub-assemblies, room had to be found for exhaust manifolds that would have been more suited to a heavy goods vehicle – tuned for power it wasn't. In a converted mill in the village of Burgstall, inhabited by 1525 lonely souls, AMG put the 300SEL 6.3 through two development programmes, which resulted in 290 and 320 bhp respectively. In May 1971 an AMG 6.3 with 320 bhp, driven by the respected Stuttgart car magazine *Auto, Motor und Sport*, reached 100 kph (62 mph) in 6.7 seconds, raced past the standing kilometre in 25.7 seconds, and reached a top speed of 235 kph (146 mph) at which point it was slowed by its wind resistance. Klaus Westrup headlined his article on it 'Smoke Bomb', referring to the torque which would so easily send its rear wheels spinning.

Before the Mercedes tuner AMG had the idea of using a 6.3-litre engine in saloon car racing, Daimler-Benz itself had already prepared three vehicles for competition. With at least 378 bhp these monsters entered the 1969 Spa 24-hour race at Francorchamps in Belgium. To the astonishment of the spectators, the powerful heavyweights recorded fantastic times, but had to be retired early due to excessive tyre wear. Afterwards, AMG tuned a 6.3 racer for the Mercedes dealer Klaus Behrmann who had a lot of fun in the German Saloon Car Championships in 1971, and still has the car today.

But the greatest impression was caused at the beginning of the '70s by the fifth 300SEL 6.3 racer, equipped with AMG's own new light-alloy wheels. AMG was then still a small and relatively unknown company, but that was soon to change. For the start of the 1971 saloon car racing season, Hans-Werner Aufrecht and Erhard Melcher took apart a damaged 6.3-litre, welded its sun roof shut, installed the recently-homologated Daimler-Benz five-speed gearbox, and zipped the large-calibre V8 engine up to around 420 bhp with delicate tuning work. Its first appearance in the Bavaria race on the Salzburgring – its driver, Erich Waxenberger, starting under a pseudonym ended with an encouraging second place. At Hockenheim, Helmut Kelleners blundered off the track but it ran magnificently in the 24-hour race at Spa in 1971. Manned by Hans Heyer and Clemens Schickentanz, what appeared to be an almost standard limousine (compared to the others) thundered around the Ardennes circuit at impressive speeds. When the AMG Mercedes passed the finishing line second after a works Ford Capri RS, only eighteen of the sixty-four saloons that had started were still in the race and the little AMG earned its standing ovation. During the race there were heavy storms, leading *Autocar* to describe the big Mercedes' performance in the following terms: 'Under the suitably Wagnerian accompaniment of thunder and lightning, the AMG Mercedes was a truly spectacular sight for the 180 000 spectators.'

The Mercedes 560SE of today, which combined the short S-class car body with the big V8 engine of the long-wheelbase 560SEL is another unostentatious and fast luxury limousine. Although its engine is at least 800 cc smaller, it is technically very similar, but its alloy V8 engine provides 29 bhp more than the old cast-iron motor, despite its catalytic converter. Admittedly, one has to accept an increased engine speed (maximum power comes 1200 rpm higher) and be satisfied with considerably less torque. Tested by *Auto Zeitung*, the 560SE blazed along at 238 kph (148 mph) and reached 100 kph (62 mph) in 7.6 seconds. In spite of that, the

560SE comfortably manages 100 km with 17 litres of lead-free petrol, where the 300SEL 6.3 would have guzzled 20 litres of leaded to feed its eight cylinders. Compared both to its racing competition and to the bread-and-butter cars of its day, of course, the 560 doesn't seem anywhere near as extreme and unusual as the 6.3 did twenty years ago. For one thing, some Japanese manufacturers have joined Mercedes and Jaguar in the luxury class, while mid-range cars of great technical sophistication today perform at levels once reserved for an élite minority. How times change.

HOW DO THEY COMPARE ?

But how does the 560SE compare with its predecessor, the 300SEL 6.3?

Bruno Sacco's design may be ten years old now but it still looks impressive, albeit rather too familiar. What is the public reaction to the 560SE, a black one say? In Germany it seems to be a mixture of respect and mistrust: with a bored expression on their faces, townspeople assume that within rides a minister, a diplomat, or an entrepreneur. And countryfolk, by comparison, expect something more, perhaps even the prime minister. If there is really something unappealing about the S-class to broad sections of the population, it is merely that politicians and middle and high-grade civil servants drive around in them at the taxpayer's expense.

Twenty years ago, chrome was much in evidence for the top range. That may be completely out of fashion today, but it still conjures a friendly smile onto the lips of anyone who sees an old S-class Mercedes. Seen from the front, the 300SEL 6.3 is bold and upright, though perhaps a little rugged by today's standards. By contrast, the 560 is broad, low and unembellished. Where the veteran flashes its ostentatious double headlamps, its successor throws far more light from its anonymous rectangular lights onto the road. But the veteran has a low, almost delicate silhouette seen diagonally from the rear – thanks to Paul Bracq's draughtsmanship. The rear lights of twenty years ago were small and narrow; today they are hefty and powerful. The 560 may appear to be tons heavier than the 300, but it is actually 18 kilograms

(40 lb) lighter. The alert reader will ask: is that all, after so many technological advances? The problem is that so much has become standard such as air conditioning, power seats and windows and anti-lock brakes.

Seen from the driver's seat, the veteran 300SEL 6.3 is low, broad and very bright. Its windows are conspicuously large, and its dashboard is low. Above all, there is no central console on its carpet-covered transmission tunnel, which is what gives it such a spacious feel. The outsized steering wheel with its thin black bakelite rim and chrome-plated disc takes some getting used to. And between the large tachometer and the combination petrol, water temperature and oil pressure gauge is the rev counter, small as a wristwatch. To be sure, a Jaguar 420G pampered its passengers to a far greater degree with hardwood, leather, and beautiful dials, but all the same, a Mercedes 300SEL 6.3 soon attains the comfort of a well-heated living room.

That's quite a contrast with the Mercedes 560SE. Its cockpit is cool and functional. Hardwood is sparingly used, and struggles to counteract the almost suffocating predominance of black plastic. Even the beautiful wood hardly makes an impression in such dull surroundings. The current car has so much equipment – heated seat, heated floor, electrically operated rear windows shades, even a CD player – that the driver is provided with a bewildering number of buttons and dials on the central console. Bewilderment continues even after a period of acclimatisation. But in one respect Daimler-Benz has stayed absolutely true to form: the steering wheel of the 560SE of 1988 is extraordinarily large, just like that of the 300SEL 6.3 of 1968. Instead of the thin bakelite rim, though, the driver holds a thick wheel covered with high-grade leather in his hands.

Whether covered in smooth bakelite or in prehensile leather, both wheels steer quite exceptionally powerful automobiles. For all its massive appearance, the 560SE is a very fast car. All the same, the torque of the old 300SEL 6.3's cast-iron engine knocks the modern alloy V8 into a cocked hat: 500 Nm at only 2800 rpm compared with 430 Nm at 3750 rpm. What difference does all this extra torque make?

The 6.3-litre engine come to life with the slurping sounds of suction. With the frivolously delicate joystick of the automatic gearbox switched to D, a shudder goes through the whole car and the frequency of the pounding idling sounds changes. Something is going on! Foot off the brakes, accelerate slightly, the fluid drive whisks up the hydraulic oil, then all 1.9 tons spring into action. The mammoth engine hums meatily with the foot half down on the accelerator, and hammers metallically when the automatic transmission kicks down. At speed. However engine noise is increasingly masked by the sound of the wind.

The 560 SE by contrast is completely quiet when idling, silkily at low engine speeds, and subdued at half throttle. One might almost imagine that a huge electromagnet was dragging the heavy luxury car through the landscape. Only at full throttle does it give voice to an angry, though by no means uncivilized, growl. It does not, however, accelerate in quite as violent and unbridled a manner as its great father. Barely perceptibly, its automatic transmission changes gears, like a knife through butter. It is helped in that by the electronic engine management retarding the ignition at just the right moment so there are no jolts during gear changes. Only at really high speed does the Mercedes 560SE leave the 300SEL 6.3 behind, and, thanks to its better aerodynamics, the 560 will only gradually lose speed. By contrast, the 6.3 slows quickly due to its own considerable wind resistance.

The driver will have good reason to be grateful to the old car if he has to slow down quickly from high speed. Although the brakes of the 300SEL 6.3 are powerful, even by today's standards, the car dips markedly at the front under braking. Then its rear swing-axle jacks up and allows the rear wheels to change their camber it is then – only too easy for the rear to slew out. In the not-so-good old days, quite a few 6.3s sailed into the crash barriers in that way . . . . At the time the VW Beetle drivers frequently underestimated the speed of an approaching 6.3. If a slow car suddenly slipped out from between two lorries to overtake, then the Merc driver could quickly get into trouble. All the same 324 SEL 6.3s can still be seen in Germany.

The story is quite different with the 560SE. Sophisticated rear suspension, anti-dive and an anti-lock braking systems are taken for granted today, not only in the luxury class.

It is in such areas that the progress of the last twenty years is most marked. All the same, the unusually low noise level and the car's effortless performance at high and top speeds hide the danger of unconsciously driving too quickly. Even driving at 230 kph (143 mph) in the 560SE on a three-lane motorway hardly feels out of the ordinary, but things get tricky when an obstacle suddenly comes out of nowhere. At that point it gets difficult to understand why everyone else is moving so terribly slowly.

Twenty years of development at Mercedes have also led to similar improvements in handling. Whereas the old favourite 300SEL 6.3 always gives the driver clear signals through the steering wheel and the rear axle, the 560SE waits a long while before indicating the limit of road adherence. Its power steering rarely beams messages from the road to the arms of the driver. On fast curves the car leans, understeers slightly, then stays neutral for a very long time. Oversteer can be provoked by harsh use of the accelerator, but no-one would want that – 1.9 tons cannot be juggled by force.

The wheelbase of the 560SE is 14 cm (5.5 in) shorter than that of the over-the-top 560SEL. Nevertheless, this Mercedes is still a princely express on the motorway transferring its passengers in comfort and silence from one city to the next. The loss of a little rear legroom may well have made the car more agile, but all the same it gives far less driving pleasure than did the 300SEL 6.3 of 1968. There is only one conclusion that I can reach: whoever can afford it should put a well kept old 300SEL 6.3 in the garage at the villa. Just for the weekend.

Above and overleaf: Mercedes-Benz 300 SL coupé 1954. What began as a technical necessity – actually getting into the sporty 'Dream Coupé' – resulted, much to the surprise of the Daimler-Benz designers, in a 'stylistic' sensation: the wing doors known as 'gull wings'. The 300 SL was originally (1952) conceived as a racing sports car, but from 1954 on there was a road-going version. From both technical and design perspectives the 300 SL represented the zenith of car-making at that time.

From 1954 to 1957 1 400 coupés were built and from then until 1963 1 858 300 SL roadsters.

Pages 196-197, 198-199: Mercedes-Benz 300 SL roadster.

Technical data: 6 cylinders, 2 966 cc capacity, 215 bhp at 5 800 rpm, maximum speed around 250 kph.

*Above: Mercedes-Benz 190 SL 1955. In 1955 the 300 SL gained a baby
brother, the 190 SL sports car. The instigator was the then USA importer
Maxi Hoffman (who had also eased the way for Porsche into the USA
after the war). The 190 SL had been presented as a prototype in New York
the previous year. It was based on the 180, but had a new engine. The 190
SL, an elegant car with a robust engine, was not designed for competitive
sport but was more of a sporty touring car. About 26 000 were built
between 1955 and 1964.*

*Technical data: 4 cylinders, 1 897 cc capacity, 105 bhp at 5 700 rpm,
maximum speed 171 kph.*

INGO SEIFF

Safety First

'Motor racing is dangerous' – that is what is printed on entrance tickets to English circuits, and the renowned Nürburgring sends its visitors home after races with the warning: *Motorsportfreunde fahren vorsichtig nach Hause!* – 'Friends of motor sport drive home carefully'. In fact, it is to the perfectly 'normal' traffic on country roads and motorways that several thousand people a year fall prey. In 1988, 8500 people died in two million traffic accidents on German roads, and the total cost incurred by these accidents ran to DM 45 billion – approximately £15 billion.

The death toll from traffic accidents in Great Britain in 1987 was 5100, and 46 000 in the USA in the same period.

There seems to be no remedy for this lamentable blood-letting – for appeals to drivers' reason have not borne fruit. It would appear that if you ask an ordinary driver to consider nothing more than the physical laws of motion, you are asking too much. He knows little of the energy involved in an impact, of the crushing zones or the extent to which the passenger space can be deformed. His sense of the harsh physical realities of driving is clouded by the emotions that always go hand in hand with possessing a car. To millions of people their car represents the most spectacular means of living out their own personal freedom – freedom to come and go as they wish. Unfortunately that freedom yearly takes a toll that only cynics can turn away from with a shrug of the shoulders. So what is to be done? Even those that have the greatest faith in progress do not believe that one day we will breed the ideal, accident-free driver. Instead, we expect manufacturers to build cars which are as safe as possible for their occupants. Man is the culprit in ninety per cent of all accidents; the human being proving truly to be the weak link between car and road and the least susceptible to change. Automotive engineers can improve the car, but not the man.

Daimler-Benz has made strenuous efforts over the last six decades to improve both the active and passive safety of its vehicles ('active safety' meaning all the characteristics of a vehicle that help to avoid accidents, while under 'passive safety' come those measures that lessen the consequences of an accident).

At first most attention was paid to improving active safety, consistent with the state of the art in motor vehicle technology. The introduction of independent suspension, double action bumpers, and the first twin-circuit power brakes were important milestones.

Development continued after the war with passive as well as active safety being improved with features, such as door safety locks, rigid tonneaus, smoother interiors, safety steering columns, crush zones and so on. With door locks it was important that they should not open on impact, but could still be opened after an accident, to save occupants from death by fire.

A significant milestone in improving car safety was the 'Memorandum of Understanding' that was signed by the German Federal Republic and the United States. The safety requirements of the USA, as one of the German car industry's most important export markets, gave a fillip to safety research and development at Daimler-Benz.

'ACTIVE SAFETY'

But it was not only the American safety initiative that led to the intensification of R & D at Daimler-Benz. The company had been carrying out experiments on impact and the results of cars overturning since 1959. Seat belts have been built in since 1961, and safety head-rests since 1968.

A high point in the development of 'active safety' came in 1970, with the introduction of ABS anti-lock brakes which enable one to brake hard without the car skidding – and thus stop in a shorter distance. The car also remains steerable during braking, which means that one can brake and drive around an obstacle at the same time. Meanwhile, automatic front seat belts became standard from 1973 onwards, and rear ones from 1979.

After a decade of development, Mercedes-Benz offered airbags in the column of the steering wheel as an additional safety device from 1981 on, together with a device for tightening the seatbelt of the co-driver.

That was in 1984 and now all Mercedes-Benz cars – from the compact 190 to the large coupé –are provided with electronically controlled belt-tighteners for both front seats. In 1987 Mercedes-Benz introduced the passenger's airbag as a logical addition to the airbag for the driver. That appeared first for all S-class limousines and coupés and, since October 1988, the mid-range too. Many Mercedes' developments have become standard safety requirements in construction across the industry.

The ingenious safety devices described here are not technical gimmicks; they save lives.

An unbelted passenger in a car continues to move forward at an almost undiminished velocity during frontal impact, until he makes contact with his own car which has already come to rest. The following figures show the energy involved: Hitting a solid wall at nothing more than walking pace corresponds to a fall from a height of over four feet. Meanwhile, as the energy of impact rises with the square of the speed, hitting that same solid wall at 51 kph (32 mph) corresponds to a fall from the fourth floor of a block of flats.

Improving active safety is crucial, but so is improving the driver's environment and increasing his 'sense of well-being'. Everything should be laid out to maximize relaxation and comfort and require the least possible expenditure of energy by the driver; allowing him calm concentration during a long, strenuous trip. The engineers at Daimler-Benz also speak of *Wahrnehmungssicherheit*, which means having a clear view, and of *Bedienungssicherheit*, that is user-friendliness.

The subject of *Fahrverhalten*, or road behaviour, also comes under the subject of active safety; where the suspension has a great deal of travel, for example, there are changes in toe-in and toe-out which are vital to the way the car behaves. In coming to come to grips with this problem, engineers always come up against the question of comfort. Solving this conflict of interests requires *Kunst der Abstimmung*, or the art of fine adjustment, as it is called by Daimler-Benz. This art lies in exploiting the kinematic properties of an axle, along with the elastokinematic properties of the steering and suspension in their rubber bushes, in order to arrive at the right compromise between handling, roadholding and comfort. This requires precision adjustment.

A largely compromise-free solution to this conflict of interests was achieved by a front axle with dampers and a multi-link independent rear suspension, which, without writing off comforts, allow only the bias effects desired.

'PASSIVE SAFETY'

The most important basis on which passive safety is developed is the analysis of real-life accidents. Accidents involving Mercedes-Benz cars, in which passengers were injured, have been systematically studied since 1969. The information gleaned is substantially different from other statistics, and for years has helped Daimler-Benz safety standards to be far above those stipulated in law in the USA and Europe.

Accident investigation also proves the effectiveness of measures taken for the protection of passengers. For example, in Mercedes' current range, the danger of injury has been reduced by more than fifty per cent compared with the models built between 1968 and 1975, which themselves were above average in terms of safety.

Approximately thirty per cent of this reduction can be accounted for by an increase in the numbers of those wearing seatbelts, but twenty per cent is due to additional measures; non-deformable body interiors; deformable crumple zones at front and rear, chassis stability that resists slewing and rolling over, locating the fuel tank above the rear axle; and reinforcement of the interior to protect the occupants as much as possible.

Just consider the safety features in the steering alone, with a collapsible steering column; a cushioned and collapsible head in the steering wheel; and an arrangement whereby the pedals tilt out forwards in the event of frontal impact.

The passenger restraining system employs the automatic safety belt along with the standard belt-tighteners at the front, not to mention the additional protection given by airbags for the driver and front passenger's.

The object of all this is to minimize the danger to passengers but Daimler-Benz pays great attention to external safety too, intended to reduce the danger of injury to pedestrians and cyclists. Accident research has shown that seventy per cent of all accidents where the passengers are injured are frontal collisions. Where previously only minimal means of collapse were available, today the front of the car, including the bumpers, radiator grille and bonnet, area are designed to be more yielding. The lighting units now slide back on impact and the lower windscreen frame and the windscreen wiper unit are largely covered.

CRASH SURVIVAL

In fifty per cent of frontal collisions with injured occupants the damage is on the driver's side, in other words, against the flow of traffic; in a further twenty-five per cent the impact is on the passenger side, and in only a quarter of cases is it head-on. That knowledge has led to crash experiments at Daimler-Benz which cover frontal impacts alone. As impact here can cause more critical damage to the body and suspension than is reflected by the legally required crash tests, new forms of construction had to be developed. In contrast to cars which are designed to withstand only a frontal collision against a flat wall, the passenger cell of every Mercedes-Benz can survive intact an offset crash at 55 kph (34mph). After trials to test the vehicle after such a crash, all the doors can be opened without any problems, the leg-room is only slightly reduced and the steering and the instrument panel are only pushed back a little.

This ability to maintain structural integrity is due to the so-called *Gabelträgerkonzept*, or fork carrier concept. It consists of a threefold connection of the front longitudinal chassis member – to the strong transmission tunnel, to the floor construction and to the stronger doors and pillars.

In today's heavy traffic where drivers follow too closely the vehicle in front, nose to tail collisions are inevitable. Here too most impacts are angled, leading to great localized deformation even with stiff rear structures. Clearly the position of the fuel tank plays an important safety role. Mercedes' fuel tanks are mounted above the rear axle, separated by at least 80 cm (30 ins) from the rear bumper. The structure remains strong, even in extreme cases, for example when the car is hit by a heavy truck, because the tank cannot end up under the wheel of any heavy goods vehicle.

The only exception is the T-series. In an estate car the need for space dictates that safety must be compromised by mounting the tank beneath the luggage space. To compensate, these vehicles have extremely stiff rear structures, formed by additional longitudinal struts under the rear floor, and extra support in the D-pillar where it joins the roof. The tank is also mounted 52 cm further forward from the rear bumper than in any rival model.

DRIVING DYNAMICS

As the risk of injury in head-on collisions has been decreased by effective vehicle design, attention has turned to the problem of protecting driver and passengers from side impacts; which frequently involve collisions with solid obstacles after the car has left the road. In these cases the design of the roads themselves is almost as important as improvement to the cars.

Also crucial is the so-called Mercedes-Benz *Fahrdynamik-Konzept* – the Mercedes-Benz driving dynamics concept. In that, the most modern automobile mechanics and hydraulics are combined with artificial intelligence to produce traction aids far beyond anything conventional devices can offer.

It consists of three hierarchical, automatic, electronically-controlled systems, adapted to the most varied driving situations: the automatic locking differential (ASD), traction control (ASR) and 4-matic. They come into their own in dangerous situations, extreme weather conditions or extraordinary road conditions. This integrated concept of automatically-adjusted vehicle behaviour and appropriate driver data now guarantees the highest degree of active safety, a concept which is unique in the car industry, and constitutes a new era in car technology.

The common factor in all three systems is that they 'think' by themselves – registering driving conditions precisely, recognizing the situation and reacting in milliseconds. Electronically-automatically they integrate with the driver. Dashboard lights inform the driver that the systems are functioning so that he can adjust his driving as necessary.

ASD is an automatic locking differential used in the four- and six-cylinder models. Where the road surface is smooth, or slippery on one side only, ASD prevents any wheel from skidding. The electronic circuit causes the differential to lock-up to a hundred per cent, depending on the situation, increasing traction impressively. As the differential lock is released during braking, driving stability remains undiminished and the anti-lock brakes can function.

ASR is a traction-control device. Even under full throttle ASR automatically applies only as much pressure to the drive wheels as they will take before skidding. Driving stability, control and hill-climbing power are all considerably increased, helping the driver to swerve out of the path of an obstacle for example, or to drive more safely in snow or on a road surface slippery on one side. Incidentally ABS (anti-lock braking) is an integral part of the ASR traction control.

4-MATIC

The final part in the jigsaw is 4-matic: electronically-controlled automatic four-wheel drive with two differential locks.

When the 4-matic switches drive to all four wheels, thirty-five per cent goes to the front wheels, sixty-five per cent to the rear. The result is greatly improved climbing power and off-the-line traction, improved road-holding and directional stability in curves. If required, the centre differential between front and rear axles can be locked; finally, in a third stage the rear differential between the two wheels can also be locked. With 4-matic, as in ASR, the driver is kept informed by a dashboard display. A better conversion of driving power into motion is difficult to imagine.

There are unique advantages to this way forward: the chance for human error to intervene in reacting to events is markedly diminished. Recognition, decision-making and reaction occur in good time and at a speed beyond the capabilities of a human being – without treating the driver like a child, distracting him or leading him to make errors. Daimler-Benz has brought automotive engineering three giant steps closer to the goal of optimal active safety by the intelligent application of electronics; electronics, that is, which will never deprive the driver of control. The main operations of steering, braking and accelerating remain in his power. Electronics only come in where they can react more quickly than a human being, for example with ABS, which slows the car more quickly and effectively than a driver could ever manage. ABS can 'pump the brakes' many times quicker than any skilled driver.

DRIVING SIMULATOR

Daimler-Benz engineers are particularly proud of the driving simulator, which has revealed new research possibilities in vehicle safety. Four years after opening the driving simulator at the Berlin-Marienfelde works it is clear the investment of 25 million DM has been worthwhile. The simulator provides, for the first time ever, a complete test bed for work on active safety.

The purpose of a simulator is to imitate, with as much precision as is possible, a specific situation, enabling theories to be tested and systems planned. Research in the simulator enables rules of thumb to be established. It should uncover more about the laws to which human beings are subject as drivers, about what constitutes a safe car and, indeed, what constitutes a safe road.

Very complex vehicle components can be judged in a simulator for their effects on driving performance even at a very early stage of their development, speeding up progress and enabling new technology to go into production earlier.

The driving simulator also aids decision-making: it helped, for example, in the decision not to have a permanent all-wheel drive, but to develop permanently available four-wheel drive with 4-matic. Test drives on the simulator showed that on uneven slippery road surfaces the drivers could compensate if the 4-matic warned of changed traction conditions. Improved forewarning led to less stressful driving; the researchers registering the lowest heart and breathing rate of any driving conditions when 4-matic was used.

The simulator's performance and research capabilities are simply unlimited. Not only does it help the development engineers in their main task of adapting vehicle technology to human capabilities, it also means the effects of individual changes and their combined effect can be tested – as often as desired, in quick succession, in various traffic conditions and – not least – as an exact simulation. It can monitor the driver alone – in such areas as his subjective sense of safety, fatigue, driving strategy, risk assessment and the effect of medicine and alcohol. The interrelationship of car and driver can be also be considered – in such matters as the ergonomics of the driver's seat, the effect of vehicle characteristics on driver/vehicle behaviour and the effect of controls designed to give extra support to the driver.

Finally, the simulator can help assess the driver/ vehicle/environment – demonstrating the interplay during interference such as side winds, and aquaplaning; in judgement of, and reaction to, traffic situations, the effect of traffic regulations and road signs, the design of the road itself and driving behaviour in general.

The circle closes: at the beginning of this chapter we viewed the human being as the weak link in the safety chain. The driving simulator will uncover instead his motives, his desires, his emotions, his capabilities, which all affect the kind of driver he is; and we will all profit from that.

RICHARD VON FRANKENBERG

The Dream Car
The 300 SL

The following article was written by the late Richard von Frankenberg for *Motorrevue* in Spring 1971:

It was on 19 November 1952 that Kling/Klenk and Lang/Grupp took their 300SLs to first and second places in the Mexican Carrera Panamericana, still one of the greatest in achievements in racing history. Not only did it demonstrate considerable driving and technical skill, but it was also of great economic significance, opening doors to the hitherto closed American markets for the entire German export industry.

On 19 January 1952, a small news item had appeared in *Auto, Motor und Sport*, mentioning for the first time the new Daimler-Benz sports car. As precise details regarding the new car were unclear, the article cautiously stated, 'at present the engineers of Daimler-Benz are working on the development of a sports car based on the Mercedes-Benz series 300S. In December, Karl Kling carried out a few test runs on the Hockenheimring in the Mercedes-Benz 300SS, reaching a lap average speed of roughly 190 kph (118 mph). The car, which is aerodynamic in design, is larger in size than the Porsche. The six-cylinder engine apparently produces a power output of 170 bhp. It also has two Weber carburettors and hemispherical combustion chambers. It is anticipated that the car could reach a maximum speed of 240 kph (149 mph). Even though the design work has still to be finalized, the car will probably take part in large international motor racing events.'

This news item ushered in a racing model that was soon to make motor racing history. Subsequent production models were to be the most fascinating and technologically advanced vehicles yet built. As suggested above, the designation 300SS was initially being considered, but the suffix was soon replaced by SL.

This 300SL range comprised three basic models and these should be properly distinguished from each other. The first, launched in 1952, was a vehicle not built for sale to the public. It had a carburetted engine, designed in fact for the endurance motor racing events in which the company participated. At that time Daimler-Benz always used carburettor-engines for long-distance events.

The second version was based on a works racer, but was for sale. It had the same swept volume of 3 litres, but had the advantage of Bosch fuel injection. This was a coupé with a high spaceframe chassis which demanded the use of lift-up doors, called 'gull wings' in America.

The third 300SL, introduced at the Geneva Salon of 1957, had a different chassis, which permitted conventional doors to be fitted and made this a more civilized car. It had the same engine as the Gullwing and was available as a roadster, a roadster/coupé and as a coupé.

This third variant is often known as the 300SLR, the R representing 'roadster', but the designation is confusing – and incorrect – because the roadster was just called 300SL. The true 300SLR was in fact the racing car that Daimler-Benz used in 1955 in sports car championships, a machine that was never offered for sale. The construction of this car has nothing in common with the 300SL. Engine and chassis were derived from the Mercedes Grand Prix car of the day; and, although it had a swept volume of 3 litres, just like the 300SL, the SLR engine was a bored-out version of the 2.5 litre GP engine.

The first 300SL was the racing model developed during 1952. Indeed, the first test vehicles had been ready since the end of 1951, for trials at Hockenheim. This was kept strictly secret, the cars being transported on a lorry, covered with tarpaulin.

Professor Nallinger, a member of the managing board with a technical background, was heavily involved in the development of the cars. He worked closely with Rudolf Uhlenhaut, who was responsible for testing, and Josef Müller, the man responsible for the construction. Later they were joined by Hans Scherenberg, who looked after motor vehicle production. 'Well', said Nallinger, 'we wanted to try a new approach to international motor racing and the best and easiest way to do this was by using the 300SL.'

The reason for this was that the engine of that first SL

had been derived directly from the 300 and the 300S engine unit. Naturally, the chassis and the bodywork were completely new, being suited to motor racing.

A STAR IS BORN

The Mercedes-Benz 300 was launched at the 1951 Frankfurt Show and went on sale in November of that year. Initially it had a 2996 cc, in-line six-cylinder engine (bore and stroke 85/88 mm), with a Solex fixed-venturi 40PBJC carburettor and a compression ratio of only 6.4:1. Power output was 115 bhp at 4600 rpm.

This engine, with its overhead camshafts driven by a Duplex chain, was the basis of the 300SL unit. There was, however, an intermediate stage; the very rare 300S (available as coupé and convertible). This car's engine was the one actually used in the first 300SL and it went into production in the summer of 1952 with a compression of ratio 7.8:1, three 40PBJC carburettors and 150 bhp at 5000 rpm. The 300S was launched at the Paris Salon of October 1952, by which time the SL was well on its way.

Following the *Auto, Motor und Sport* news item concerning a new sports car and the subsequent rumours regarding the use of these cars in competition, Daimler-Benz announced the first details of the secret car in March. A later copy of *Auto, Motor und Sport* carried the following statement: 'The long-anticipated Mercedes-Benz 300SL sports car has arrived! Its six-cylinder in-line engine, with a cylinder capacity of 2996 cc produces 175 bhp at 5200 rpm. The overhead-camshaft unit has a compression ratio of 8:1, an automatically adjustable Duplex timing chain and a full-flow fine-gauge oil filter to enhance its continuous high performance. The maximum speed is about 240 kph (149 mph). The fact that the hydraulic brakes of the 300SL are especially large is self-explanatory, and with an overall height of 1265 mm (49.8 in) the car is even lower than the Porsche. Its four-speed gearbox is fully synchronised, the fuel tank takes 170 litres (37.4 gallons) and the special tyres are mounted on 15-inch wheels.'

The technical data related here was more or less

correct. Racing cars did not generally develop more than 175 bhp in 1952; even early on there were some 172 bhp engines. Also, the compression ratio was generally higher than 8.1:1. This relatively low ratio – today 'better' touring cars have a higher ratio – is easily explained. While the fuel for Formula One races was specially prepared, sports-car competitions, from the Mille Miglia to Le Mans, demanded sump fuel, whose octane rating was much lower than it is today. An octane rating of only ninety or just over was anticipated, so a higher compression ratio would have been an unwise choice. Even 8.1:1 was only possible with very carefully shaped combustion chambers. Above all, this engine was to be used in major long-distance races; at Daimler-Benz the three most important events were the Mille Miglia, Le Mans and the Carrera Panamericana in Mexico. Thus, the engine required not only enough power, but it had to supply it flat-out over long periods.

TECHNICAL MASTERPIECE

A streamlined shape had to compensate for a lack of outright power. By the end of 1951, the first 300SL had already been tested in a full-size wind tunnel, at the research institute of the Technische Hochschule, Stuttgart. (This institute was known even before the war, for the experiments and designs of Professor Wunibald Kamm ['K-form'].) The ratio of power to speed suggests that from 1952 the 300SL had a drag coefficient of less than 0.38.

The engineers also tried to achieve the best possible acceleration with 175 bhp. It was a well known fact that the 3-litre Ferrari, the 4.1-litre Ferrari, the 4.5-litre Talbot, and the Gordini sports car would be the toughest opponents. The Ferrari and the Talbot obviously had much more than 175 bhp, so the weight of the 300SL had to be kept as low as possible by using an aluminium chassis, giving the racing model a weight of 840 kg (1852 lb). This weight was remarkable for a 3-litre coupé. The power/weight ratio was 213 bhp/tonne and acceleration from 0 to 100 kph (62 mph) took less than 7

seconds – excellent by 1952 standards.

The rear-mounted racing fuel tank was built in various sizes and fitted to suit the course. The 170-litre version was the common one, but the capacity varied between 150 and 220 litres. It is obvious why such big fuel tanks were installed: each refuelling stop would take valuable time during a long-distance race and there was plenty of space in the rear, since there was no need for a boot. Continental tyres ('Monza' or 'Nürburgring') were most commonly used, 6.50-15 front and 6.70-15 rear, but occasionally Englebert tyres of the same size were fitted.

The 1952 works cars did not have a limited-slip differential, which is surprising, since it was later possible to buy the 300SL with such a device. However, different final drives were used from track to track.

Three different types of chassis were available for the 300SL in 1952. Initially, the car was only used as a coupé, at the Mille Miglia and Le Mans, but in shorter events, such as those on the Nürburgring, it was decided to use a convertible. It seemed sensible to give drivers cars with an improved field of vision, particularly on tracks with a large number of corners.

THE 'GULL WING'

There were two types of coupé. The first had lift-up 'Gull wing' doors; if doors is really the right term! The lift-up flaps on the side only opened the window and part of the roof leaving a sill 887 cm (34.7 in) high for the driver to climb over. It is surprising that the regulations permitted this. In events where it was necessary to swap drivers, a modified lift-up door was used, also installed in later production versions of the 300 SL. In this, the hinges were located higher on the roof and the door itself extended below the window, right down to the spaceframe chassis. Now the sill was only 56 cm (22.1 in) high. The first car with these enlarged doors appeared in 1952 at the Berne circuit, driven by Fritz Riess. All the works cars had these larger doors from Le Mans onwards. The replacement car was revealed at Le Mans, too. This had an air brake – an adjustable surface on the roof top operated by rods – tested during practice.

The plexiglass panels on the sides of the 1952 works 300SL had small sections which could be opened but the main ventilation came from an air vent in the middle of the roof. Such a primitive arrangement was of course unsuitable for the production 300SL.

The car was equipped with integral moulded seats and the dashboard was dominated by a large 270 kph (168 mph) speedometer with a neighbouring rev-counter whose red line was at 5800 rpm; speeds of more than 6000 rpm were not possible with this relatively long-stroke engine. Beneath these were gauges for oil and water temperatures, oil pressure and fuel level. This last indicated the exact content of the fuel tank, although for the later production 300SL the usual petrol gauge, indicating full, half-full and reserve, was installed.

There were two versions of the works engine. One had a power output of 175 bhp and, contrary to the original published specification, had a Solex carburettor, not a Weber. The second variant, which was super-charged, was tested on the Nürburgring but never used in competition.

In April 1952, the Daimler-Benz team was ready to compete. Neubauer's idea was to use three cars in all competitions, in line with tradition, which had dictated three or even four GP cars; if you want success you cannot afford to cut corners. At two races, Nürburgring and Berne, four 300SLs took part.

The drivers for the 1952 Mille Miglia were Rudolf Caracciola, Hermann Lang and Karl Kling. Each driver had one or two 'mulettos', which were used during practice and served as replacement cars. The same cars were always used for each competition, albeit slightly modified, and in all there were ten 300SLs.

THE MILLE MIGLIA

The 300SL marked the official return by the company to international motor racing and this comeback explains why the Mille Miglia was watched with great interest all over Europe, particularly since Caracciola and Lang were both experienced 'old guard' drivers. It was evident from the outset that success was not deemed to be about winning a class, but about overall victory.

The Italians were enthusiastic about Daimler-Benz's return to motor racing in the Mille Miglia. It was remarkable that Rudi Caracciola was to drive in the event at the age of fifty-one, almost two decades after winning the 1932 Mille Miglia with a Mercedes-Benz SSK. Insiders knew that his come-back was simply too late: his accident at Indianapolis in 1946, which rendered him unconscious for eleven days, had left its mark on the aged driver. It had been a glorious achievement taking fourth place in his last Mille Miglia, but, although he was experienced in not over-taxing himself or the car, he was simply not fast enough any more to get to the front.

For forty-two-year-old Hermann Lang, the Mille Miglia was over at quarter-distance, with his visit to a ditch. The only chance of victory now rested with the thirty-two-year-old 'youngster', Karl Kling.

Every year the Mille Miglia route was altered, but for 1952 it covered a distance of 1564 km (972 miles). Check points were set up in Ravenna, Aquila, Rome, Siena, Florence and Bologna, with the start and finish being, as usual, in Brescia. After 1224 km (760 miles), Kling was ahead of the 3-litre-Ferrari driver, Giovanni Bracco, who had two advantages: first of all he knew the route better than Kling, and secondly he was to benefit during the wet last quarter of the race, since the field of vision in rain is obviously superior in an open car such as the Ferrari. It is likely too that the tyres on the Ferrari were better than those on the Mercedes. Nevertheless, Bracco was a most skilled road driver and proved faster over the last stretch, especially when crossing the Futa and Raticosa passes, coming home to win with Kling second, Fagioli, in a souped up Lancia Aurelia GT, third and Caracciola fourth.

Second place in the Mille Miglia was not a bad performance; the motor racing world was once again talking about the cars which had been produced by Mercedes and above all about the new 300SL. The team's appearance at Le Mans on 14 June was thus eagerly anticipated by the fans.

THE PRIX DE BERNE

Prior to this there was an interlude in racing at the Bremgarten circuit, Berne, during the Swiss GP on 18 May 1952. In the early afternoon a trial event was organized, 'for international racing cars with a cylinder capacity of more than 1500 cc', called the Prix de Berne ('Victory in Bremgarten'). Although there were only eleven cars which lined up on the grid, amongst these there were three major attractions. First of all, Daimler-Benz had entered three of the same type of car, one of which was again made available to Rudolf Caracciola. Secondly, Ferrari had given Willy Peter Daetwyler, the Swiss motor racing champion, a 4.1-litre, twelve-cylinder sports car, clearly superior to the 300SL. Third, Geoffrey Duke, the motor cycling world champion made his continental four-wheeled debut with a 2.6-litre Aston Martin, although this Aston was not thought to be powerful enough to be a serious threat and Duke did not have the same degree of expertise as Surtees was later to demonstrate.

Daetwyler, driving a Ferrari, was fastest in practice, his lap time of 2m 55.6s being nearly 5 seconds better than that of the fastest 300SL driver, Karl Kling. Caracciola was third quickest followed by Lang, with Riess substantially slower in the fourth Mercedes. Questioned about the large time difference between him and Daetwyler, Riess claimed that his Mercedes was too low geared, so, during the night before the race, the gear ratios were changed, in the hope of gaining 3 or even 4 seconds.

As things turned out Daetwyler's Ferrari did not figure in the race. A joint broke at the start and the car managed only the few yards to the edge of the circuit. Caracciola took the lead at first, but then Kling moved ahead, closely followed by Lang, leaving Caracciola nearly half a minute behind. Then disaster struck: shortly before a sharp right-hand bend just before the start/finish straight, Caracciola's car left the track and crashed into a conifer, which then fell on to the road. This really did prove the end of the maestro's motor racing career; he was hospitalized, suffering from several breaks and other injuries. Only the spaceframe chassis of the 300SL protected him from more serious damage.

Kling won from Lang, with Riess following in third place. Lang had the satisfaction of turning in the fastest lap, in 2m 56.1s, and almost matched Daetwyler's practice time. The higher gearing had indeed made the 300SL almost as fast as the big Ferrari.

LE MANS 1952

At Le Mans in 1951, a 3.4-litre Jaguar had beaten a 4.5-litre Talbot and it was known that these two cars were amongst the toughest Mercedes opponents, particularly as they had faster acceleration than the 300SL. The Talbot had a power output of almost 260 bhp and was certainly faster than the 300SL. In addition to that, Ferrari had entered not just a 3-litre car, but a powerful 4.1-litre machine as well.

Le Mans was definitely not to be an easy race for Mercedes. The hope was that the reliability of the 300SL might tip the balance, with faster cars not having the endurance to last for 24 hours.

The first lap did not look very promising. After the long Mulsanne straight, it was a 5.4-litre Cunningham, driven by American Phil Walters, that rounded Mulsanne corner in the lead, followed by the two Jaguars of Moss and Rolt, Simon's Ferrari, another Cunningham, a Ferrari and a third Jaguar.

Ascari/Villoresi's incredibly fast 3-litre Ferrari broke down, although Ascari had already achieved a lap record of 4m 40.5s. The two fastest Jaguars, in the hands of Moss and Whitehead, also dropped out during the first 3 hours due to overheating engines. Two 4.1-litre Ferraris, driven by Dreyfus and Trintignant, also failed to finish, as did the fastest Mercedes-Benz, that of, Karl Kling and Hans Klenk. During the night, a faulty generator caused them to retire in the pits.

Towards midnight, with 8 hours gone, a 2.3-litre Gordini was leading followed by Levegh's 4.5 Talbot and two 300SLs. These Mercedes entries were piloted by Lang/Riess and Helfrich/Niedermayr, hired especially for the 24-hour race on the strength of their good showing in the Veritas in past years. Riess, who came from Nuremberg, Helfrich, from Mannheim, and the very fat Niedermayr, from Berlin, proved to be ideal choices for Le Mans, They drove quickly and precisely and were very careful not to over-stress their engines. Hermann Lang was in fact the only driver from the 'Old Guard' who was participating in this race, as Rudolf Caracciola was still in hospital.

It was foggy and thus exhausting during the early hours of the morning. The Gordini had long-since dropped out, but Levegh now had a clear lead and was at times two laps ahead. He intended to drive the 24-hour race without a break – a tactic which was still allowed then, but was soon to be banned. The Helfrich/ Niedermayer 300SL pairing was second and the Lang/ Riess car third. After a pit-stop, second and third positions changed hands, but the Talbot held its lead. The public and the press had almost made up their mind; second and third places for Mercedes at Le Mans would be a glorious success. Yet a dramatic change came just 1 hour 45 minutes before the end of the race.

Levegh dropped out with his Talbot, the oil supply and a push-rod having failed. The two 300SLs were now seperated by one lap and they went on to take first and second places. A British journalist wrote: 'they deserved it in view of their excellent preparatory work, but were also lucky.'

The two SLs were driven back on the road to Stuttgart, where the engineers proudly concluded that the turbo-cooled drum-brake pads would have lasted for another 1500 km. The winning car had achieved an average speed of 156.3 kph (97.13 mph), a new record for Le Mans.

ON THE 'RING'

Next in the Mercedes calendar was a sports car race during the German Grand Prix weekend, at the Nürburgring. This also gave the team an ideal opportunity to show off the 300SL to the German public, which would benefit the organizing clubs as well as Daimler-Benz.

Mercedes had already been to the Nürburgring to test the new supercharged engine for the 300SL, which was an obvious progression in design, since the company had gained valuable experience with supercharged engines during the 1920s and '30s. The performance of the existing 300SL unit was relatively low, so it was thought that a supercharger would substantially increase its 175 bhp power output.

The original competition 300SL engine was known in the factory as the M194, whereas the new supercharged unit was called the M197. The supercharger was entirely re-designed for this engine. It was a single-stage Roots blower, with two three-locked rotors, and was mounted between carburettor and cylinder, housed in a magnesium casing. The usual Solex fixed-venturi carburettor was replaced by a Weber 45DOM of a similar type with magnesium manifolding.

The supercharger drive was taken from the camshaft; the camshaft sprocket had a spur wheel attached, which drove, via another gear, a pinion and, via a torsion rod, the blower. Different gear wheels were designed, so that the ratio of the supercharger speed to the crankshaft speed could be either 1:1.13 or 1:1.68. The compression ratio was reduced from 8.1:1 to 7.2:1. The tests were carried out using pump petrol, with an octane rating of 90, as required by the sports-car-racing regulations. This type of fuel is less than ideal for supercharged engines since it has inadequate cooling properties, hence the reduction in compression ratio. Earlier supercharged racing cars had always used special fuel, enriched with alcohol.

The engine was inclined to the left at an angle of 40 degrees, in order to keep the car's frontal area small. This attitude remained for the M197, in which the supercharger was mounted above the crankshaft, to the right of the canted engine. The test car in which the M197 was installed had a scoop in the bonnet to allow for the engine's extra height.

Karl Kling was the only team driver to try the M197-engined car on the Nürburgring, although Uhlenhaut also had a try. The car was never used in a race; on normal petrol it was not possible to make the most of the supercharger, although compared to the normal output of 170–175 bhp this unit showed a remarkable increase in power. The M197 had a power output of 230 bhp, and the reduced speed of 5800 rpm, with improved torque to match. At 3000 rpm the older engine developed 93 bhp and the supercharged unit 115 bhp, while at 4000 rpm the ratings were 143 bhp and 165 bhp respectively.

Why wasn't this promising supercharged engine developed further? There were three reasons. First, when it was tested the first experiments with fuel injection were already under way – the second production 300SL being equipped with this – and fuel injection was seen as a 'natural' method to increase performance. Second, in the autumn of 1952 Daimler-Benz had already started on the design of the W196, for the 2.5-litre Grand Prix formula of 1954, and Formula One took priority over sports-car racing. Thirdly, Daimler-Benz did not intend to take part in any motor racing events with the M197 engine; having achieved such sensational victories with the 300SL, the company wanted to wait until it produced another sure winner. As a matter of interest, Daimler-Benz no longer possesses a M197, although a supercharged engine still exists.

TRIUMPH IN MEXICO

At the Nürburgring, the drivers could not use the Coupé, as the field of vision was too limited for the winding track. Thus, the roadster came into being. In those days it was permissible to drive a racing car with a covered co-drivers's seat and a windscreen, so the Roadster was appropriately equipped. Owing to the excellent power/weight ratio and roadholding, these cars achieved nearly 175 kph (109 mph), a high speed on the Nürburgring. The fastest race lap was driven by Lang, at an average of 131.5 kph (81.7 mph).

Four roadsters had been prepared by Daimler-Benz for the 'Ring'. Karl Kling took the lead, but Hermann Lang eventually passed him to win the race. It was the last win for this magnificent driver. Fritz Riess took third place and Helfrich fourth.

When this race took place, the Daimler-Benz had already prepared the 300SL for the Carrera Panamericana in Mexico. Three cars were to enter the race, including two Coupés, for Kling and Lang, and a Roadster for the American, John Fitch. Fitch was not just a concession to the important American market. He was a fast, reliable driver.

The Carrera Panamericana was the most popular motor racing event in the world at that time. It was considered an adventure to take part in a race in an exotic country, especially since this one lasted several days. It made front page news, as an elite of American and European sports car drivers participated in the event. A well known American motoring magazine of the day, The World's Greatest Sporting Events, is quoted as saying that at this race in 1952, the Daimler-Benz 300SL was seen by an estimated six to eight million people along the course.

Although the 300SL appeared at the event in Mexico, it was neither the most powerful nor the fastest car, but it was perhaps the best prepared entrant. At the end of the first stage, covering a distance of 530 km (329 miles), Jean Behra had astonishingly taken the lead with a 2.3-litre Gordini. He was 6 minutes ahead of Bracco, driving a Ferrari, followed by Karl Kling, as the best Mercedes driver, 2 minutes further behind. John Fitch was seventh and Hermann Lang eighth. Günther Molter was the press spokesman for the Mercedes team and he reported the dramatic events of the race.

'Only 1 kilometre after the start the misfortune began: Lang ran over a dog at a speed of 200 kph (124 mph) and a resulting hole in the light-alloy bodywork was very noticeable at high speeds, working like an air-brake and reducing performance. Kling was at the outskirts of Tehuantepec when a vulture sitting next to the road was suddenly frightened and hit the windscreen with the car travelling at nearly 200 kph (124 mph). It was lucky that the bird hit the screen on the co-driver Hans Klenk's side. Klenk, who had taken off his crash-helmet at the last wheel-change, was knocked unconscious and suffered cuts. Kling stopped, managed to revive his co-driver and continued the race, but due to the sudden air-pressure within the car the rear window was pushed out.'

Considering the circumstances, third place was an excellent achievement. At the halt, the mechanics fixed seven steel tubes across the windscreen of Kling's car, to prevent any recurrence.

During the second stage, the leading car, driven by Jean Behra, ran wide on a bend and fell down a ravine, luckily without serious injury to the driver. Behra drove alone, while the Mercedes entries had driver and co-driver. Prior to the race the co-drivers had taken note of the most dangerous points on the route. Hermann Lang drove with an experienced engineer called Grupp, while John Fitch shared his car with Eugen Geiger.

The low average speed on this phase was due to the many bends and it was here that Fitch was able to prove his driving skill. He came second in the roadster, behind Luigi Villoresi in a Ferrari, but 1½ minutes ahead of Kling. During the third stage, covering a distance of 130 km (81 miles) from Puebla to Mexico City, the powerful Ferraris of Villoresi and Bracco were first and second closely followed by Kling, Fitch and Lang. The race still had a long way to run.

The fourth stage covered the 430 km (267 miles) from Mexico City to Leon, a much faster section than any so far. Kling was unlucky to suffer a puncture, while Villoresi had lost a great deal of time in the first stage, so his subsequent times did not take him into the lead. Bracco, with his Ferrari, was well ahead of Kling during the first half.

The fifth stage, covering a distance of 537 km (334 miles) between Leon and Durango, saw Villoresi dropping out with broken front suspension. In order to make up time, he had driven too quickly over the uneven road surface. With an average speed of 170 kph (106 mph) Kling was quicker than Bracco for the first time, although he was at that point no threat to the Italian.

Stage six, from Durango to Parral – 404 km (251 miles) – and stage seven from Parral to Chihuahua –

300 km (186 miles) – were qualifying sections. Between the two stages there was a break of 30 minutes for tyre changes, re-fuelling and any essential repairs. John Fitch was unhappy because he had not been able to finish all his repairs and indeed he slowed to a halt after 100 metres. With the permission of the commissioner, he returned to the garage to have his car checked again and restarted: 13 minutes later. He was disqualified nevertheless, because he had received outside assistance. Karl Kling was 2½ minutes quicker in the sixth stage than Bracco and even Lang had achieved a better time than the Ferrari when he arrived in Parral.

At the start in Parral, Bracco dropped out with a faulty differential. During this fast stage Kling drove at an average speed of 204 kph (126.8 mph) and won unchallenged, ahead of the two Ferraris of Chinetti and Maglioli. Lang crossed the finishing line 9 minutes behind Kling. He had had to change a wheel, after which the gullwing door was apparently not closed properly and was flung across the road at a speed of 200 kph (124 mph). After stage seven, Kling had a clear lead, which he kept during the next stage.

He unexpectedly gained an even greater advantage on the flat stretch between Chihuahua and Ciudad Juarez, covering a distance of 358 km (222 miles) in 1 hour 44 minutes 20 seconds, an amazing average of 218.49 kph (135.46 mph). Chinetti, driving the best Ferrari, was two minutes behind, followed by Lang lagging by another minute. So Kling had chalked up a remarkable victory, covering the course in 18hr 51m 19s – average speed 165.16 kph (102.63 mph) – Hermann Lang, in 19hr 26m 30s, came second and the Ferrari of Chinetti third, in 19hr 32m 45s.

Also worth mentioning is the emergence of the then completely unheard of Phil Hill, who came sixth driving his own Ferrari. He was subsequently hired for the Ferrari racing team and won the World Championship in 1961. Fürst Metternich came eighth with a 1500 Porsche. Graf Berckheim, also with a 1500 Porsche, came in seventh, but dropped out before Puebla when a stone damaged the transmission.

That the production 300SL is, even today, seen as a

desirable vehicle, and collectors are prepared to pay out substantial amounts for it, is not only a comment on the extraordinary design and performance, it is due also to such extraordinary victories as this, victories that made the 300SL almost a legend.

Theodor Heuss, then the President of the Federal Republic of Germany, sent, shortly after the announcement of the victory, a telegram to Daimler-Benz in his inimitable style: 'To you and Messrs Kling, Lang and Neubauer, with whom I sympathise and congratulate on their successes in Mexico!'

Kling's car, with its steel-tube vulture screen, can be seen at the Daimler-Benz Museum in Stuttgart-Untertürkheim. If you have a chance to visit the museum, it is worth taking a close look at the rear wheels; even the Rudge joints had been drilled into in order to remove any excess weight, just as in the GP cars. One of the test cars meanwhile, the first 300SL, is on loan to the Motor Museum at Castle Langenburg, near Hohelone.

A 'CIVILIZED' SPORTS CAR

One year and three months after its success in the Carrera Panamericana, in February 1954, the 300SL, now available to the public, was launched to the public in New York. This was only a prototype, but production started in autumn. The chassis, bodywork and the engine position were identical to those of the racing cars; even the designation remained unchanged. The interior, however, was no longer so spartan. The new model was a 'civilized' sports car, equipped with a useful heating and ventilation system and comfortable seats, although the sporty integral moulded seat-design was retained.

The two significant changes concerned the engine and the chassis. Following lengthy experiments, the engine had been fitted with fuel injection – developed in close co-operation with Bosch – making this probably the first sports car in the world to have injection. The bore/stroke ratio of 88/85 mm remained unchanged,

resulting in a cylinder capacity of 2996 cc. The canted in-line six was still dry-sumped (total oil content was 12 litres!) and had an increased compression ratio of 8.55:1 and generated 215 bhp at 5800 rpm (in the USA, the power output was put at 240 bhp SAE). The 'civilized' model thus in fact produced a much greater power output than the competition car of 1952.

A few compromises had had to be made. Although the power output was up by twenty per cent, the total weight had been substantially increased, due to the more comfortable interior, a mass-produced steel chassis in place of the hand-made alloy item, and steel instead of alloy for the gullwing doors. The spaceframe consisted of a number of triangles, the corners of which were joined at certain points like a knot, thus the lift-up door was still necessary and by now had become an accepted design feature. While the race model had a weight of 840 kg (1848 lb), the production 300SL weighed 1200 kg (2640 lb).

This was not too much for a 3-litre car, but despite the increased performance, the power/weight ratio had deteriorated to 178 bhp/tonne. In competition in 1952 it stood at 213. Acceleration was then considered exceptional and is still impressive today: 0–100 kph (62 mph) in less than 9 seconds, 0–160 kph (99 mph) in 18 seconds. Also noteworthy is the fact that the car could achieve 120 kph (74 mph) in second gear. Above all, the engine was distinguished by exemplary flexibility, partly thanks to the fuel injection.

The production 300SL had a final drive ratio of 3.64:1 which at the red-line speed of 6000 rpm produced speeds of 64 kph (40 mph), 108 kph (67 mph), 155 kph across (96 mph) and 235 kph (145.7 mph) across the gears, all of which had synchromesh. Two higher final drives were available to order, with ratios of 3.42:1 or 3.25:1. With the higher of these, intermediate gear speeds of 72 kph (45 mph), 121 kph (75 mph) and 173 kph (107 mph) were possible, with a theoretical maximum of 260 kph (161 mph) in fourth; the true tested maximum of the production gullwing SL being 246 kph (153 mph) – an excellent speed, bearing in mind the standards of 1955.

These results indicate that the production car was not as streamlined as its competition cousin, although at a glance the two looked much the same. In fact solid bumpers had been attached front and rear, the radiator slope was steeper and the grille was topped with a large Mercedes star. The headlights were also slightly different, there was an additional chrome strip and two additional sections over the tyres. In view of these 'luxuries' the drag coefficient (Cd) was still very favourable at 0.397. The resulting ratio between 215 bhp and a top speed of 246 kph (153 mph) is even today an extraordinary achievement which has not been surpassed.

The weak point of the 300SL was its rear axle. Although the front had wishbones and coil springs with an anti-roll bar, rear suspension took the form of double-jointed swing-axles, something which was also used in the 300 saloon, a vehicle which was not only much heavier but was not used for racing like the 300SL. That swing-axles were deemed unsatisfactory for touring became clear from the fact that the succeeding model, the 300SL roadster, was equipped with a different kind of rear suspension.

The original had a tendency to oversteer slightly and, if driven recklessly or with abrupt movements, the rear swerved sharply. Roadholding was particularly poor in wet conditions. In a drive on the Nürburgring, when the road surface was wet, the author found this a great problem, especially when the brakes were applied fiercely. The rear axle track changed; the car was lifted up on its springs at the rear, the wheels acquiring positive camber. To avoid swerving, the car had to be steered with great care. However, at high speeds the SL performed well.

The brakes were large (braking area 1664 square centimetres/258 square inches) and the production vehicle also retained the turbo-cooling. Despite this, with a dry weight of 1200 kg (2640 lb) – with a full 130-litre (28.4 gallon) fuel tank roughly 1300 kg (2860 lb) – drum brakes were no longer adequate. Hence, the Roadster later acquired disc brakes. Unlike the racing version, the production 300SL had a servo unit, which reduced the otherwise high pedal pressures. Racing tyres were used

on the road car, the 6.70–15s coming from Continental, Englebert or Dunlop and being mounted on 5K–15 rims. The dimensions were as follows: wheelbase 2.40 m (94.5 in), overall length 4.46 m (175.6 in), width 1.79 m (70.5 in) and height 1.30 m (51.2 in). Interestingly, the front track was laid down at 1.385 m (54.5 in) and the rear track at 1.435 m (56.5 in), while the turning circle was 11.5 m (452.8 in). The price of the production 300SL, with its gullwing doors, was set at a remarkable DM 20 000. Between autumn 1954 and spring 1957 1400 such cars were produced.

ROADSTER

The 300SL roadster followed. First shown at the Geneva Salon in 1957, the model went into production in May of that year, DM 32 500 standard or DM 33 250 with an optional hard-top. This version was also sold as a fixed-head coupé.

Although this third variant offered the greatest comfort and had moved away most noticeably from the original design, sales were not as high as originally anticipated. In two and half years only 1400 300SL roadsters and coupés were produced. The chassis of this 'Mark III' had been altered to accommodate ordinary doors, the boot was much larger and arm-chair-type seats had been fitted. Its roadholding was much improved. By the time production ceased, in autumn 1962, about 1850 coupés had been produced.

The 300SL roadster was an extremely comfortable sports-car weighing 1420 kg (3124 lb) (1460 kg [3212 lb] including the hard-top), which aerodynamically had little in common with the 'old' 300SL, despite the fact that few alterations had been made. The enlarged headlight and the new roof resulted in an increase in the drag coefficient, although the dimensions had not considerably altered. The track was increased by 1 cm (0.4 in) and the overall length by 5 cm (2 in), but wheelbase, height and width remained unchanged.

The 215 bhp fuel-injection engine was the same, with its remarkable 202 lb ft of torque at 4600 rpm, but the compression ratio was increased from 8.55 to 9.5: generating a power output of 225 bhp (DIN) or 250 bhp SAE. During tests an SL roadster with a 215 bhp engine and suitable gearing reached a speed of 230 kph (143 mph). Moreover, a driver for the Swiss *Automobil Revue* magazine managed to reach a speed of 237 kph (147 mph) with a 225 bhp engine.

The 300SL roadster was available with four different final drive ratios; apart from the three gullwing cars, there was another, especially low ratio of 3.89:1, for America, where maximum speed was restricted but good acceleration was of great importance. Unlike the gullwing with its 130-litre (28.4-gallon) fuel tank, the roadster had a 100-litre (21.9-gallon) tank, which increased the available boot space.

Between 1957 and 1960 the car was sold with 300SL drum brakes, which were replaced in 1961 by servo-assisted discs. Although the weight of the 300SL roadster seemed unsuitable for motor racing, the roadster participated a few times in national hill-climbs, in the large GT category, with some success. These successes were due to the improved handling and roadholding ability, brought about by the new rear axle design. The swing-axles now had a coil spring positioned at an angle above the final drive casing, in addition to the slightly slanted coil springs at the sides; thus the rear suspension was softer and more weight was transferred to the front in cornering.

The SL designation was hardly appropriate to the roadster, standing as it did for 'Sport Leicht' (Sport Light'), but the company had undoubtedly kept to its tradition.

Page 217 (top): Mercedes-Benz 220 coupé, 2 Seater 1954. The 220 was a classic product of the German economic miracle. It was premièred at the Frankfurt Car Show, April 1951. Striking features included a new engine and the chassis and bodywork of the 170 S (although the headlights were no longer free-standing). The 220 also came in a variety of superb bodywork that today's car buyers can only dream of. The coupé in the picture is of a very rare type.

Technical data: 6 cylinders, 2 195 cc capacity, 80 bhp at 4 850 rpm, maximum speed 140 kph, cabriolet 145 kph.

Page 217 (bottom): Mercedes-Benz 220 SE coupé 2/2 Seater 1958. After Daimler-Benz had introduced ponton bodywork on the 180 which made the cars more spacious and wind-resistant, the more elegant series of the 220 a, 219, 220 S and the 220 SE were developed on the same basis, the 220 SE being the only one with direct injection.

Technical data: 6 cylinders, 2 195 cc capacity, 115 bhp at 4 800 rpm, maximum speed 160 kph.

Previous page: Mercedes-Benz 300. The 300, with its variants built from 1951-1962, was the first car of pomp, circumstance and prestige of the infant Federal Republic of Germany. The nation's Chancellor, Konrad Adenauer, was chauffeured daily in a 300 from Rhoendorf to his office in Bonn. For this reason the 300 is also called the 'Adenauer'. President Theodor Heuss also valued the 300 because there was so much headroom that he did not have to remove his hat when inside.

Technical data of the 300 (W 186 II): 6 cylinders, 2 996 cc capacity, 115 bhp at 4 600 rpm, maximum speed 160 kph.

Right: Mercedes-Benz 300 S, Cabriolet A 1954. The 300 S was a dream car of the fifties either as a cabriolet or coupé. Stylistically, its relation to the elegant supercharged cars of the thirties is unmistakable.

Technical data: 6 cylinders, 2 996 cc capacity, 150 bhp at 5 000 rpm, maximum speed 176 kph.

Previous page: Mercedes-Benz 600 1965. The 600 represented the ultimate in car technology of its time. Built from 1964 to 1981 it was the vehicle preferred by heads of state throughout the world. But this mighty flagship of the Mercedes-Benz company was never in fact a sales hit: 2 190 limousines, 428 Pullmans, with their strikingly long wheel base, and 59 landaulets, with hoods collapsible over the rear seat, have been built since 1964. Of the 250 bhp this eight-cylinder was capable of, 50 bhp was syphoned off to power the many supplementary units that provided its unique comfort, such as the 'Ease Hydraulics'. These open and close the windows, allow one to open and shut the boot at the press of a button, adjust the seats and control the vents on the automatic heating and cooling systems.

Technical data: 8 cylinders, 6 332 cc capacity, 250 bhp at 4 000 rpm, maximum speed 200 kph.

Above: Mercedes-Benz 300 SEL 6.8 1971 – an even more powerfully built 6.3 litre Mercedes from AMG Motorenbau. The picture shows the car at the Spa 24 hour race in 1971, driven by Hans Heyer and Clemens Schickentanz.

Technical data: V8 cylinders, 6 800 cc capacity, 428 bhp output, maximum speed 285 kph.

Opposite: Mercedes-Benz 300 SEL 6.3 1967. The 300 SEL 6.3 can be regarded as the Daimler-Benz engineering team's coup de main. They implanted the 6.3 litre from the '600' in the 'normal' 300 SEL 3.5 litre and offered the series with halogen headlights on the main and dipped beams. (Air suspension was already standard on the 3.5 litre car.) This created one of the fastest and safest touring limousines in the world. The picture shows it on the steep curve at the Daimler-Benz test track.

Technical data: V8 engine, 6 300 cc capacity, 250 bhp output at 4 000 rpm, maximum speed 221 kph.

Pages 226-227: Mercedes-Benz 230 SL 1963-67; 250 SL 1966-68; and 280 SL 1968-71 embodied an elegance which had nothing to do with the Teutonic solidity so typical up to that point of the Mercedes-Benz sports car. The so-called 'pagoda roof' was particularly exciting – it was more than just a designer's gimmick, providing a surprisingly easy way of getting into the car.

Technical data (280 SL): 6 cylinder fuel-injection engine, 2 778 cc capacity, 170 bhp output at 5 750 rpm, maximum speed 200 kph.

Pages 228-229: A Mercedes-Benz 560 SE 1988 (left) and a Mercedes-Benz 300 SEL 6.3 1971 (right). A comparison of these two luxury cars is the subject of the chapter Hitting the Heights.

Previous page and above: Mercedes-Benz 280 SE 3.5 Cabriolet (1971). Although from the outside this model is almost indistinguishable from the 280 SE, because of its totally new 3.5 litre V8 engine it is in a completely different class. An outward hint of the increased power output is given by the elegantly styled '3.5' at the rear.

Technical data: V8 engine, 3 499 cc capacity, 200 bhp output at 5 800 rpm, maximum speed 210 kph.

Hans Scherenberg
A Creative Influence

Ingo Seiff talks to Prof. Hans Scherenberg, from 1965 until 1977 a member of the managing board of Daimler-Benz.

Looking back on your long career at Daimler-Benz, which achievements are you particularly proud of?

This is a rather difficult question to answer. What has always fascinated me, was the way in which the 'creative process' worked with the team and myself. By that I mean the combination of research, development and engineering which finally resulted in the creation of a new model, where matters of design and style also had to be considered. There were good reasons why important staff meetings always took place at Sindelfingen, near Stuttgart. There, the design department has rooms large enough to accommodate without difficulty models to the scale of 1:5 or even 1:1. This enabled us to take a good look at them and to discuss them. This interplay of the various 'creative elements' which led to a finished new model, plus the extensive test drives, have always been a special fascination for me.

Which of the Mercedes-Benz cars built after the war was, in your opinion, the most impressive?

Every model has its own special appeal. Whether it was the series production of the 300SL or the long, impressive list of models in our normal production-line output . . . . Our criterion for quality always has been to provide our series production cars with the very best engineering, and to ensure that all vehicles meet high standards. We, as engineers, always liked our most advanced model best . . . .

How important is the recognition of the company and its achievements to you?

The appreciation of our customers and the long waiting list – in my time three years – are very satisfying. So too is the admiration of leading technical journalists.

To what extent has your expertise in the development of aero engines influenced your work with Daimler-Benz since the Second World War?

Fuel injection would be part of that, but so would high capacity, light-weight construction and the use of aluminium . . . plus a great deal of technical know-how. The 300SL and, from 1952 onwards, the racing models of the new formula have all profited from fuel injection. **You just mentioned sports cars. The golden years of the formula racing car, and of the 300SL, ended at Daimler-Benz abruptly in 1955. Were you shocked by this decision of the board? And what were the reasons for pulling out of racing?**

It was an enormous turning point for all of us, though rather less for myself, since from 1956 I became responsible for the large engines and aero engines sector. But I shared responsibility for that decision – a disappointment to millions of racing fans – because Professor Nallinger always consulted us before such an important decisions would be made. What were the real reasons? They were that we had come to realize that our best designers and test engineers were intensively employed in the racing car sector.

And not only that; the workshops, too, which made the parts for test cars and pre-production models, had to be enlisted for racing car activities. Of course, it was our ambition to be the *best* on the racing circuits of the world. To keep up with the competition, we constantly looked for improvements and technical innovations in our racing cars. It was Fritz Nallinger who one day warned his fellow directors about the problem: that development of our series production was suffering because of our racing activities, however successful these had proved to be.

This was nothing new, of course. It had been the same before World War II. In the meantime, BMW, for instance, not having its own racing car production, was building very good, very fast modern cars, while we were somewhat lagging behind as far as new development was concerned.

The board of directors realized that Daimler-Benz could not afford to let this situation get any worse. The technical demands of racing cars had increased enormously so that it would have been impossible for us to accommodate this programme in our normal research and development work. We needed our best designers and test engineers for the series production which also made more and more demands: lower fuel consumption, improved safety, better roadholding, more comfortable driving conditions and reduced noise levels.

In 1970, we set up the research department, where our best teams were needed. The fact that we won every single race in 1955 made our decision to stop our involvement somewhat easier.

Would you have been able to utilize the know-how gained in racing car production?

Yes, but to a much lesser extent than it is widely believed. Which manufacturer, for instance, could afford to use titanium for its series production – as we did for our racing cars – or have a lattice frame for the bodywork? Some of the know-how in areas such as light metal engineering, roadholding and testing methods for parts and systems with specially developed testing equipment proved to be invaluable.

The psychological benefit in the motivation of staff, which occurred because of the successes of Mercedes-Benz racing cars was also important. But what really mattered was this: with every victory we demonstrated to the entire world the ability of our development team to produce first rate engineering.

Were there important findings from racing which were useful for the production of engines in production cars?

Directly, very few.

At Daimler-Benz, the turbo principle is only used in diesel engines. Why is it not possible to use turbocharging in at least some of the normal petrol engined cars? And how about the supercharger which Paul Daimler already used for his aircraft engines during World War I . . . ?

Most of the World War I aircraft engines had to be supercharged, even at high altitudes, because of the level of performance required. The technical expertize gained at that time lead to the development of supercharged engines in the 1920s. As early as 1885, Gottlieb Daimler included an 'Over and Supercharge' in his patent No. 34926 of 3 April. The principle was first used by Paul Daimler in his supercharged racing engine in 1921 and his successor, Porsche, continued it with models S, SS and SSK.

You were asking about turbocharged engines for 'normal' passenger cars. There are many other ways of increasing the performance, and turbo would make a car very expensive. It makes sense, though, to use a super-charger with diesel . . . diesel engines need more air than petrol engines because they have fewer revolutions and their hauling capacity is bigger; a diesel is virtually predestined to have a supercharger.

We always used them for commercial vehicles and large engines. Modern tank engines, like the Leopard for instance, have turbo-superchargers. This was the beginning of a totally new design development for engines, including those for civilian use, for example boats and stationary engines. 'Otto'-engines are today so highly developed that they can operate without having to be supercharged, especially if their cylinder capacity is high. **For many years now, there has been an extensive advertising campaign by Japanese competitors for a four-valve system. Is this something very new? Even the new SL will have engines with 24 or 32 valves.**

There is nothing new at all about it. Racing cars and aircraft engines used the system before World War I. In 1909, Benz designed a four-valve concept racing model which was tested a year later and competed in the Prinz-Heinrich-Fahrt. The winning Mercedes cars in the motor races of 1914 had four-valve engines, as did many others. Today's trend reflects the old experience that a greater number of valves help the engine to 'breathe'; they speed up the filling-up of the cylinder and its emission, and aid the air intake which, together with the added fuel, will give a better performance. Technically, it is a very simple affair and Daimler-Benz has been in the forefront in its development. The four-valve design for the smaller 190 class was a 'first' for a production car and has proved successful. It makes the performance of the 190E 2.5–16 (the new sixteen-valve), comparable to that of a powerful racing car.

When you introduced the multi-link independent rear suspension in the 190 in 1982, it was rumoured that its development had cost about one billion Deutsche Marks . . . .

Generally speaking this figure is correct. During the early stages of the axle design we set up a competition in our own design department. Eight different designs were entered, four of which were selected for further testing. The 'Staengele-axle', as it is popularly called, won the contest and has proven to be most successful.

Can you describe its advantage over the previously used axles?

One of our most expensive research and engineering projects led to the construction of a rear axle which absorbs in an optimal way any forces exerted on the back of the car by excess luggage – stabilizing the handling and holding the track. For each rear wheel there are five wishbones connected to flexible bearings, so you do not get an unwelcome steering effect from the action of the back wheels.

Gas-pressurized shock absorbers, coil springs, the flexible rear axle joined to the frame base at four points, the low noise level and the starting and braking torque are other advantages.

I have always been fascinated, and at the same time irritated, by the diesel policy of the Daimler-Benz group. There has been a lot of talk about compression ignition which seems to be a flop – undeservedly say the experts . . . .

There have been times when diesel engines constituted more than forty-eight per cent of our passenger car output. Diesel was still popular when there was talk of exhaust fumes emission control with petrol engines which needed to have converters and at a later stage catalytic converters. The diesel did not need these cleansing processes because the analysis for carbon monoxide and hydrocarbon were very low to start with . . . even lower than those of an Otto engine with a catalytic converter.

The only disadvantage so far has been the higher nitric oxide ratings, compared with those of the Otto engine, though no doubt that problem is answerable as well. What has alarmed me about diesel is the question of soot particles. Some claim that the benzpyrene in soot particles are carcinogenic. Together with other motor manufacturers, we had tests carried out by independent research institutes in the 1970s. They could not find any danger in the low concentration of diesel emissions from the car which is much less dense than, for example, in cigarette smoke. All the same filter systems have been tested now for several years and will be included in the near future.

What has made diesel passenger cars so successful is their unrivalled low fuel consumption. In the United

States they even had a kind of snob appeal – though it was not just for this reason – which led me to equip the first supercharged diesel for the American market with an American-made exhaust gas turbine so that there was an American element present in the car. The turbocharged diesel became a sales winner in the USA.

Earlier, we described at length the 'safety principle' at Daimler-Benz. I would like to ask you about it because you were responsible for the development of passenger cars. You, too were bound by the slogan: 'Daimler-Benz puts safety first in the development of their passengers cars'. To start with there is four-wheel steering: has this been promoted by Daimler-Benz?

As part of its 'image-grooming', Daimler-Benz places the accent very much on safety in construction. Apart from ABS (anti-lock brakes) there is the electronic propulsion ASD (automatic slip differential), ASR (automatic actuation slip regulator) and 4 matic (electronic automatic four-wheel propulsion with two differential and integrated ABS).

Does this mean that safety takes precedence over speed and performance at Daimler-Benz?

It's like this: on the one hand, all our cars – even the small models – are capable of reaching a good speed. But on the other, there have been moves towards the introduction of a speed limit, as in other member states of the EC. In the Federal Republic, such legislation might be passed one day. TV discussions about the pros and cons seem to favour the introduction of a speed limit. There is a reason for this attitude, and we have to prepare for the day when we will have to comply with European speed restrictions. Of course we would like to maintain the freedom of driving. We have the safest cars and the safest motorways. It would be a shame to have a speed limit – but you have to be realistic. From this we must draw the conclusion that we should be *less* concerned about performance and more concerned with safety.

Safety engineers use the term 'functional safety'. What does it mean?

The driver should be able to rely totally on the proper functioning of all important systems without having to worry about faults and break-downs.

And what is meant by 'conditional safety'?

Translated from engineering jargon, it means that a Mercedes-Benz car is designed for relaxation, well-being, effortless driving – just for quiet concentration even on long strenuous journeys.

In my opinion this 'conditional safety' aspect is undermined by chassis designers aiming for an extremely low drag coefficient, and therefore using a very slanted windscreen, sometimes also at the rear. The test reports tend to sound like this: 'The interior is strongly overheated and imposes turkish bath-type conditions on the occupants . . . '. In other words, this has an adverse effect on the driver.

You see, this is the reason why we do not put too much emphasis on streamlining. I remember well, when we first drove the new NSU Ro80 which was highly praised because of its favourable drag coefficient. I was horrified by the way the sun mercilessly roasted the occupants. That was a warning for us and it taught us how important it is not to put the windscreen too near to the driver's head but to utilize the roof as a sun screen. If you have to have a heavily slanted windscreen for better streamlining it should be positioned further forward towards the bonnet. In my opinion, we have solved that problem very well.

Car accidents are costing the economy billions every year. Is it not depressing for development and test engineers to have to make allowances for inadequate driving behaviour and ability when they design new cars? Statistically, ninety per cent of all accidents are due to human error.

That is because, on the whole, drivers do not know enough about the physical laws governing cars and driving. They cannot control their cars in a critical situation without ABS. There are still many cars, especially in the smaller range, which are not equipped with it and problems are bound to arise. Some drivers still think they can do without ABS.

At Mercedes-Benz, all series production cars have ABS – with the exception of the so-called compact class where it can be added at a reasonable price. After we first used the ABS system ten years ago, its excellent safety record was welcomed, and today it is more and more in demand. I hope that the same will happen with ASR. Anybody who has driven a car with ASR in difficult winter conditions will never want to do without it. ASR was pioneered by Daimler-Benz which also developed and introduced ABS to the public nineteen years ago.

Daimler-Benz never believed in keeping its safety innovations strictly to itself.

That's right. We engineers always felt that our competitors and therefore every driver should be able to benefit.

One quite often hears the criticism that the interior of a Daimler-Benz car has all the charm of a Prussian army barracks. All the instrumentation is there, everything is in its place and is functional. But the overall impression is one of joylessness. Why is that?

'Functional' is the right term. The introduction of plastic in car manufacture was very tempting for designers like us; it was cheaper and much easier to use for part production. While on the subject of lower cost structure, one soon has to decide where the priorities are, on the fittings or the engineering (efficiency, safety, performance). This question is especially relevant to the lower price range, but there is only one answer: even a 'Baby-Benz' has to have Mercedes-style engineering.

Austerity also has its advantages as it means less distraction and fewer gimmicks.

Quite so. Gadgets can be dangerous, too.

You said that engineers have to be cost-conscious. Does that mean that they have to bow to the laws of marketing? Do marketing people have a say in the development of a new model?

In my time, hardly at all. Whatever came from that direction had very little to do with technical design. But our sales department always had the right idea about the Mercedes image, and knew that it originated from the high standard of engineering. And of course, it is not at all easy for a marketing man to recognize future technical requirements, though modern market research methods might have made it easier to spot a trend.

Maybe we should have taken the question of the twelve-cylinder engines more seriously. We did discuss the subject at great length and carried out tests, but as we had excellent V8 engines which were nearly as good as

the twelve-cylinder, we did not pursue the matter. Actually, this race for higher cylinder figures seems to be largely for reasons of prestige.

To what extent are you influenced by your competitors?

We are always aware of what the competition is doing. We spend days at motor shows wandering from stand to stand to gather information about new developments and trends. Though we never copied others when we worked on new engineering developments. We also do not just drive our competitors cars; we take them apart as well and during important test drives we always include comparable models of other manufacturers. What we are striving for, of course, is that our models are quite different from any other car: that they are completely 'Mercedes-like'. That must be obvious as soon as you shut the car door.

. . . as though you are in a safe . . . .

Yes, when first driving . . . the feel of the interior: solid, functional, with everything it its place . . . it is hardly surprising that the chief designers of the competition are always trying to reach the standards of Mercedes-Benz. Of course, they buy our cars, dissect them, test-drive them, in the same way we do with their models.

What you call 'image' is the sum of all the creative processes that designers and engineers contribute to the conception of a new model, though with Daimler-Benz emotional factors and our tradition, too, play an important role. That is why I talked about 'our traditional progress for a progressive tradition' at the end of my farewell speech in January 1978.

May I ask you about new materials and fuels. Will plastics be used for chassis? One famous example is the 'baked body' of the Corvette . . . .

The C111 which we used as a rolling laboratory for many years had a plastic body. But crash tests have shown that plastics do not absorb impact very well. You can toughen it but it cracks relatively easily and does not have the denting property which makes sheet metal such an ideal material. The repair of plastic car bodies also presents many problems and they are much more difficult to recycle than the traditional metal ones.

Two or three years ago, during a symposium, I put

forward the argument that if we had had nothing else but plastic, the invention of metal would be hailed as a great sensation. It will be a very long time – if ever – until we will develop a synthetic material with the same qualities and versatility of metal, meeting the required safety standards at the same time.

Will ceramics be used more and more in the motor industry?

There are many signs which point to more ceramics under the bonnet. They have their application in the turbo sector – in the lining of the exhaust-driven turbo-supercharger and in rotors. Ceramics have a great level of heat resistance and a much better resistance to wear and tear than metals.

Also worth mentioning is their excellent heat insulation. At the same time ceramics are highly inflexible and corrosion resistant, and are therefore ideal for those components which require a high degree of rigidity. But it will be a long time before a complete ceramic engine will be on the market, as there are quite formidable problems yet to be solved. For example, the brittleness of ceramic materials compared to metals, which means they are much more susceptible to the stresses of compression and tension.

There was a headline in a newspaper, some months ago, proclaiming: 'The fuel of the future is hydrogen!' What is your opinion on that?

We started experimenting with hydrogen as a fuel very early. There are many reasons why hydrogen is ideally suited to replace petrol and diesel. Not only is there a near inexhaustible supply of water, but also the only pollutant emitted would be nitrogen oxide in very low concentration.

Unfortunately, while it seems to be possible to adapt the engine to use hydrogen, there is a problem to produce a large enough number of engines to make it economically viable. There is also the problem of storing a sufficient supply of hydrogen in the car because, after all, it should be able to cover a reasonable distance.

When hydrogen cars were extensively tested in Berlin, many questions remained unanswered. How was the hydrogen to be stored? Should it be kept as gas in pressurized cylinders; as a liquid in vacuum-insulated tanks, or as a chemical compound?

It cannot be a matter of indifference to the driver that a hydrogen tank would weigh 20 times as much as a petrol tank. Also there is the question of the infrastructure: roads would have to have a network of fuel stations and so on. All these arguments show that it will be a long time before we will see the hydrogen engine.

Professor Scherenberg, thank you very much.

Maybe I could just add one thing: you asked at the beginning which achievement I was particularly proud of when looking back at my time with Daimler-Benz. I am retired now, but when I drive in Germany or abroad and notice all the Mercedes-Benz cars on the road which were built while I was responsible for their development, I have a feeling of great satisfaction.

STANISLAW PESCHEL

The Diesel Revolution

The diesel engine is a combustion engine, invented by the German Rudolf Diesel. This engine differs from the petrol-driven engine in that it ingests pure air, and the fuel injected into the combustion chamber is not electrically ignited by a spark plug. The fuel ignites itself on the highly-compressed hot air which has a temperature of roughly 800 degrees Celsius.

When the captain of the *Dresden* started up his steam engines for the channel crossing from Antwerp to Harwich on the afternoon of 29 September 1913, he had an important passenger on board.

He was a man whose declared intention it had been to bury the engines that were driving the ship on that day. His name was Rudolf Diesel, and he was travelling to England with business friends to set up a factory to manufacture the Diesel engines named after him. The crossing, however, was to be his last trip . . . .

Diesel was born in Paris, to German parents, on 18 March 1858, appropriately at a time when the petrol industry came into being and the first oil derrick was erected on Lüneburg Heath. He spent his first years in Paris, years that were overshadowed by the harsh discipline imposed on him by his father. But soon the Diesels had to leave France: the German victory in the battle of Sedan in September 1870 made it impossible for them to remain in France. They moved to London, where little Rudolph could visit the famous Science Museum and tend the flame of his passion for steam engines that had developed in Paris. Here he learned the names of the luminaries of the steam age, men like Savery, Newcomen, Watt and Trevithick.

Due to his family's lack of money Rudolf was unable to remain in London and was sent to an uncle in Augsburg. Luckily this uncle was a professor of mathematics, who was able to teach Rudolf the principles of science. The course of Diesel's life was determined in Augsburg where he went to business industrial schools before moving to Munich in 1875, where he graduated from the polytechnic with excellent grades. By the time he had graduated as a fully-trained engineer, he already had the idea at the back of his mind to which he dedicated all his later work.

He recognized that in the age of explosive industrial-isation, the steam engine, with its low efficiency, had to be replaced by a better source of power. But before he could put his plan into operation he had to have a job, and so offered his services to Carl Linde, the inventor of air liquefaction. He was sent to Linde's company head-quarters in Paris where Linde's ice machines were pro-duced, and Diesel soon became the director.

Back at his birthplace Diesel developed his interest in engines. He skilfully made use of his knowledge of the circular processes of refrigerators and heat engines, and constructed small experimental machines driven by superheated ammonia vapours.

Diesel expected the ammonia vapours to improve the efficiency of the steam engine, but this ultimately proved impossible. Yet the experiments were not fruit-less, as Diesel himself reported:

'The parallel theoretical investigations demonstrated the necessity of a simultaneous application of very high pressure to exploit the properties of superheating.

Such vapours under extremely high tension and superheated to an extreme degree are in an almost gaseous state. I do not know how the main idea develo-ped of replacing the ammonia by a real gas, air, under extremely high pressure and superheated, gradually in-troducing finely dispersed fuel, and allowing it to ex-pand simultaneously with the combustion of the indi-vidual fuel particles, so that as much as possible of the heat generated is transformed into external work. But by incessantly striving after the desired goal, by investigat-ing the relationships between countless possibilities, the right idea was sparked off, something that filled me with a joy beyond words.'

This was the basis for a completely new type of engine, which Diesel had running for the first time on 17 February 1894, in the machine factory in Augsburg. It did not require a separate ignition because the temperature necessary for igniting the fuel at the end of the third cycle was attained by compressing the air sucked in during the second cycle; this new engine was patented No. 67207 in Diesel's name in 1893.

Unfortunately, he cited in the patent description a process for combustion at constant temperature that is not applicable in this context -- the so-called Carnot cycle. This error made him the target for the rest of his life of both critics and the envious, a lot which has befallen many a genius.

Above all, it was the envious who raised their voices when Diesel made himself a fortune by selling his patents. But it was his poor luck that most of his money was in shares which soon proved worthless, as is so often the case in stock market history. Diesel plunged into reckless deals concerning oil fields in Galicia and overpriced properties – and lost money hand over fist. And although his name spread far and wide – above all, in the USA – his financial position went from bad to worse.

Eventually he realised that he was utterly impover-ished, and incapable of making new technological breakthroughs. It was the end.

On 10 October 1913, Dutch fishermen dragged a corpse out of the sea. The sailors found some papers and private possessions that identified the deceased as Rudolf Diesel. Following time-honoured tradition, they returned the corpse to the sea. They were the last to see Rudolf Diesel.

HIGH EFFICIENCY

But Diesel did not live in vain. He bequeathed to the world his engine, which was in certain respects superior to the already established and more developed Otto engine. The diesel's main advantages were its greater efficiency compared with the Otto engine and the wide range of fuels on which it could run. But at that time, the advantages it displayed were theoretical – the state of the diesel art did not allow its universal employment. Its handicaps were its great weight and size and relatively low engine speed. And so the Diesel engines of the age, apart from stationary ones, were only to be found in ships and locomotives.

Nevertheless, by 1897 Diesel was already convinced of a future for his engine in cars. His vision was to be fulfilled: 'The car is underway, and so soon will be the diesel engine. The steam engine, which had to disappear anyway, due to its steam boiler, coal firing and other reasons, will not lead to the decisive breakthrough for the car. In contrast, my engine is coming onto the scene at precisely the moment of victory of the combustion engine, even if it is first in the form of the petrol engine. In a few years, the diesel engine will take the place of the petrol engine, because it does not have the undependable apparatus for gasification of the fuel, and for ignition, and can be run on cheaper fuel, of which it also uses far less; neither does the fuel create the risk of explosions . . .'.

Today we know where Diesel was wrong, and we also know why the first diesel engine to be fitted to a vehicle – a Benz-Sendling tractor – was only started up in 1923.

The greatest problem in fitting a diesel into a road vehicle was getting fuel into the combustion chamber. Because there were no injection nozzles as we would understand the term today, the fuel had to be pumped in by compressed air before the end of the third stroke. It was an involved process that took approximately ten per cent of the power generated to drive a compressor.

The fact that it was almost impossible to regulate engine speed was a major problem. In 1907 Diesel himself attemped to build an engine for a heavy goods vehicle, but soon gave up.

PROSPER L'ORANGE

The laurels for driving the first motor vehicle with a diesel go to the engineer Prosper L'Orange, who – despite his name – was a German who had become involved with the diesel engine in 1906. L'Orange, employed at the time as director of the test department at the Deutz engine factory, had been given the task of making the diesel process applicable to smaller engines of up to 35 bhp. He soon recognized that the key was overcoming the uncontrolled introduction of fuel. He searched for a technique that would allow him to determine exactly when the fuel was injected and when combustion took place. The solution lay in abandoning the compressor and using a precise injection pump, and

that's what L'Orange set out to develop.

The next step involved finding a process that would effectively enable the fuel to be mixed into the compressed air.

The desired effect was partly achieved by the construction of a so-called *Nachkammer*, or 'post-chamber' which was patented in 1908. This was only a partial success because the combustion processes were insufficiently controlled and an automobile engine that could function by this method was inconceivable. On the other hand the engine's capacity to burn even the heaviest of fuels was of a very high order.

Such was the state of the art when L'Orange left Deutz to join Benz & Cie in Mannheim in early 1909. There he built an engine to test various cylinder-head designs. The most important detail was to find the correct combustion chamber design. The breakthrough came in placing an extra, or pre-, chamber between the injection nozzle and the combustion chamber itself. The point of this arrangement was that part of the fuel in the chamber, or rather the antechamber, was combusted. The resulting high pressure ignited the fuel in the combustion chamber itself. As in the post-chamber process, the direct-fire compressor became superfluous, and furthermore the engine was made to run smoothly. The culmination of this sequence of experiments was a continuous run lasting eight days. Although this engine too was far from being suitable for a motor vehicle, it did have the characteristic features needed for the later development of diesel high-speed engines. At this point further experiments had to be cut short when World War I intervened and L'Orange's company had more pressing tasks.

L'Orange resumed diesel development in 1919. First he investigated every combustion machine since the granting of his antechamber patent 1909. That designed by Leissner was the most advanced, built by the Swedish firm of Ljusna Woxne-AB and called the 'Ellwe engine'. L'Orange evaluated the properties of this engine painstakingly and what he learned from it helped him to improve his 1909 design considerably.

This time L'Orange really had solved the problem – the solution was a funnel-shaped insert in the antechamber, which guaranteed safe ignition and also good combustion under all loading conditions. The path-breaking *Trichter* (or funnel) patent (397142) was granted in September 1919. Shortly afterwards another patent followed, relating to a novel, and far more accurate, needle injection nozzle. The three further patents, which followed up to 1921, covered the regulation of the fuel injection pumps.

Research into basic principles was complete with the third of the patents ('the reverse-pressure free-fuel pump for combustion engines'); the path to production of a fast-running diesel was clear. Now the effective stroke of the pumping piston (and thus its and the engine's performance) could be changed smoothly – an essential precondition for a car or truck engine.

In 1922 Benz and L'Orange went their separate ways – he became the director of the newly founded *Motoren-Werke Mannheim* and turned to new tasks, but his achievements were successfully followed up at Benz.

THE FIRST DIESEL TRUCK

As far as the motor industry was concerned, the diesel age began in 1923, on fields if not on the roads. In that year, Benz & Cie signed a contract with Benz-Sendling in which the former agreed to build the new twin-cylinder engines (producing 25 bhp at 800 rpm) for Sendling's tractors, the first true diesel-powered vehicles in the world.

Benz & Cie took the next step that same year, and built the first four-cylinder antechamber diesels, for 5-ton heavy goods vehicles. The first test drive of 103 km (66 miles) over difficult, hilly terrain was a great success, particularly in fuel consumption which was reduced by 86 per cent compared with an identical lorry with a conventional petrol engine.

Only three weeks before the Benz test run Daimler's first diesel truck took to the road, driven by a four-cylinder engine, which used the complicated and un-suitable method of compressed-air direct fuel-firing. Despite the Daimler test run, by 1925 the battle between the two rival systems had been decided in favour of the superior antechamber process. That was just before the amalgamation of Daimler and Benz.

The next step, in the early thirties, was to fit a diesel engine to a passenger vehicle. The driving force behind that project was director of development Hans Nibel, who attacked the problem with the help of Albert Hess, a consummate engine-builder. What was required was a balanced blend of elements – power without too much weight and noise – a very difficult problem, especially considering the vibration levels of a diesel. The result of these efforts was the OM134 (OM for *Oel-Motor*, or oil engine), a three-cylinder in-line engine, with a considerable performance of 30 bhp from its 1796 cc.

Mercedes-Benz 160 Vs fitted with either limousine or car bodies, served as test vehicles for the six engines. The result was the new but short-lived MB175, the vibration problems proving insurmountable. The engine's shortcomings were also demonstrated by a second test series, in which twelve MB130Hs were fitted with the three-cylinder engine, from that point called the 175H.

Next, Daimler-Benz turned to the four-cylinder, which was expected to perform far better. The new engine was the OM141, displaced 1752 cc and produced 35 bhp at 3000 rpm. Like its predecessor, this engine was tried in a W134 chassis, producing four Mercedes-Benz 175DXs.

All of these vehicles came into being under Nibel's direction. After his death in 1934, Max Sailer took over, developing the MB 175DXs into the OM141 I. Its displacement was 1940 cc, which generated 40 bhp. Six MB 190D test vehicles were powered by these engines.

THE FIRST DIESEL TAXI

By 1935, the design of what became the standard passenger vehicle diesel engine had been determined. Its development was completely independent of the earlier three-cylinder engine: it was directly descended from a 3.8-litre six-cylinder M20 petrol engine of 1933. Power was 50 bhp at 3200 rpm, and much was expected of it, expectations which came to naught when it was fitted to two Mannheim W10s, as its non-independent suspension exacerbated the vibration of the diesel engine.

Four W20s with far superior suspension, fared no better. As a result, no diesel cars were displayed at the 1934 Berlin Motor Show.

In spite of the setbacks it suffered the OM20 was not simply abandoned; it underwent surgery, having two of the original six cylinders improved. In particular, it was found to be necessary to lose some of its very considerable weight and to get rid of the vibration. The injection pump developed at Bosch went a long way to solving this problem, working as it did at relatively low pressures and allowing for the development of a smooth running engine that did not cause excessive wear and tear to the bearings.

By the end of 1935 everything was ready, and the OM138 was fitted to the Mercedes-Benz 230 to form the 260D, the first production diesel car and the sensation of the Berlin Show in 1936.

It was, in fact, taxi drivers who were the first to recognize the advantages of the 260D, chiefly its economy and their acceptance was sufficient to finally still the chorus of sceptics who could only see the diesel's negative characteristics.

Nevertheless, diesel-powered cars were to remain exotic birds in the automobile aviary; only 1967 were built before the outbreak of World War II. The diesel, however, came into its own during the lean postwar years. In 1949, while ration cards were still in use, Daimler-Benz brought out the MB 170D, building 61 695 such cars in five versions by 1955. By this time motorists had become divided into two camps – a community of committed diesel fans having emerged. They began to think of their car as nothing more than transport, something to move them as cheaply and dependably as possible from A to B. And for that purpose the diesel is ideal. Unlike a petrol engine it is built to withstand significantly higher internal stress. A diesel also has to cope with higher temperatures and the engine components are therefore built correspondingly larger and stronger. That alone, however, is not the reason the diesel is a by-word for longevity. The decisive factors are that engine speeds are relatively low, and diesel drivers, being more fuel conscious, rarely drive their cars at top speed, tending to glide through the countryside in a stately and dignified manner.

TURBO DIESEL

What is the state of the art of diesel technology today? Gone are the times when drivers performing a cold start had to put in the famous 'minute's silence for Rudof Diesel', to allow the glow plugs the time they required for starting up.

A crucial milestone in the history of the diesel engine was the first production turbo diesel shown at the IAA in Frankfurt in 1977. It was designed for the 300 SD developed for the United States market. Power was increased by over 40 per cent by the turbo, making it every bit as fiery with its 125 bhp as the petrol engine.

Another of the diesel's advantages is that it, unlike the petrol engine, is unaffected by variable fuel quality. For this reason diesels can be used in all parts of the world without modification or adjustment, which is certainly not the case in catalytic-converter vehicles.

Diesels are extremely economical, thanks to their high efficiency. They do not need the fuel-intensive warming-up phase of the petrol engine with an over-rich fuel mixture during cold-starting, and that's beneficial both to the driver's pocket and to crude oil reserves.

Diesel engines are also superior to petrol engines in exhaust emission. Even petrol engines with catalytic converters cannot rival the low levels of carbon monoxide, nitric oxides and hydrocarbons that a diesel engine emits.

D '89

Unfortunately, due to the nature of the fuel and the manner of its combustion, diesels unavoidably produce soot. Although there is no clear scientific evidence of damage to human health caused by soot particles, some people are not convinced.

According to the Chairman of the managing board of Mercedes-Benz, Dr Werner Niefer, 'The three-way catalytic converter in a car with an Otto engine unquestionably represents the most effective form of exhaust purification. But it is just as unquestionable that our cars produce a level of exhaust emission comparable to that same low level.

'As Mercedes-Benz is absolutely convinced of the advantages of diesel technology, we will continue development in this area and with our new diesel concept, called Diesel D '89, we have introduced new measures that will overcome discrimination against diesel on environmental grounds. These measures represent a genuine alternative to the soot filter. Lower cost and improved consumption are further advantages.

'The outstanding innovation in the D-'89 concept is the further development of the existing antechamber design with indirect fuel injection; while the noise and exhaust emitted immediately after cold-starting were also improved. In addition, the Diesel '89 contains an injection pump with automatic level adjustment for all normally-aspirated engines. By acting upon the regulator, a reduction of the full injection load appropriate to the decrease in air density is achieved.

'If one compares the power of our new Diesel '89 with that of earlier engines, one will see what tremendous progress has been made, in particular in fuel consumption, exhaust and noise emission, and power and comfort.

'As far as the question of fuel consumption is concerned, even in this age of apparent energy surplus, it is important that we remember that there remains no more economical way that one can run a motor vehicle than a diesel engine.

'In order to reduce particle emission, we were the first manufacturer to install a soot filter as standard in a car, in 1985. It is known that we have had setbacks in this technology; but we have succeeded in the Diesel '89 in passing the strict European and American particle-emission standards which are scheduled. Particle emissions were reduced by around forty per cent with the D '89 concept.

'As far as driving is concerned, the time when compromises had to be made in buying a diesel has long gone and turbo diesels are equal to a driver's most rigorous demands. There is still considerable development potential in this diesel, due among other things to advances in electronics, which may help more than the petrol engine. And those are grounds enough for continuing to travel vigorously down the path of diesel development.'

W E R N E R   N I E F E R

The Star will Continue to Shine

Chairman of the managing board of Mercedes-Benz, Dr Werner Niefer was asked to take stock of the state of Mercedes-Benz today and to consider what he thought would be the most critical developments in the years to come. In the mind of Werner Niefer there are seven good reasons for being optimistic about the future.

1. Every year a new model
2. A four-valve engine for the middle-series W124
3. The new SL; the R129
4. The V12 engine
5. Car electronic/car 2000
6. Synergy
7. Even in one hundred years the star will still shine

1 Every year a new model

The motor car has been the origin and main concern of Daimler-Benz in the past and will remain so in the future. We have started an investment programme which is unique in the history of the company.

Half of the funds made available are earmarked for new projects. The production cycle, which is now 10 years, will be reduced to eight and our designers and engineers will create better and more ingenious cars with the help of computers.

New design and production techniques in conjunction with the application of electronic methods, such as CAD/CAM (computer aided design and computer aided manufacturing) will allow the design of new models or variants each year. New ideas are constantly adapted for series production, safeguarding the principle that our models should be characterized by advanced automobile technology.

Without crystal ball gazing, I can see some revolutionary innovations, especially in vehicle and engine technology. Four-valve engine technology will receive a decisive impulse through adjustable camshafts. New materials will be used for the construction of engines and chassis. We will continue to plan new safety elements, such as active suspension systems and/or rear-axle steering.

2. A four-valve engine for the middle-series W124

At the Frankfurt Motor Show in 1989 many models in the middle-class series had their debut. In this way we gave the popular and successful medium range Mercedes car a futuristic engine technology. The transmission, the transmission shaft, the tyres and the brakes of the T-model limousine and coupés were adapted for a greater engine performance.

The concept of using four valves per cylinder already has a tradition eighty years old. Daimler used one at the 1914 French Grand Prix; Benz in 1910 at the Prinz-Heinrich-Fahrt. Though in the main, this concept had only been used for racing and high performance sports cars, multi-valve technology has become a feature of many engines. Four valves for each cylinder not only improves the exchange of gas whereby the content will be increased, but also allows a central position of the spark plugs with short ignition distances permitting a greater compression ratio. The four-valve engine has changed from a pure power unit for motor racing to an excellent high technology engine, with improved performance and torque and better exhausts.

The 3-litre, six-cylinder engine with twenty-four valves was already launched in spring 1989 in the new SL sports car and represents a special solution to technical problems. This 217 bhp engine (in the SL, the output is higher, 231 bhp) is the solution to the classic four-valve dilemma: higher performance but little torque at lower revs. Apart from multi-valves, there is another technological innovation: an electronically-controlled hydraulic-unit at low revs which alters the partially-loaded area of the inlet camshaft so that the time for allowing air into the cylinder is shortened. The result of this variable opening means greater torque and lower emission of pollutants.

The medium-range Mercedes car is more than ever a motor car for the driver who demands style and performance and does not want to forego the proven virtues of a Mercedes.

3 The new SL; the R129

With the R129, as it is called by the in-house engineers, Mercedes-Benz continues its successful concept of the open roadster in the exclusive 'cultivated' class of sports car, where particular attention has been paid to improved performance and 'classy' appeal.

The new SL sports car follows in the legendary tradition of the 300SL of the 1950s. The tradition of the Mercedes-Benz roadster dates back thirty-five years. Following the basic concept of 1950s sports cars, so successful then in motor racing, the 300SL gullwing coupé was further developed into a high performance roadster. This 300SL received the project designation W198 and was produced between 1957 and 1963.

This was a classic sports car. The motor sport engine possessed an enormous power output of 215 bhp at 5800 rpm and reached a maximum speed of up to 250 kph (155 mph). Its 'great-grandchild', the new SL, still complies with this requirement and is a truly innovative product among our large sports cars.

The new SL series is established at the top end of the market segment even more significantly than the 230SL (pagoda roof) and the preceding series of the 300SL with its technical extravagance. This series appeals to a particular consumer who desires an exclusive, and, in many aspects, a unique vehicle.

In the areas of motorization, comfort, safety, driving for fun and prestige, the new SL sets new standards. First of all, the concept of a new twelve-cylinder engine will be launched and carry on beyond the year 2000. The twelve-cylinder will be introduced with the 600SL which has an output of approximately 400 bhp, and will represent the top engine development of modern engine design.

Until then, the scale of SL engines will comprise three variants. There will be the 300SL with the well-proven six-cylinder 3-litre unit with two valves per cylinder; the 300SL 24 with the new four-valve cylinder head and an output of 231 bhp and the 500SL with the new eight-cylinder, four-valve engine and 326 bhp.

Second, there is the concept of comfort to which Mercedes-Benz has paid particular attention in the development of the SL. The adaptable ADS suspension system controls the response of the car to the shock absorber depending on road conditions and driving behaviour. The scale ranges from comfortably soft to sporty-smooth. In borderline situations, the sporty smooth suspension is automatically selected in order to attain the highest possible degree of safety.

Mercedes-Benz considers the electro-hydraulically operated standard collapsible roof top as the most comfortable. One push of the button and 'open, sesame!', the fabric roof top moves upward after the hinge on the windscreen has opened. It then folds backwards and it clicks as if by magic into its anchorage.

Third, with regard to the safety of the new SL, it is worth noting that the roadster has never before been equipped in a similar way. With the hard-top, the SL reached the same excellent results in in-house crash-tests as the 124 coupé. Recent findings in the area of active or passive safety have been addressed with this series, establishing new standards as a pioneer in the highly advanced safety technology.

An entirely unique safety element is the standard automatic roll-over bar. In an open vehicle the passengers are more endangered than in a closed one in the event of an accident which results in the car overturning. Firmly installed roll-over bars are often not aesthetically pleasing and are restrictive when driving an open car. This has resulted in the development of an automatic roll-over bar for the roadster which is normally folded away and can be accommodated in the compartment for the convertible roof, leaving the contours of the vehicle streamlined.

In the event of the car overturning – this will be detected electronically through various sensors – the roll-over bar will be folded out within 0.3 seconds and, in conjunction with other safety measures, particularly the stiffened frame of the windscreen, reduces the risk of injury to passengers. By pressing a button, the roll-over bar can be folded out at any time.

Especially noteworthy are the integral seats which are electrically adjustable as standard. These have been completely redesigned to optimize comfort and safety. The three-point-automatic-safety belt with a safety belt tightener and the belt feed are completely integrated in the seat. The top fitting of the belt can be adjusted simultaneously with the headrest so that the seat belt can always be adjusted to the passenger's body height. Additional protection is provided by airbags for the driver and the front passenger as an extra.

This construction method is particularly costly as the underfloor of the car has to be strengthened. Only then can the vehicle withstand the energies which are distributed by the usual seat belt anchorage through the point where the webbing is fed at the B-column.

I am not only infatuated with the new sports car simply because I am the head of Mercedes-Benz AG, but also because I am an engineer and motor enthusiast. The drag-coefficient of the new SL is 0.32, making it one of the most streamlined roadsters. For reasons of road safety we have curbed the maximum speed: this is 250 kph (155 mph), at which point an electronic override is actuated.

The new SL sports car is a brilliant and unparalleled achievement in automobile construction. The shape alone highlights its character: dynamism, a sporty flair, comfort, elegance and exclusivity.

This model is just as unique in today's market as the 300SL with lift-up doors was thirty years ago. I believe you will see the often-quoted 'new beginning of a legend'. Although the SL is not the car for everybody, it is everyone's dream.

4 The V12 engine

Mercedes-Benz believes that top German cars of the future must come from Stuttgart.

The massive line-up of technology which the company will look at is a Herculean twelve-cylinder engine. The V12 is not a magic number for us as our group already produces thirty-two cylinder engines. However, a new power unit is in preparation. If a well-designed engine is cast in a light metal, a sufficient cylinder capacity can produce enough torque. Our engineers worked first of all with a swept volume of six litres; a good swept volume being the best prerequisite for powerful and comfortable propulsion.

The top priority of the Mercedes twelve-cylinder engine is a low noise level. The engine is still being developed and naturally has four valves per cylinder producing a powerful torque. The engine designers estimate a power output of nearly 400 bhp for the 6-litre engine. As for torque, more than average standards are available: 550 Nm is a realistic figure which underlines the top performance of today's suction engines. In this respect the company has followed in its traditional footsteps. So it is worth remembering not only the mighty V8 engines of the 1960s and 1970s (in the 300SL 6.3 and the 450SEL 6.9), but also the prestigious pre-war models or the legendary 600 limousine.

5 Car electronic/car 2000

Cars built now by Mercedes-Benz have an average life expectancy of ten to twelve years. That means, of course, that cars built by the company today will still be on the roads in the year 2000.

The car of the next generation will be characterized by the extended application of microelectronic regulation and control systems and an increased use of new materials with the aim of better comfort, safety, ecological benefits – and, yes, profitability.

New technologies, particularly microelectronics will ultimately serve mankind. The reliability and easy maintenance of the car is further increased by integrating electronic systems and computerized fault-finding equipment.

6 Synergy

Key technology offers new possibilities in the interrelationship of mankind, the environment and new technology. The application of microelectronics and the increased use of new materials result in an increased demand for synergy which will be satisfied through our involvement in the areas of electronic, aeronautics and astronautics.

The technology subsidiaries AEG (electrotechnology), Dornier (aero and astronautics), MTU (propulsion for aircraft and ships) and MBB (aero and astronautics) will be conducive to the technological advancement of the automobile in the near future.

The new know-how of the additional business areas will benefit Mercedes-Benz vehicles. The change from leading automobile manufacturer to technology group allows us to benefit from the opportunities arising in these future industries.

7 Even in one hundred years the star will still shine

The Americans might sell the best computers in the world and the Japanese might design the most efficient chips. With the exclusive Mercedes-Benz motor car, robust lorries and buses the Germans can proudly claim to build the world's best cars.

'The best or nothing at all' was Gottlieb Daimler's motto and Karl Benz thought along similar lines. The engines and automobiles they constructed had to stand up to this principle or they would be lost forever. The star today embodies both tradition and progress. This combination of qualities gives the company an unique appeal.

It is not a coincidence that both Daimler and Benz came from south-west Germany. Ingenuity coupled with perseverance are part of the local character. Even today, these qualities persist at Mercedes-Benz, which is still identifiable by the German virtue of thoroughness.

If you want quality you have to accept competition; Mercedes-Benz has always been a private business enterprise and has also adhered to the principles of free-enterprise and free world trade. And if you have a track record of 100 years behind you, short-term advantages are less important than profit in the long-term.

One of the board's basic principles is that a Mercedes motor car must only be manufactured in Germany and in Mercedes-Benz plants. It is certainly fair to say that the secret of its success is success itself. However, there is more to this than meets the eye. The shine of the star is the reflection of many varied day-to-day endeavours. To maintain this alone is company policy and the duty of any individual working for Mercedes. In 100 years something great has been created and preserved.

Previous page: Coupé Parade. Left: Mercedes-Benz 280 CE (1971), right: 280 CE (1977), 6 cylinder fuel-injection engine, 185 bhp, centre: 300 CE (1987), 6 cylinder fuel-injection engine, 180 bhp.

Right: A 300 CE on a so-called 'fan-course'.

Technical data: 6 cylinder fuel-injection engine, 2 962 cc capacity, 180 bhp output at 5 700 rpm, maximum speed around 228 kph.

Overleaf: Mercedes-Benz 500 SE Cabriolet 1987. The design and construction of this cabriolet come from an independent German bodywork manufacturer. This model is not supplied by the works.

Pages 254–255: Mercedes-Benz 190 E (as of 1982) also known as the 'Baby' Benz. Famous primarily for the 'multi-link independent rear suspension', presented for the first time ever on this model with its five flexible-mounted links on each rear wheel designed to neutralize any self-steering effect, whatsoever the driving conditions.

Technical data: 4 cylinders, 1 997 cc capacity, 118 bhp output at 5 100 rpm, maximum speed around 195 kph.
(Other models: 190/190 E 2.3/190 E 2.6/190 E 2.5-16.)

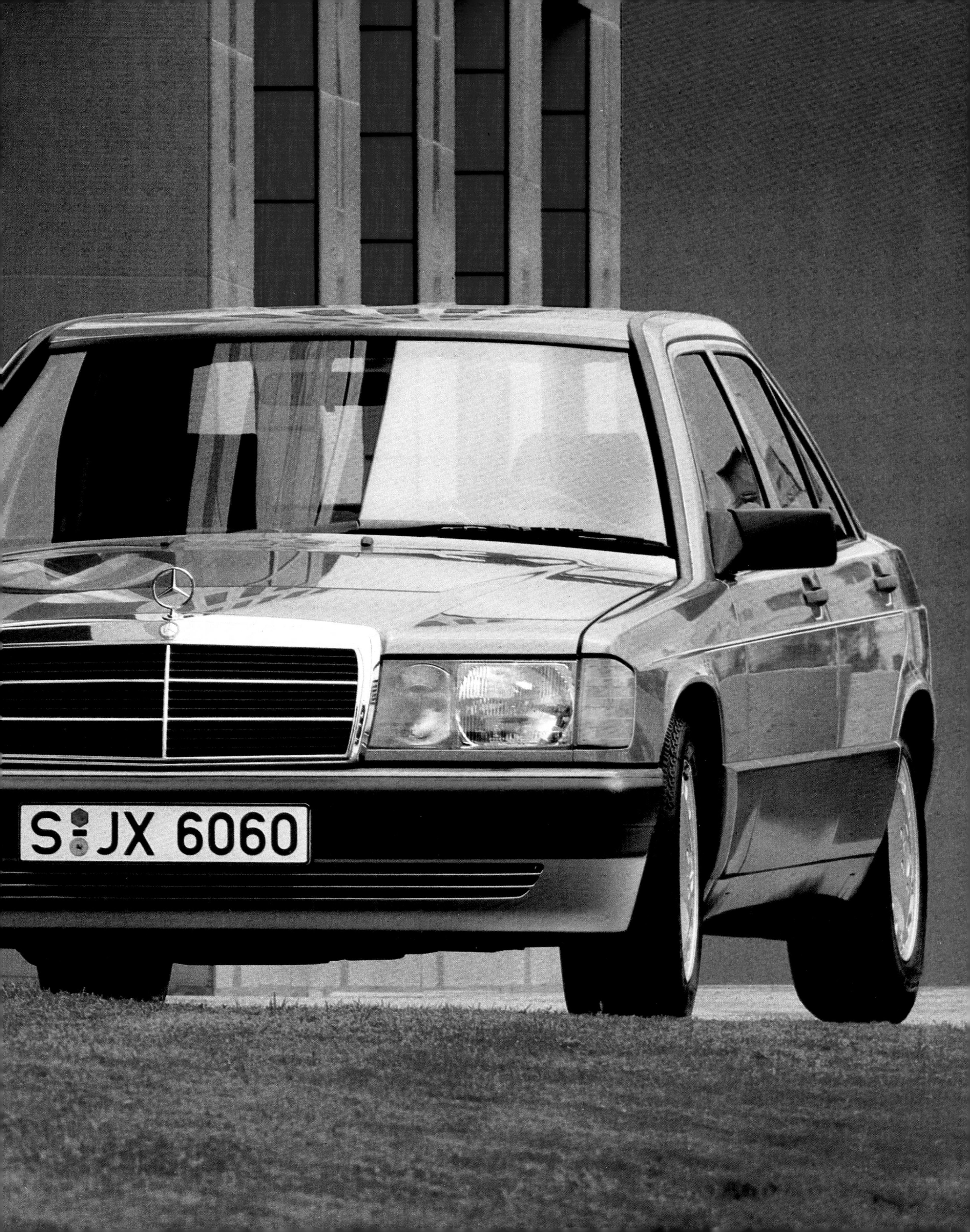
S JX 6060

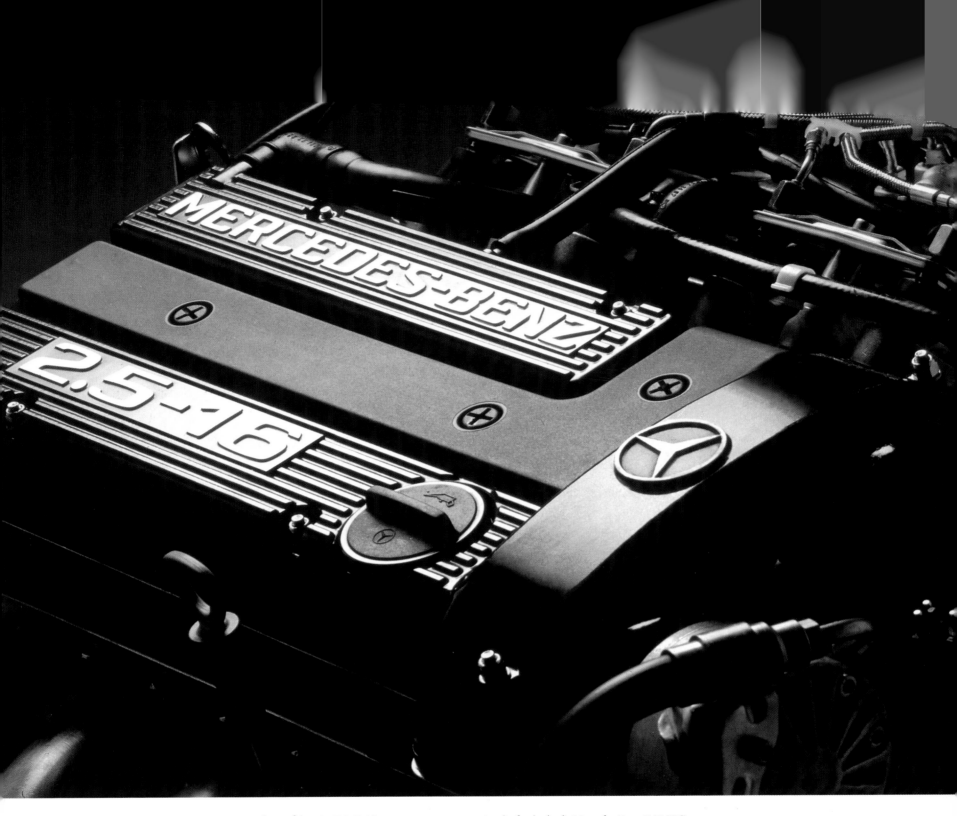

Opposite: 'Cockpit' of the 190 E 2.5-16.

Above: Engine of the 190 E 2.5-16, 4 cylinders, 2 498 cc capacity, 195 bhp at 5 500 rpm.

Overleaf (left): Brabus 190 E 3.6. A version of the Mercedes-Benz 190 E six cylinder designed and built by the Brabus team. In this modified version the car has an output of 245 bhp at 5 750 rpm, with a capacity of 3 588 cc, maximum speed 260 kph.

Overleaf right (top): Mercedes-Benz 560 SEC 'Gemballa', 1989. This 'wide version' of the 560 SEC was designed and built by the Gemballa team who specialize in modified luxury cars.

Overleaf (bottom): An independent 'tuner's' souped-up sports version of the 300 CE.

Previous page: Mercedes-Benz 560 SEC coupé (1985).
This model is considered the crowning glory after almost
60 years of coupés designed by Daimler-Benz.

Technical data: 8 cylinder fuel-injection engine, 5 547 cc capacity,
279 bhp at 5 200 rpm, maximum speed around 250 kph.

Opposite and above: Mercedes-Benz 300/500 SL 1989. The letters SL have a legendary sound. It was the 300 SL (especially the SL with the 'gull wing' doors from 1954 on) that founded the tradition that continues today. The new 300/500 SL (a roadster with a standard hard top) made poets out of motoring journalists: 'This sweet object of desire' they called it, or a car that, 'like all

crown jewels, is reserved for the few'. To date there are three engines on offer: the three litre engine from the limousine programme with power increased to 190 bhp, then the four-valve version of the six cylinder which can generate 231 bhp, and finally the eight cylinder engine, likewise with four-valve technique, which produces 326 bhp.

Above: With its 6 litre capacity, 12 cylinders, 48 valves and 400 bhp the Daimler-Benz 'Dream Engine' should point the way to the future in the new S class. However, this series is certainly unlikely to go into production before 1991.

Afterword

Whenever you approach West Berlin on a clear night by air, you can see a gigantic Mercedes sign – the star – in blue fluorescent light turning on top of the Europa Centre. Like a bright landmark, it towers over Berlin, the star of Bethlehem of the age of technology. Here, the publicity slogan about the 'guiding star on all roads' comes to life.

Indeed, the omnipotence of Daimler-Benz manifests itself impressively on a Berlin night sky. Somehow, the Mercedes sign has become sacrosanct. To drive a Mercedes in order to get from A to B, to drop in on Uncle Fred or simply to impress clients is not enough to do justice to this most German of all German marques.

Mercedes and Benz, and from 1926 Mercedes-Benz, have always been marques for the rich, powerful, beautiful, bad and ugly of this world. However much effort Rolls-Royce puts into it: 'a Merc is the greatest car on earth', according to the bold imprint on an American businessman's card. Journalist Jürgen Lewandowski wondered whether there was an affinity between money, power and cars. Men like Reichspräsident von Hindenburg, Field Marshall Mannerheim of Finland, King Ahmed of Albania and many others demonstrated their power in an ostentatious 'Mighty Mercedes', model 770. And if it was not the 'Mighty' itself, the model below it would prove to do just as well. It itself conjures up some illustrious names, such as Gustav Krupp von Bohlen und Halbach, Richard Tauber, Edouard Rothschild, Al Jolson . . . .

After World War II, the 'beautiful people' were once again inevitably attracted by Mercedes-Benz cars. 'The 300 soon became the one and only car for heads of state, film stars and businessmen. Its list of proprietors included among many others; Bundespräsident Theodor Heuss, Errol Flynn, Shah Reza Pahlevi, Jean Marais, King Idris of Libya, Haile Selassie and King Gustav of Sweden . . . ', writes Jürgen Lewandowski.

The 300SL, still deemed by insiders to be the most exciting post-war model made by Mercedes-Benz , fascinated such well known celebrities as Sophia Loren,

Juan Domingo Peron, Prince Ali Khan, Herbert von Karajan, Zsa Zsa Gabor, Rafael Trujillo, Clark Gable, Curd Jürgens, Elvis Presley, the Maharaja of Jaipur . . . .

The 190SL even took on a note of demi-monde and villainy, when a highly paid call girl, Rosemarie Nitribitt from Frankfurt, gave chase to affluent clients in her 190SL – before she was murdered. In modern folklore, Nitribitt and her Mercedes are remembered as one.

However, such society talk still does not shed any light on the mystique which surrounds Mercedes-Benz. For many people, cars are an expression of their way of life and represent the fashion in which they live. Often, such people compensate for shortcomings of say character and personality by adopting the trappings of power. In that case a Mercedes-Benz may be a substitute for moral support.

In his remarkable book, *A Critique on Cars*, Otl Aicher ponders over the car as a status symbol: 'Throughout the centuries, artists have dealt with the subject of people – stationary or in motion. However, a president who walks is not a real president. He has to be carried – as in ancient China – or driven, be it in a six-horse-drawn carriage or in a Mercedes. Not even the Pope can repudiate that truth, although Jesus in a Mercedes is a contradiction which is so absurd that it could hardly even have been the brainchild of a dadaist. Nothing against cars – thank God there are wheels – but driving as transcendental compulsion either generates derision or homage among the watching crowd.'

'BIG MERCEDES'

And these cars have to lend themselves to being polished. 'Having a shining car makes people assume that one has the staff to polish it. The aesthetics of privilege put shine only one step down from grandeur' (Aicher). For centuries, a Mercedes has been a symbol of success and power. I remember well how stunned we used to be as children every time the richest man in our little town, a wily cattle-dealer, drove past in his Mercedes-Benz. For the Sunday church trip the car was painstakingly polished, although it served as transport for young pigs during the week. We soon learned what

the notion of 'big Mercedes' meant and what it stood for: 'The Führer drives a big Mercedes', our father explained, 'and so does Rudolf Caracciola!'

The word 'car' was always associated by us kids with 'Mercedes-Benz'. Horch and Maybach, two other German top marques, were second-rate to us. The fact that Adolf Hitler almost totally identified himself with the brand-names Mercedes and Mercedes-Benz must have left a strong mark on the American car industry. 'How else could you explain why in 1935 the American car manufacturer Studebaker introduced a model called Dictator, to join the existing President and Commander ranges, announced in 1931 and 1932, respectively. The name of this series later fell into disrepute, since the catalogues for the year 1938 merely show the names State Commander and State President' (excerpt from *The Automobile and Art*).

Does it not appear to be of macabre symbolic significance that Field Marshall Rommel, after having revolted against Hitler, committed suicide as ordered by the Führer on 14 October 1944, not in a Mercedes-Benz, but in a Horch 853 – that is to say, not in a state car symbolizing state power . . . ?

THE WAY OF LIFE

It has long been an established fact that cars are central to the art of technology. Their design reflects what millions of car buyers consider as being chic and good looking. But cars also reflect the way of life of whole eras. Thus there is a British expression 'Edwardian Cars' and the art and motoring historian D.B. Tubbs speaks about 'Cars of the Jazz Age'. According to him that period, the '20s, was represented by brand names such as Hispano-Suiza, Voisin, Bentley, Isotta-Fraschini, Bugatti, Rolls-Royce, Salmson, Sizaire-Berwick, Delage, Duesenberg – but not Benz, Mercedes or Mercedes-Benz. The roaring sound of supercharged engines by Paul Daimler, Hans Nibel and Ferdinand Porsche did not seem to go with the jazz bands, cabarets or the songs of Mistinguette or Josephine Baker. Mercedes-Benz instead conjures up Richard Wagner, alpine horns, kettle drums, military music, exactitude, order, perfection, reliability, or German craftmanship.

Did any Mercedes-Benz model ever have such a human touch as Henry Ford's Model T, affectionately known as the 'Tin Lizzie'? Thanks to Ford, the United States had millions of cars before they had a large enough road-network. Tin Lizzie became something of a national mascot representing the pioneering spirit of millions of Americans. It would be unthinkable that any German poet could ever enthuse about a Mercedes-Benz car in the same way as John Steinbeck did in his book 'Cannery Row' about the Tin Lizzie: 'Someone should write an erudite essay on the moral, physical and aesthetic effect of the Model T Ford on the American nation. Two generations of Americans knew more about the Ford coil than the clitoris, about the planetary system of gears than the solar system of stars. With the Model T, part of the concept of private property disappeared. Pliers ceased to be privately owned and a tyre pump belonged to the last man who had picked it up. Most of the babies of the period were conceived in Model T Fords and not a few were born in them.'

Today, Mercedes-Benz cars still radiate dignity, detachment, elitism and superiority and allow you to distinguish social groups at a stroke. This is demonstrated by a London estate agent describing the neighbourhood in which he offers his properties as a domain of the 'wine-drinking, Mercedes-driving class', and the

sad husband of a murdered wife being referred to in the London popular press as 'Mercedes owner' XYZ. But the times when the ownership of a Mercedes was a privilege of the wealthy, and powerful of 'high society' are drawing to a close. When Pope Pius XI took delivery of his Mercedes-Benz Nürburg in 1930, Daimler-Benz director, Dr Hans Nibel sent a telegram to his colleagues in Stuttgart: 'His holiness praised the performance of the car'. Although the Pope still passes his cheering crowds of followers in a – often bullet-proof – Mercedes-Benz, he now shares his preference for these luxury cars with second-rate politicians, chairmen, arms-dealers, pimps, farmers from the mid-west and TV personalities. It is not by mere chance that J.R. Ewing most often plans his infamous intrigues in a Mercedes-Benz. Many Germans were quite moved when Frank Sinatra flirted with Grace Kelly in a Mercedes in the unforgettable comedy *High Society* and the American singer Janis Joplin picked her desire for a Mercedes into the Blues line: 'Oh Lord, won't you buy me a Mercedes-Benz?'

The Soviet General Secretary, Leonid Brezhnev, who received a Mercedes-Benz 450SLC from the government in Bonn during his state visit to West Germany in 1973, subsequently smashed the back of the luxury car when on a run near the capital; Willy Brandt simply sent another 450SLC to Moscow . . . .

It is a never-ending story . . . .

Major Landmarks in Automobile History

PRE-PETROL PIONEERS

c.3500 BC First recorded use of the wheel on Sumerian chariots.

c.500 BC 'Sicilian' surface oil (petroleum) used for lighting by Romans.

308 BC Demetrios (Greece) builds an enclosed 'war wagon' occupied by two men, one steering, the other treading a wheel driving the rear wheels.

1420 Giovanni Fontana (Italy) builds one-seater four-wheeled 'sedan,' propelled by occupant pulling on endless rope working a drum and gears.

1649–63 Hans Hautsch (Germany) builds 'wonder' horseless carriages, operated by men concealed within, working cranks.

1673 Christiaan Hüygens of Holland demonstrates possibilities of internal combustion by exploding gunpowder in a cylinder, thereby raising a piston and causing a vacuum, atmospheric pressure then forcing piston down and lifting a weight.

1689 Legless cripple Stefan Farffler of Altdorf, Germany, builds hand-operated three-wheeler 'for going to church'.

1694 Elie Richard (France) proposes a carriage treadled by a footman behind passenger's seat.

1771 Nicolas Cugnot (Lorraine) builds working three-wheeled, high-pressure steam-powered gun tractor.

1784 James Watt (Britain) patents specification for steam road carriage with three-speed variable transmission.

William Murdoch (Britain) builds working model steam vehicle.

1787 Oliver Evans (USA) patents a high-pressure steam wagon.

1788 Pistons on articulated connecting rods first prescribed in an engine by Robert Fourness in a steam engine design.

1791 Nathan Read (USA) projects a twin-engined, rack-driven steam car.

1801 Richard Trevithick (Britain) builds full-scale working high-pressure steam road vehicle.

1803 Charles Dallery (France) patents four-wheeled steam car with selectable gear ratios.

1807 Isaac de Rivaz (Switzerland) makes a working vehicle propelled by gas electronically fired in a cylinder.

1815 Josef Bozek (Bohemia) builds Watt low-pressure steam-powered four-wheeler.

1823 Samuel Brown (Britain) successfully climbs Shooter's Hill, London, with two-cylinder 'gas-vacuum' powered four-wheeler.

1825–c.1840 First steam carriage era brings working vehicles by Gurney, Burstall & Hill, Hancock, Nasmyth, Napier, James, Fraser, Ogle & Summers, Heaton, Macerone, Scott Russell and others of Britain; Dietz (France); Bordino (Italy); Fisher (USA) and others.

1828 Onésiphore Pecqueur (France) patents four-wheeled steam wagon with differential drive.

1858 Thomas Rickett (Britain) builds first of several light passenger-carrying steam carriages, one being used to tour the Scottish Highlands by Earl of Caithness.

1863 J-J Etienne Lenoir (Luxembourg) builds and runs a three-wheeled 'break' on coal gas.

1873 Amédée Bollée Snr (France) completes *L'Obéissante*; first of several practical, working steam carriages, driving it 135 miles to Paris without mechanical mishap two years later.

1858–85 Second steam carriage era; vehicles built by Yarrow, Cooke, Tangye, Thompson, Carrett & Marshall, Inshaw, Prew, Mackenzie, Todd, Blackburn, Grenville and others of Britain; Dudgeon, Roper, Reed, War, Carhart, Copeland and others of USA; Ravel, Bollée, De Dion-Bouton and Trépardoux of France; Nussberger of Sweden.

1876 Nicolaus Otto (Germany) patents four-stroke cycle, only to lose rights ten years later on grounds that principle was propounded in 1862 by Alphonse Beau de Rochas (France).

1881 Jeantaud (France) builds and runs electric car powered by twenty-one Fulmen batteries.

1883 Daimler patents DRP 28 022 and 28 243 of 16 and 22 December 1883; basis for a light, fast-running petrol engine.

THE VETERAN ERA

1886 Karl Benz builds first practical petrol-powered tricar; single-cylinder, single speed, belt drive.

Daimler patents DRP 34 926 of 3 April 1885; an encased, standing engine suitable for mounting; revolutionary in motor vehicle technology.

Gottlieb Daimler builds first four-wheeled petrol car with fast-turning single-cylinder engine, two speeds, and belt-cum-gear drive.

Benz patent DRP 37 435 of 29 January 1886; basis for the development of the motor car as a universal unit. Daimler engines are installed in motor-driven carriages and motor boats.

1888 Frau Berta Benz and two sons complete first extended motor drive (125 miles).

1889 Daimler introduces twin-cylinder engine and sliding pinion four-speed transmission.

Panhard and Levassor acquire licence to manufacture Daimler engines.

1890 First Peugeot and Panhard-Levassor cars, both Daimler-engined.

First four-cylinder engine (by Daimler).

1891 Peugeot car covers 1280 miles, following the Paris—Brest—Paris cycle race.

1892 Panhard-Levassor build the first front-engined petrol car.

Wilhelm Maybach of Daimler introduces constant-level float-type jet carburettor.

1893 First four-wheeled Benz car, the *Viktoria* is introduced.

1894 Panhard-Levassor and Peugeot share first prize in Paris—Rouen 'Concours', the world's first motoring contest.

Panhard introduce countershaft sliding gear system.

Frank and Charles Duryea found first American motor manufacturing company at Peoria, Illinois.

1895 Emile Levassor in a Panhard-Levassor, with 1.2-litre Daimler Phoenix in-line twin-cylinder engine and enclosed gearbox, wins world's first motor race, the 732-mile Paris—Bordeaux—Paris.

First pneumatic tyres used on a car by Michelin brothers.

Rudolf Egg of Switzerland develops lever-controlled gearless variable transmission.

1896 De Dion-Bouton market proprietary air-cooled, single-cylinder 1500 rpm engines from 1hp upwards for use in light two-, three- and four-wheeled vehicles.

Léon-Bollée produce 650 cc tandem-seated three-wheeled voiturette.

British Daimler Motor Company founded at Coventry. Henry Ford builds first experimental car.

1897 First petrol-engined car with two-speed epicyclic gearbox and shaft final drive to live axle made by F. W. Lanchester.

Mors of Paris produce 45-degree V4 air-cum-water-cooled car with low tension coil and dynamo ignition.

First front-wheel-drive car built by Graf und Stift in Vienna, using De Dion engine.

Low tension magneto introduced by Bosch in collaboration with F. R. Simms.

Benz introduces 5 bhp 'Kontra' horizontally opposed twin-cylinder engine.

1898 Louis Renault builds prototype small car with front-mounted De Dion engine, direct-drive top gear and universally jointed shaft final drive.

Decauville *Voiturelle* has independent front suspension by transverse leaf spring.

Daimler-designed four-cylinder engine used in touring Panhard-Levassor.

1899 Four-cylinder German Daimler Phoenix has honeycomb-type radiator, pressed-steel frame and gate-type gearchange.

First monobloc four-cylinder engine made by Amédée Bollée Jnr.

Automatic advance and retard ignition control used by Hiram Maxim and Packard in USA.

1900 Acetylene (carbide) lighting supplements oil and kerosene.

Honeycomb radiator; an important prerequisite for producing motor vehicles with an improved performance. Mercedes cars are characterized by a combination of fine engine performance, chassis, bodywork and other components of the vehicle.

1901 First Daimler aircraft engine.

Daimler's first Mercedes car has throttle-controlled engine, improved honeycomb radiator, twin side camshafts operating inlet and exhaust valves, and gate gearchange.

Oldsmobile Curved Dash is America's first car to go into high quantity production.

1902 Bosch introduce high-tension magneto.

Spyker of Holland build six-cylinder four-wheel-drive car.

First straight-eight-engined car (two four-cylinder units coupled together), with single-speed gearbox, built by CGV of Paris.

Truffault of Paris introduce friction-type shock absorber.

Disc brake patented by F. W. Lanchester of Britain.

Single-overhead-camshaft engine with pressurized lubrication marketed by Maudslay in Britain.

1903 Ader of Paris build V8-engined car.

1904 Napier of Britain market first successful six-cylinder car.

Sturtevant of Boston, USA, market first car with automatic three-speed transmission.

Engine and gearbox in one unit on French Motobloc and American Stevens-Duryea cars.

Riley of Coventry introduce detachable centre-lock wire wheels.

Introduction of Schrader needle-type tyre valve.

THE INTERIM YEARS

1905 Moseley of Britain produce detachable wheel rim for easier tyre-changing.

Renault of France patent a hydraulic shock absorber.

Pipe of Belgium make a twin-high-camshaft engine with inclined overhead valves.

The first Rolls-Royce, the in-line twin-cylinder 10 bhp, is marketed.

First car by Rover of Coventry has cast-aluminium backbone frame embodying engine, clutch housing and gearbox.

Simms-Welbeck car is fitted with pneumatic rubber front bumpers.

1906 Front-wheel brakes fitted experimentally to a Mercedes.

Michelin introduce press-on tyre gauge.

Rudge-Whitworth market detachable wire-wheel.

Electric lighting by accumulator becomes an optional extra.

1907 Rolls-Royce adopt one-model policy with 40/50 six-cylinder 'Silver Ghost'.

Chadwick of Pittsburgh, USA, introduce supercharged sporting model.

1908 Ford Model T ('The Universal Car') is introduced (over 15 million built by 1927).

First coil-and-distributor ignition system introduced by Delco, USA.

First V12 engine by Schebler, USA.

Car heating by exhaust (USA).

Formation of General Motors, USA, the world's first big motor combine.

Sankey of Britain market steel artillery wheel.

1909 Aquila-Italiana introduce aluminium pistons on sporting models.

Isotta-Fraschini standardize front-wheel brakes.

Christie of USA build transverse-engined, front-drive taxi with independent front suspension (the Mini layout).

First dipping device by Blériot, France, for acetylene lamps.

1910 Hydraulic tappets patented by Amédée Bollée Jnr.

1911 De Dion V8-engined car marketed.

Delahaye V6-engined car marketed.

1912 Cadillac of USA standarize coil ignition, electronic starting and electric lighting.

Hupmobile and Oakland (USA) produce all-steel bodywork.

Triplex introduce splinterproof glass in France.

1913 William Morris (later Lord Nuffield) markets Morris Oxford, using proprietary engine and other major components.

Reo of USA employ centrally positioned gearchange.

Lagonda of Britain employ unitary construction of chassis and body.

Cable-operated direction indicators introduced in USA.

1914 Loughead of USA (later Lockheed) develop hydraulic braking system.

Adjustable driving seats offered in France and USA.

1915 Cadillac market first American series-production V8-engined car.

Packard of USA market world's first production V12-engined car, the Twin-Six.

Dipping headlights and suction-operated windscreen wipers introduced in USA.

1916 Brake lights introduced in USA.

1917 First use of torsion bars in suspension on the Spanish Diaz-y-Grillo car.

THE VINTAGE ERA

1919 Hispano-Suiza of France and Spain pioneer use of servo-assisted four-wheel brakes. Isotta-Fraschini of Italy market world's first in-line eight-cylinder (straight-eight) engined car.

Citroën of France introduce American-type mass-production methods to Europe.

New Bentley 3-litre sparts car is announced.

1920 Duesenberg of USA employ hydraulically-operated four-wheel brakes.

Leyland Motors of Britain announce new 7.2-litre straight-eight luxury model.

1921 The supercharger is used for the first time to increase the performance of catalogued cars (Mercedes).

1922 Integral chassis/body construction, vertical coil independent front suspension and narrow-angle mono-bloc V4 engine in new Italian Lancia Lambda car.

British prototype North-Lucas car has all-independent suspension by swinging arms, coil springs and coaxial hydraulic dampers. First British four-cylinder, four-seater, four-wheel braked 'baby' car, the Austin Seven, is introduced.

Trico of USA produce first electrically operated screen wipers.

Mercedes of Germany market first European supercharged sports car.

Fast-running diesel engine; the Benz pre-combustion chamber method – the opposite number to the fast-running petrol engine.

1923 Pratt's 'Ethyl' leaded fuel introduced in USA to reduce engine detonation.

Ferdinand Porsche becomes chief engineer and a member of the board of directors of Daimler-Benz AG in Stuttgart. His best known models are the S and SS.

1924 Japan takes up motor manufacture with the 10 bhp air-cooled Lila light car.

The first MG sports car, based on the Morris Oxford, is marketed in Britain. Introduction of the low-pressure balloon tyre by Goodyear, USA.

'Duco' quick-drying cellulose car finish pioneered by Du Pont, USA.

1925 Electric direction indicators marketed by Bosch of Germany.

General adoption in USA of front and rear bumper bars.

1926 Two major German makes, Mercedes and Benz, combine to form Mercedes-Benz.

Silentbloc oilless rubber bushes are introduced in USA.

1927 Ford USA replace Model T, after nineteen years' production, with the Model A.

World's largest production road car, the 12.8-litre Bugatti Royale, with 14 ft 2 in wheelbase and weight of 2½ tons, is announced.

Epicyclic preselector 'self-change' gearbox developed by Wilson of Great Britain.

Triplex of Great Britain market laminated safety glass.

Tracta of France market 1100 cc front-wheel-drive sports car.

1928 Widespread adoption by US manufacturers of chromium plating in place of nickel.

Cadillac adopt the synchromesh gearbox. New Morris Minor 'baby' car with overhead-camshaft engine is announced in Britain.

The first MG Midget, using the Morris Minor engine, is introduced.

Piloting the Porsche-designed Mercedes SS with supercharger, Rudolf Caracciola wins the German Grand Prix at the Nürburgring.

Foot headlight dipping introduced in USA.

1929 Car radios offered as optional extras in USA.

1930 Shell-type quickly replaceable 'thin-wall' engine bearings developed by Cleveland Graphite, USA.

World's first V16-engined production car by Cadillac, USA.

'Fluid flywheel' hydraulic clutch and epicyclic gearbox adopted by Daimler of Britain.

Wolseley Hornet Light 6, using Morris Minor bodywork, is announced.

British rear-engined Burney Streamline all-independently sprung car developed by designer of R101 airship. Britain's first quantity-production £100 car, the Morris Minor, is introduced.

1932 Auto-Union AG (Horch, Wanderer, DKW, Audi) is established.

THE HITLER ERA

1934 New racing car concepts appear from Auto Union and Mercedes-Benz.

1935 Introduction of self-supporting chassis for large-scale passenger car production (Opel Olympia).

1938 Laying of the foundation stone of the Volkswagen factory.

1939 World War II begins.

1940 Introduction of the automatic transmission for passenger cars. Start of production of the jeep in the USA.

PHOENIX FROM THE ASHES

1945 Production of the Volkswagen 'Beetle' starts at Wolfsburg.

1948 Production of the Citroën 2 CV begins.

1952 Introduction of fuel injection for sports and racing cars.

1956 West Germany becomes the world's leading automobile exporter and the second largest car producer.

1957 The rotary piston is designed by Felix Wankel.

1959 Production of the Mini starts.

'Compact cars' from General Motors, Ford and Chrysler go onto market.

1964 First passenger car with rotary engine (NSU Spyder).

1965 Strict safety regulations laid down for the passenger car production in the USA.

1969 Europe outstrips US automobile production.

1971 Japan outstrips the Federal Republic of Germany's automobile production.

1972 The number of 'Beetles' produced exceeds that of the Model-T Ford ('Tin Lizzie').

1973 First general oil crisis.

1977 Saab is the first company which constructs a turbo-engine for its production passenger cars.

1979 US car manufacturers turn away from petrol guzzlers and introduce more economic passenger cars.

1980 Japan becomes the world's biggest motor car manufacturer.

1981 The 20 millionth 'Beetle' is produced.

1987 Honda introduces the first series-produced vehicle with four wheel steering ('Prelude') in the world.

1989 Four wheel drive has established itself in almost all types of cars, particularly in Europe and Japan.

Multiple valve-technology becomes more and more established worldwide, ranging from small cars to luxurious automobiles.

Major Landmarks in the History of Benz, Daimler, Mercedes and Mercedes-Benz

EARLY BREAKTHROUGHS

1868 Gas engine by Otto and Langen.

1876–8 Daimler and Maybach work together in Deutz to develop the gas engine further.

1883 Benz establishes Benz & Cie Rheinische Gasmotorenfabrik in Mannheim.

1885 The Daimler *Reitrad* is patented, the first motor cycle in the world to reach a speed of 18 kph (11 mph).

The *Standuhr* is developed by Daimler; it is an upright single-cylinder four-stroke engine with a power plant output of 1/4 bhp at 600 rpm.

THE ARRIVAL OF THE AUTOMOBILE

1886 Karl Benz introduces his *Patent-Motorwagen*.

Gottlieb Daimler presents his motor-driven carriage. Test drives begin.

The first Daimler motor boat.

Daimler constructs his engine in Draisine, as well as a tramcar which runs over a course of 1 km in Cannstatt.

1888 Daimler equips a balloon, a fire-engine, and a locomotive with engines.

Having taken out patents for the USA,

William Steinway sets up the Daimler Motor Company on Long Island, New York.

1889 Daimler and Maybach design a 2 bhp two-cylinder vee-engine to run at 600 rpm.

Daimler exhibits his tubular framed *Stahlrad wagen* at the Paris World Exposition.

1890 Daimler constructs a four-cylinder in-line engine, the basic design for today's engine construction.

The Daimler Motoren Gesellschaft (DMG) is founded in Cannstatt.

1891 The first usable American vehicle engine is constructed in Hartford,

Connecticut, following original plans by Gottlieb Daimler.

1892 Rudolf Diesel announces his invention of an 'efficient combustion engine'.

1893 The Benz *Viktoria*, with axle-pivot steering, arrives.

1894 Limited production at Benz of the small *Velo*, which, at 2000 Marks, was the first inexpensively manufactured vehicle in the world.

Vehicles with Daimler engines win the first motor car competition in the world (Paris-Rouen-Paris).

Benz constructs his first bus, delivery van and touring car.

1895 While Benz sells 120 motor cars in the course of this year, DMG mainly supplies engines and, between November 1894 and June 1895, delivers only four 2 bhp motor cars.

The capital of DMG is increased to 900 000 Marks.

1896 The Daimler taxi and lorry (the latter with an engine mounted under the floor for the first time) are introduced. The entire range of Daimler Motoren Gesellschaft comprises twenty-four models (cars, trams, boats).

Daimler establishes the *Motorwagen Kutscherei* in Stuttgart, which is the first taxi service in the world.

DMG constructs the first truck in the world, which is delivered to the British Motor Syndicate Ltd.

DMG produces thirty-three vehicles, twenty-eight of which are for clients abroad.

1897 Robert Bosch introduces his low-tension magneto in Stuttgart.

1898 The first Benz car with pneumatic tyres.

1899 Daimler works on airship and aircraft engines.

The name 'Daimler' becomes a registered trademark.

THE TWENTIETH CENTURY

1900 (6 March) Gottlieb Daimler dies.

Emil Jellinek is elected a member of the supervisory board in April.

Apart from stationary engines, Benz produces 603 automobiles, 341 of which are for customers abroad. This makes the company the largest manufacturer of motor vehicles in the world.

1900–1 The first Mercedes cars; new landmarks in the construction of cars.

1902 The name 'Mercedes' becomes a registered trademark.

1903 A large fire in Bad Cannstatt destroys nearly ninety finished and semi-finished cars (9–10 June).

The Mercedes Company New York is

established with a capital of US $2.7 million.

1907 Wilhelm Maybach resigns from the board of directors of DMG. His successor is Paul Daimler, who is appointed manager of design and technical development.

1908 The new factory of Benz & Cie in Mannheim-Waldhof is completed at a total cost of 600 000 Marks. All motor vehicle production is moved there.

1909 DMG acquires the exclusive right to manufacture in Germany the sleeve-valve engine invented by the American Charles J. Knight.

Benz & Cie has orders which will keep the 'production line' busy for the next six months.

DMG begins to manufacture four-cylinder, 60 bhp engines for aircraft.

Benz begins development of the pre-combustion chamber layout for diesel engines.

The Mercedes star becomes a trademark.

1910 Daimler engines are used by the navy.

1911 The streamlined *Blitzen Benz* racing car with a 200 bhp engine achieves a world speed record of 228.1 kph (141.7 mph).

1913 Benz & Cie begins production of its aircraft engine, which is awarded the *Kaiserpreis*.

1914 Benz & Cie and DMG switch to war production.

1915 DMG acquires land to build an aircraft factory in Sindelfingen, near the military airport of Böblingen. There the company builds the large four-engined RII aircraft.

Benz and Cie extend the limits of their production capacity to fulfil orders from the army for motor vehicles, trucks, aircraft and boat engines.

1918 The management of DMG is put under military supervision and is accused of charging excessive prices.

1920 Within eight months, DMG's capital trebles and reaches 100 million Marks. The size of its capital makes the company Germany's largest industrial enterprise.

THE ROARING '20s and '30s

1921–22 The first Daimler car with a supercharged engine.

1922 Benz produces his first 30 bhp diesel engines with precombustion chambers, for the Sendling motor plough.

1924 The two oldest motor car manufacturers, Benz and DMG, decide to pool their resources (1 May). Dr Emil Georg von Stauss of the Deutsche Bank heads the committee set up for this purpose.

1926 Merger between Daimler and Benz to form Daimler-Benz AG.

1928 Mass-production of commercial

vehicles with diesel engines at Daimler-Benz.

Switch from manual to series production in the Sindelfingen chassis factory. First application of the *Weingarten* body press.

1929 The deaths of Karl Benz (4th April) and Wilhelm Maybach (29th December) are announced.

1930 To make production more efficient motor cars are manufactured in Untertürkheim, trucks in Gaggenau and chassis in Sindelfingen.

A quarter of the annual production is stockpiled, a sign of the Great Depression.

1932 Sales of motor vehicles reach their lowest levels since 1927. The annual loss is about 5 million Reichsmarks after write-offs.

The number of people employed by Daimler-Benz has dropped by more than half since 1927.

To use the full capacity of the workshop, chassis for the 3/20 PS BMW and other BMW models are manufactured in Sindelfingen until 1934. Subsequently, work is also carried out for Wanderer, a part of Auto Union.

DBAG doubles its market share in Germany, reaching 14 per cent for cars and 16 per cent for trucks.

1933 With a market share of 11 per cent, DBAG becomes the third largest motor vehicle manufacturer in Germany.

1936 The first diesel motor car in the world is introduced: the Mercedes-Benz 260 D.

Nearly one third of all exported German cars are made by DBAG.

The aircraft engine factory of DB-Motoren GmbH is built in Genshagen.

Vehicle and engine exports rise by forty-three per cent compared with the previous year.

1938 Since the beginning of 1933 DBAG has invested more than 100 million Reichsmarks in the extension of its plants.

A down-draught carburettor is introduced by Daimler-Benz.

Construction of army vehicles, aircraft engines, marine engines and a coal generator.

WORLD WAR II

1939 At the outbreak of war, orders are twice as high as in the previous year. They amount to 600 million Reichsmarks and exceed the previous year's turnover by half.

1940 DBAG switches to war production.

Since the introduction of the 170V, 100 000 of these cars have been built.

1944 Berta Benz dies (5 May).

During two raids by American and British aircraft, eighty per cent of the buildings of the plant in Sindelfingen, and over fifty per cent of the machinery and installations are destroyed (10 and 13 September).

RECONSTRUCTION AND PROGRESS

1945 Production of the 3-ton truck (under licence) starts again in Mannheim as well as that of the 5-ton Mercedes-Benz truck in Gaggenau.

1946 Motor vehicle production restarts at the Sindelfingen plant. Annual production output: 214 cars of the pre-war 170V type.

1949 For the first time since the war, monthly production reaches 1000 motor cars (February).

1952 Daimler-Benz establishes itself in the American market by signing an agreement for representation by Maximilian Hoffman.

1953 Daimler-Benz is the biggest exporter among German motor car manufacturers, with exports amounting to 244 million DM.

The first ponton-shaped car, the Mercedes-Benz 180, is designed.

1954–5 Mercedes-Benz 300SL, the first passenger car with fuel injection appears.

1959 Daimler-Benz becomes the third largest German company, with a group turnover of DM 3.15 billion.

1961 Automatic transfer line for manufacturing passenger cars.

1964 After contracts with Studebacker-Packard are terminated, Daimler-Benz carries out its own distribution and sale in America. For this purpose Mercedes-Benz of North America is established (14 December).

1968 The two-millionth Mercedes-Benz passenger car since the war is produced.

1969 France becomes the biggest export market for Daimler-Benz in Europe.

1972 The new S-class (types 280S, 280SE and 350SE) is introduced.

1973 An agreement with the USSR about scientific and technological cooperation is signed (27 February). A well attended Mercedes exhibition is held in Moscow (20 February to 9 March).

Shares are issued to the staff for the first time.

For the first time the turnover abroad is larger than the domestic turnover.

1974 Distribution and sales in Great Britain are handled by Daimler-Benz itself (1 January) for the first time.

The 300D – the first five-cylinder diesel car in the world.

1977 The first mass-produced car with a turbo-diesel engine (300D).

The Mercedes-Benz T-series (for tourism) is introduced.

The board of directors decide to produce the newly developed *Kombi-Wagen* (T-model) in Bremen, which becomes solely a car plant (Spring).

Hanns Martin Schleyer, a member of the board of directors, is brutally murdered by terrorists (18 October).

1978 Every other vehicle from Mercedes-Benz has a diesel engine.

1979 Mercedes-Benz off-road car, the GE-type.

The S-class is upgraded.

1982 The Daimler-Benz of North America holding company is founded and a clear group organization in North America is created (1 January).

The first cars of the compact class (Mercedes 190) are shown to the public.

1983 The new Mercedes diesel 190D car has its engine enclosed to reduce noise levels.

The Mercedes 190E 2.3–16, a new model, establishes three long-distance world records, driving over a distance of 50 000 km (31 070 miles) and reaching a speed of 247.9 kph (154.1 mph).

1984–5 The new middle-class Mercedes 200D to 300E.

1985 New models for the Mercedes compact class: 190D 2.5 and 190E 2.6

New, stronger and more economic engines for the Mercedes-Benz S-class introduced.

Three electronic-automatic transmission devices introduced: MB 4-matic, ASR and ASD.

1986 Re-opening of the newly designed Daimler-Benz museum.

Daimler-Benz is involved in the development of PROMETHEUS ('Programme for European Traffic with Highest Efficiency and Unprecedented Safety').

1989 The long-awaited new Mercedes-Benz SL is introduced.

The Passenger, Sports and Racing Cars of Benz, Daimler, Mercedes and Mercedes-Benz

On the following pages are illustrations and specifications of all but a few, less significant, cars which have emerged from the workshops of Benz, Daimler, Mercedes and Mercedes-Benz since 1885.

The cars have been divided into passenger, sports and racing models, the entries providing information on first year of production, number of cylinders, bore, stroke, cubic capacity, bhp and maximum speed.

PASSENGER CARS

Benz Vis-à-Vis, 1893
1 cylinder / bore 150 mm / stroke 165 mm
2.92 litres / 5 bhp at 700 rpm / 25 kph max speed

Paul Daimler Phaeton, 1901
2 cylinders / bore 88 mm / stroke 116 mm
1.14 litres / 6.7 bhp at 800 rpm / 40 kph max speed

Daimler Motorrad, 1885
1 cylinder / bore 58 mm / stroke 100 mm
0.26 litres / 0.56 bhp at 600 rpm / 12 kph max speed

Daimler Riemenwagen Vis-à-Vis, 1894
2 cylinders / bore 75 mm / stroke 118 mm
1.04 litres / 3.7 bhp at 670 rpm / 18 kph max speed

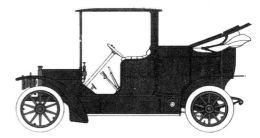

Mercedes Simplex, 1902
4 cylinders / bore 90 mm / stroke 120 mm
3.05 litres / 22.6 bhp at 1200 rpm / 70 kph max speed

Daimler Motorwagen, 1886
1 cylinder / bore 70 mm / stroke 120 mm
0.46 litres / 1.1 bhp at 600 rpm / 18 kph max speed

Benz Velo, 1894
1 cylinder / bore 110 mm / stroke 110 mm
1.05 litres / 1.5 bhp at 700 rpm / 21 kph max speed

Benz Tonneau, 1902
2 cylinders / bore 100 mm / stroke 110 mm
1.73 litres / 12 bhp at 1280 rpm / 50 kph max speed

Benz Patent-Motorwagen, 1886
1 cylinder / bore 91.4 mm / stroke 150 mm
0.99 litre / 0.89 bhp at 400 rpm / 15 kph max speed

Daimler Riemenwagen Viktoria, 1897
2 cylinders / bore 100 mm / stroke 140 mm
2.2 litres / 7.91 bhp at 720 rpm / 40 kph max speed

Mercedes Simplex Tonneau, 1903
4 cylinders / bore 100 mm / stroke 130 mm
4.08 litres / 18 bhp at 1200 rpm / 60 kph max speed

Daimler Stahlradwagen, 1889
2 cylinders / bore 70 mm / stroke 126 mm
0.97 litres / 1.65 bhp at 920 rpm / 18 kph max speed

Benz Landaulet-Coupé, 1899
2 cylinders / bore 115 mm / stroke 110 mm
2.28 litres / 9 bhp at 1000 rpm / 30 kph max speed

Mercedes Simplex Tourenwagen, 1903
4 cylinders / bore 120 mm / stroke 150 mm
6.78 litres / 40.3 bhp at 1040 rpm / 70 kph max speed

Benz Viktoria, 1893
1 cylinder / bore 150 mm / stroke 165 mm
2.92 litres / 5 bhp at 700 rpm / 25 kph

Erster Mercedes, 1901
4 cylinders / bore 116 mm / stroke 140 mm
5.93 litres / 35 bhp at 1000 rpm / 72 kph max speed

Mercedes Simplex Phaeton, 1903
4 cylinders / bore 140 mm / stroke 150 mm
9.23 litres / 60 bhp at 1060 rpm / 90 kph max speed

Mercedes Simplex Doppeltonneau, 1904
4 cylinders / bore 100 mm / stroke 130 mm
4.08 litres / 18 bhp at 1200 rpm / 50 kph max speed

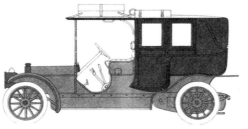

Mercedes Landaulet, 1908
6 cylinders / bore 120 mm / stroke 150 mm
10.18 litres / 70 bhp at 1280 rpm / 95 kph max speed

Mercedes 16/40 Knight, 1911
4 cylinders / bore 100 mm / stroke 130 mm
4.08 litres / 43 bhp at 1800 rpm / 80 kph max speed

Benz Parsifal Tonneau, 1904
4 cylinders / bore 90 mm / stroke 110 mm
2.8 litres / 18 bhp at 1280 rpm / 50 kph max speed

Mercedes 14/30 Tourenwagen, 1910
4 cylinders / bore 90 mm / stroke 140 mm
3.56 litres / 30 bhp at 1600 rpm / 80 kph max speed

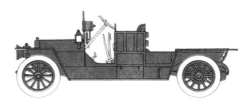

Mercedes 16/40 Jagdwagen, 1911
4 cylinders / bore 100 mm / stroke 130 mm
4.08 litres / 40 bhp at 1800 rpm / 85 kph max speed

Benz Doppel-Pheaton, 1905
4 cylinders / bore 90 mm / stroke 110 mm
2.8 litres / 14 bhp at 1200 rpm / 60 kph max speed

Mercedes 28/60 Landaulet, 1910
4 cylinders / bore 120 mm / stroke 160 mm
7.24 litres / 60 bhp at 1250 rpm / 80 kph max speed

Mercedes 22/50 Limousine, 1911
4 cylinders / bore 110 mm / stroke 150 mm
5.7 litres / 54 bhp at 1400 rpm / 89 kph max speed

Mercedes Reiselimousine, 1906
4 cylinders / bore 120 mm / stroke 150 mm
6.78 litres / 45 bhp at 1200 rpm / 85 kph max speed

Mercedes 28/60 Doppelphaeton, 1910
4 cylinders / bore 120 mm / stroke 160 mm
7.24 litres / 62.4 bhp at 1250 rpm / 85 kph max speed

Mercedes 22/40 Tourenwagen 1912
4 cylinders / bore 110 mm / stroke 148 mm
5.62 litres / 40 bhp at 1250 rpm / 80 kph max speed

Benz 28/50 Tourenwagen, 1907
4 cylinders / bore 130 mm / stroke 140 mm
7.43 litres / 50 bhp at 1350 rpm / 90 kph max speed

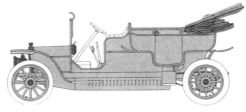

Mercedes 28/60 Landaulet, 1910
4 cylinders / bore 120 mm / stroke 160 mm
7.24 litres / 62 bhp at 1250 rpm / 85 kph max speed

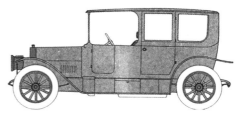

Benz 29/60 Limousine, 1912
4 cylinders / bore 125 mm / stroke 150 mm
6.76 litres / 60 bhp at 1400 rpm / 95 kph max speed

Benz Limousine, 1907
4 cylinders / bore 105 mm / stroke 130 mm
4.5 litres / 28 bhp at 1300 rpm / 70 kph max speed

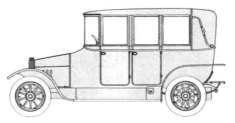

Mercedes 14/30 Limousine, 1910
4 cylinders / bore 90 mm / stroke 140 mm
4.08 litres / 35 bhp at 1500 rpm / 80 kph max speed

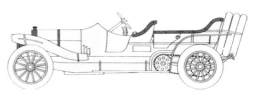

Mercedes 38/70 Sportphaeton, 1912
4 cylinders, / bore 140 mm / stroke 160 mm
9.85 litres / 95.8 bhp at 1200 rpm / 85 kph max speed

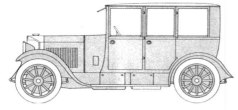

Benz 16/50 Limousine, 1921
6 cylinders / bore 80 mm / stroke 138 mm
4.16 litres / 52 bhp at 1950 rpm / 95 kph max speed

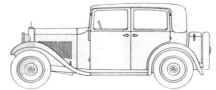

Mercedes-Benz Limousine Type 170, 1931
6 cylinders / bore 65 mm / stroke 85 mm
1.69 litres / 32 bhp at 32 rpm / 90 kph max speed

Mercedes-Benz Limousine Type 170 V, 1935
4 cylinders / bore 73.5 mm / stroke 100 mm
1.7 litres / 38 bhp at 3200 rpm / 108 kph max speed

Mercedes 10/40/65 Tourenwagen, 1922
4 cylinders / bore 80 mm / stroke 130 mm
2.61 litres / 66 bhp at 2800 rpm with supercharger / 135 kph max speed

Mercedes-Benz Limousine Type 130 (with rear engine), 1933
4 cylinders / bore 70 mm / stroke 85 mm
1.3 litres / 26 bhp at 3300 rpm / 92 kph max speed

Mercedes-Benz Cabriolet Type 170 V, 1936
4 cylinders / bore 73.5 mm / stroke 100 mm
1.7 litres / 38 bhp at 3200 rpm / 108 kph max speed

Mercedes 24/100/140 Tourenwagen, 1924
6 cylinders / bore 94 mm / stroke 150 mm
6.25 litres / 142 bhp at 3000 rpm with supercharger / 125 kph max speed

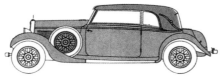

Mercedes-Benz Cabriolet Type 290, 1933
6 cylinders / bore 78 mm / stroke 100 mm
2.85 litres / 68 bhp at 3200 rpm / 108 kph max speed

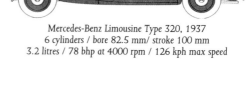

Mercedes-Benz Limousine Type 320, 1937
6 cylinders / bore 82.5 mm/ stroke 100 mm
3.2 litres / 78 bhp at 4000 rpm / 126 kph max speed

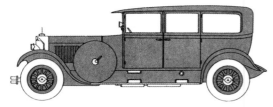

Mercedes 15/70/100 Pullman Limousine, 1924
6 cylinders / bore 80 mm / stroke 130 mm
3.92 litres / 100 bhp at 3100 rpm with supercharger / 104 kph max speed

Mercedes-Benz Cabriolet Type 380, 1933
8 cylinders / bore 78 mm / stroke 100 mm
3.8 litres / 140 bhp at 3600 rpm with supercharger / 140 kph max speed

Mercedes-Benz Cabriolet 230, 1938
6 cylinders / bore 72.5 mm / stroke 90 mm
2.3 litres / 55 bhp at 3500 rpm / 116 kph max speed

Mercedes-Benz Type 200 Stuttgart, 1926
6 cylinders / bore 65 mm / stroke 100 mm
1.98 litres / 38 bhp at 3500 rpm / 80 kph max speed

Mercedes-Benz Limousine Type 170-(with rear engine), 1935
4 cylinders / bore 73.5 mm / stroke 100 mm
1.7 litres / 38 bhp at 3200 rpm / 110 kph max speed

Mercedes-Benz Limousine Type 170 S, 1949
4 cylinders / bore 75 mm / stroke 100 mm
1.8 litres / 52 bhp at 4000 rpm / 120 kph max speed

Mercedes-Benz, 'Grosser Mercedes', 1930
8 cylinders / bore 95 mm / stroke 135 mm
7.66 litres / 200 bhp at 2800 rpm with supercharger / 160 kph max speed

Mercedes-Benz Limousine Type 260 Diesel, 1936
4 cylinders / bore 90 mm / stroke 100 mm
2.55 litres / 45 bhp at 3000 rpm / 95 kph max speed

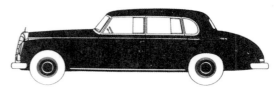

Mercedes-Benz Limousine Type 300, 1951
6 cylinders / bore 85 mm / stroke 88 mm
3 litres / 115 bhp at 4600 rpm / 155 kph max speed

Mercedes-Benz Cabriolet Type 220, 1951
6 cylinders / bore 80 mm / stroke 72.8 mm
2.2 litres / 80 bhp at 4600 rpm / 145 kph max speed

Mercedes-Benz Limousine Type 180 a, 1957
4 cylinders / bore 85 mm / stroke 83.6 mm
1.9 litres / 65 bhp at 4500 rpm / 136 kph max speed

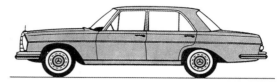

Mercedes-Benz 250 S, 1965
6 cylinders / bore 82 mm / stroke 78.8 mm
2.5 litres / 130 bhp at 5400 rpm / 182 kph max speed

Mercedes-Benz Limousine Type 180, 1953
4 cylinders / bore 75 mm / stroke 100 mm
1.8 litres / 52 bhp at 4000 rpm / 126 kph max speed

Mercedes-Benz Cabriolet Type 220 S, 1957
6 cylinders / bore 80 mm / stroke 72.8 mm
2.2 litres / 106 bhp at 5200 rpm / 160 kph max speed

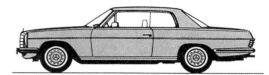

Mercedes-Benz 280 CE, 1971
6 cylinders / bore 86 mm / stroke 78.8 mm
2.75 litres / 185 bhp at 6000 rpm / 200 kph max speed

Mercedes-Benz Limousine Type 220 a, 1954
6 cylinders / bore 80 mm / stroke 72.8 mm
2.2 litres / 85 bhp at 4800 rpm / 150 kph max speed

Mercedes-Benz Limousine Type 220 b, 1959
6 cylinders / bore 80 mm / stroke 72.8 mm
2,2 litres / 95 bhp at 4800 rpm / 155 kph max speed

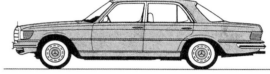

Mercedes-Benz 350 SE, 1972
8 cylinders / bore 92 mm / stroke 65.8 mm
3.5 litres / 200 bhp at 5800 rpm / 205 kph max speed

Mercedes-Benz Coupé Type 300 Sc, 1955
6 cylinders / bore 85 mm / stroke 88 mm
3 litres / 175 bhp at 5300 rpm / 180 kph max speed

Mercedes-Benz Coupé Type 220 SE, 1959
6 cylinders / bore 80 mm / stroke 72.8 mm
2.2 litres / 115 bhp at 4800 rpm / 160 kph max speed

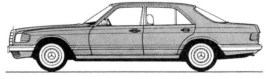

Mercedes-Benz 500 SE, 1979
8 cylinders / bore 96.5 mm / stroke 85 mm
4.97 litres / 240 bhp at 4750 rpm / 220 kph max speed

Mercedes-Benz Limousine Type 219, 1956
6 cylinders / bore 80 mm / stroke 72.8 mm
2.2 litres / 85 bhp at 4800 rpm / 148 kph max speed

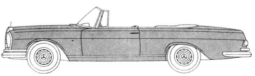

Mercedes-Benz Cabriolet Type 220 SE b, 1961
6 cylinders / bore 80 mm / stroke 72.8 mm
2.2 litres / 120 bhp at 4800 rpm / 170 kph max speed

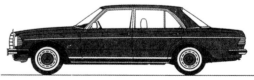

Mercedes-Benz 230 E, 1979
4 cylinders / bore 95.5 mm / stroke 80.3 mm
2.3 litres / 136 bhp at 5100 rpm / 180 kph max speed

Mercedes-Benz Limousine Type 300 d, 1957
6 cylinders / bore 85 mm / stroke 88 mm
3 litres / 160 bhp at 5400 rpm / 160 kph max speed

Mercedes-Benz Limousine Type 190, 1961
4 cylinders / bore 85 mm / stroke 83.6 mm
1.9 litres / 80 bhp at 5000 rpm / 150 kph max speed

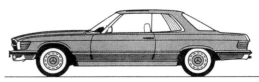

Mercedes-Benz 500 SLC, 1980
8 cylinders / bore 96.5 mm / stroke 85 mm
4.97 litres / 240 bhp at 5000 rpm / 220 kph max speed

Mercedes-Benz 300 TD Turbodiesel, 1980
5 cylinders / bore 90.9 mm / stroke 92.4
3 litres / 125 bhp at 4350 rpm / 165 kph max speed

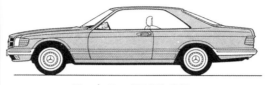

Mercedes-Benz 500 SEC, 1981
8 cylinders / bore 96.5 mm / stroke 85 mm
4.97 litres / 240 bhp at 4750 kph / 225 kph max speed

Benz 28/80 Sportwagen, 1909
4 cylinders / bore 115 mm / stroke 175 mm
7.27 litres / 104 bhp at 2050 rpm / 134 kph max speed

Mercedes-Benz 190 E, 1982
4 cylinders / bore 89 mm / stroke 80.3 mm
2 litres / 118 bhp at 5100 rpm / 195 kph max speed

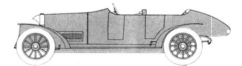

Mercedes14/30 Sportwagen, 1910
4 cylinders / bore 90 mm / stroke 140 mm
3.56 litres / 30 bhp at 1600 rpm / 70 kph max speed

Mercedes-Benz 200 T, 1984
4 cylinders / bore 89 mm / stroke 80.3 mm
2 litres / 105 bhp at 5500 / 187 kph max speed

Mercedes 38/80 Sportwagen, 1910
4 cylinders / bore 140 mm / stroke 160 mm
9.85 litres / 75 bhp at 1280 rpm / 90 kph max speed

Mercedes-Benz 260 E, 1984
6 cylinders / bore 82.9 mm / stroke 80.3 mm
2.6 litres / 160 bhp at 5800 rpm / 218 kph max speed

Mercedes 10/20 Sportwwagen, 1911
4 cylinders / bore 80 mm / stroke 130 mm
2.61 litres / 20 bhp at 1500 rpm / 65 kph max speed

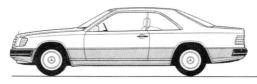

Mercedes-Benz 300 CE, 1984
6 cylinders / bore 88.5 mm / stroke 80.3 mm
2.96 litres / 180 bhp at 5700 rpm / 228 kph max speed

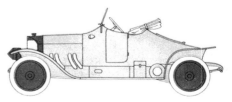

Mercedes 37/90 PS Sportwagen, 1911
4 cylinders / bore 130 mm / stroke 180 mm
9.55 litres / 90 bhp at 1300 rpm / 114 kph max speed

Mercedes 14/35 Sportwagen, 1913
4 cylinders / bore 90 mm / stroke 140 mm
3.56 litres / 35 bhp at 1700 rpm / 90 kph max speed

Mercedes-Benz 26/120/180 Model S, 1927
6 cylinders / bore 98 mm / stroke 150 mm
6.79 litres / 180 bhp at 3000 rpm with supercharger / 160 kph max speed

Mercedes-Benz Sportwagen 300 SL Coupé, 1954
6 cylinders / bore 85 mm / stroke 88 mm
3 litres / 215 bhp at 5800 rpm / 260 kph max speed

Benz 6/18 Sportwagen, 1921
4 cylinders / bore 68 mm / stroke 108 mm
1.57 litres / 18 bhp at 3200 rpm / 120 kph max speed

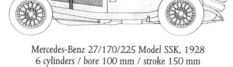

Mercedes-Benz 27/170/225 Model SSK, 1928
6 cylinders / bore 100 mm / stroke 150 mm
7.1 litres / 225 bhp at 3200 rpm with supercharger / 175 kph max speed

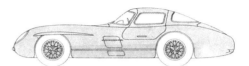

Mercedes-Benz Rennsportwagen 300 SLR, 1955
8 cylinders / bore 78 mm / stroke 78 mm
2.98 litres / 300 bhp at 7450 rpm / 290 kph max speed

Mercedes 28/95 Sportwagen, 1921
6 cylinders / bore 105 mm / stroke 140 mm
7.27 litres / 95 bhp at 1800 rpm / 110 kph max speed

Mercedes-Benz 26/120/180, 1928
6 cylinders / bore 100 mm / stroke 150 mm
7.02 litres / 180 bhp at 3300 rpm with supercharger / 185 kph max speed

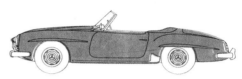

Mercedes-Benz Sportwagen 190 SL, 1955
4 cylinders / bore 85 mm / stroke 83.6 mm
1.9 litres / 105 bhp at 5700 rpm / 175 kph max speed

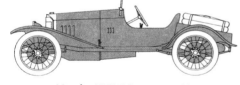

Mercedes 6/25/40 Sportwagen, 1921
4 cylinders / bore 68 mm / stroke 108 mm
1.57 litres / 43 bhp at 2800 rpm with supercharger / 135 kph max speed

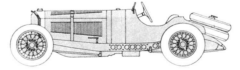

Mercedes-Benz Rennsportwagen SSKL, 1931
6 cylinders / bore 100 mm / stroke 150 mm
7.1 litres / 300 bhp rpm with supercharger / 235 kph max speed

Mercedes-Benz Sportwagen 300 SL Roadster, 1957
6 cylinders / bore 85 mm / stroke 88 mm
3 litres / 215 bhp at 5800 rpm / 260 kph max speed

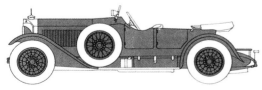

Benz 16/50 Sportwagen, 1924
6 cylinders / bore 80 mm / stroke 138 mm
4.16 litres / 50 bhp at 1950 rpm / 90 kph max speed

Mercedes-Benz Roadster 500 K, 1934
8 cylinders / bore 86 mm / stroke 108 mm
5.02 litres / 160 bhp at 3400 rpm with supercharger / 165 kph max speed

Mercedes-Benz 230 SL, 1963
6 cylinders / bore 82 mm / stroke 72.8 mm
2.28 litres / 150 bhp at 5500 rpm / 200 kph max speed

Mercedes-Benz 24/110/160 Model K, 1926
6 cylinders / bore 94 mm / stroke 150 mm
6.24 litres / 160 bhp at 3000 rpm with supercharger / 145 kph max speed

Mercedes-Benz Roadster 540 K, 1936
8 cylinders / bore 88 mm / stroke 111 mm
5.4 litres / 180 bhp at 3600 rpm with supercharger / 170 kph max speed

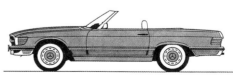

Mercedes-Benz 500 SL, 1980
8 cylinders / bore 96.5 mm / stroke 85 mm
4.97 litres / 240 bhp at 5000 rpm / 225 kph max speed

RACING CARS

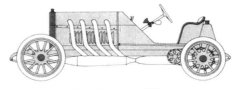

Benz Rennwagen, 1909
4 cylinders / bore 185 mm / stroke 200 mm
21.5 litres / 200 bhp at 1500 rpm / 210 kph max speed

Benz Rennwagen, 1900
2 cylinders / bore 120 mm / stroke 120 mm
2.7 litres / 10 bhp at 1000 rpm / 50 kph max speed

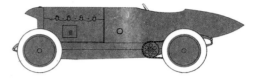

Benz Rennwagen 'Blitzen-Benz', 1911
4 cylinders / bore 185 mm / stroke 200 mm
21.5 litres / 200 bhp at 1500 rpm / 228 kph max speed

Mercedes Rennwagen, 1903
4 cylinders / bore 140 mm / stroke 151 mm
9.29 litres / 65 bhp at 1100 rpm / 128 kph max speed

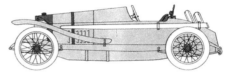

Mercedes Grand Prix Rennwagen, 1914
4 cylinders / bore 93 mm / stroke 164 mm
4.45 litres / 117 bhp at 3180 rpm / 180 kph max speed

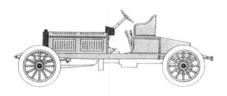

Benz Parsifal Rennwagen, 1903
4 cylinders / bore 160 mm / stroke 140 mm
11.26 litres / 60 bhp at 1200 rpm / 120 kph max speed

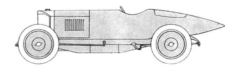

Benz 10/30 Rennwagen, 1921
4 cylinders / bore 80 mm / stroke 130 mm
2.61 litres / 30 bhp at 3100 rpm / 130 kph max speed

Mercedes Grand Prix Rennwagen, 1908
4 cylinders / bore 155 mm / stroke 170 mm
12.8 litres / 130 bhp at 125 rpm / 155 kph max speed

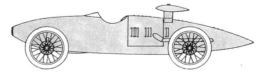

Benz Rennwagen Tropfen-Benz, 1922
6 cylinders / bore 65 mm / stroke 100 mm
2 litres / 90 bhp at 5000 rpm / 160 kph max speed

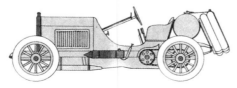

Benz Grand Prix Rennwagen, 1908
4 cylinders / bore 155 mm / stroke 160 mm
12.08 litres / 150 bhp at 1500 rpm / 160 kph max speed

Mercedes-Rennwagen Targa Florio, 1923
4 cylinders / bore 70 mm / stroke 129 mm
1.98 litres / 120 bhp at 4500 rpm with supercharger

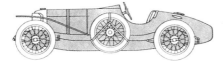

Mercedes Rennwagen, 1923
4 cylinders / bore 65 mm / stroke 113 mm
1.5 litres / 65 bhp at 3600 rpm with supercharger

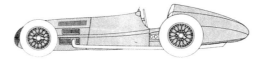

Mercedes-Benz W 154/M 154 Rennwagen, 1938
12 cylinders / bore 67 mm / stroke 70 mm
2.96 litres / 468 bhp at 7800 rpm with supercharger / 315 kph max speed

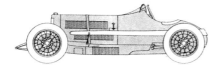

Mercedes Rennwagen Monza, 1924
8 cylinders / bore 61.9 mm / stroke 82.8 mm
2 litres / 160 bhp at 6000 rpm with supercharger

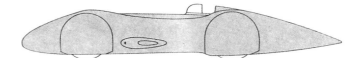

Mercedes-Benz W 125 Rekordwagen, 1938
12 cylinders / bore 82 mm / stroke 88 mm
5.57 litres / 736 bhp at 5800 rpm with supercharger / 433 kph max speed

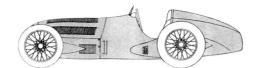

Mercedes-Benz W 25 Rennwagen, 1934
8 cylinders / bore 78 mm / stroke 88 mm
3.36 litres / 354 bhp at 5800 rpm with supercharger / 280 kph max speed

Mercedes-Benz W 154/M 163 Rennwagen, 1939
12 cylinders / bore 67 mm / stroke 70 mm
2.96 litres / 483 bhp at 7800 rpm with supercharger / 320 kph max speed

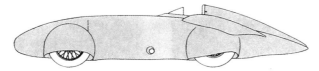

Mercedes-Benz W 25 Rekordwagen, 1936
12 cylinders / bore 77.5 mm / stroke 88 mm
4.98 litres / 540 bhp at 5800 rpm with supercharger / 372 kph max speed

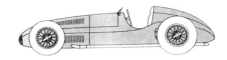

Mercedes-Benz W 165 Rennwagen, 1939
8 cylinders / bore 64 mm / stroke 58 mm
1.49 litres / 254 bhp at 8000 rpm with supercharger / 245 kph max speed

Mercedes-Benz W 125 Rennwagen, 1937
8 cylinders / bore 94 mm / stroke 102 mm
5.66 litres / 592 bhp at 5800 rpm with supercharger / 320 kph max speed

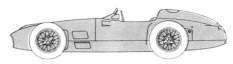

Mercedes-Benz W 196 Rennwagen Monoposto, 1954
8 cylinders / bore 76 mm / stroke 68.8 mm
2.5 litres / 280 bhp at 8500 rpm / 265 kph max speed

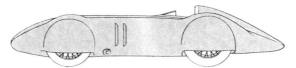

Mercedes-Benz W 125 Avus-Rennwagen, 1937
8 cylinders / bore 94 mm / stroke 102 mm
5.66 litres / 646 bhp at 5800 rpm with supercharger / 380 kph max speed

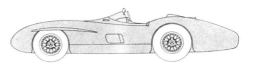

Mercedes-Benz W 195 'streamlined body', 1954
8 cylinders / bore 76 mm / stroke 68.8 mm
2.5 litres / 280 bhp at 8500 rpm / 275 kph max speed

Selected Bibliography

Aicher, Otl: Kritik am Auto. Munich 1984

Antonik, M.: Illustrated Mercedes-Benz Buyer's Guide

Automobile Quarterly. Mercedes-Benz: A Century of Invention and Innovation

Barthel, Manfred/Lingnau, Gerold: 100 Jahre Daimler-Benz. Die Technik. Mainz 1986

Bell, R.: Great Marques: Mercedes-Benz

Benz, Karl: Lebensfahrt eines deutschen Erfinders. Die Erfindungen des Automobils. Erinnerungen eines Achtzigjährigen. Leipzig 1943

Bishop G.: Mercedes – Auto Color Library

Bladon, Stuart: Mercedes-Benz

Boddy, William: Mercedes-Benz 300 SL

Boesen, Victor/Grad, Wendy: The Mercedes-Benz-Book. New York 1981

Bols, Udo: Mercedes Personenwagen. Brilon 1988

Brooklands Books. Mercedes-Benz Cars 1949–1954.

Brooklands Books. Mercedes-Benz Cars 1954–1957.

Brooklands (ed.). 'Road & Track' on Mercedes 1952–1962

Brooklands (ed.). 'Road & Track' on Mercedes 1963–1970

Brooklands (ed.). 'Road & Track' on Mercedes 1971–1979

Brooklands (ed.). 'Road & Track' on Mercedes 1980–1987

Buergle, Klaus/Frankenberg, Richard von: Autotypen gestern und heute. 2 über-arbeitete Auflage. Stuttgart 1970

Busch, Fritz B.: Das Daimler-Benz-Museum. Konstanz 1987

Casucci, P.: Mercedes-Benz 560

Cimarosti, Adriano: Autorennen. Bern 1986

Clarke, R. (Ed.): Mercedes-Benz Competition Cars 1950–1957

Clarke, R. (Ed.): Mercedes 230/250/280 SL 1963/71

Clarke, R. (Ed.): Mercedes 350/450 SL & SLC 1971/80

Daimler-Benz AG. 75 Jahre Motorisierung des Verkehrs 1886–1961. Stuttgart-Untertükheim 1961

Daimler-Benz AG: Das Werk Untertürkheim. Stuttgart 1983

Diesel, Eugen/Goldbeck, G./Schildberger, Friedrich: Vom Motor zum Auto. Fünf Männer und ihr Werk. Stuttgart 1958

Diesel, Eugen: Rudolf Diesel – sein Leben, sein Schicksal. Stuttgart 1953

Diesel, Eugen: Rudolf Diesel. In: 'Die großen Deutschen'. Band IV 1957

Diesel, Eugen/Strößner, Georg: Kampf um eine Maschine (Die ersten Dieselmotoren in den USA)

DMG. 1890–1915. Zum 25 jährigen Bestehen der Daimler-Motoren-Gesellschaft. Adapted by G. Braunbeck. Stuttgart-Unterürkheim 1915

Dracket, P.: Classic Mercedes-Benz

Fersen, Hans Heinrich von: Autos in Deutschland 1885–1920. Eine Typengeschichte. Stuttgart 1968

Fersen, Hans Heinrich von: Sportwagen in Deutschland. Eine Typengeschichte. Eine Typengeschichte der deutschen, öster-reichtschen und tschechischen Sportwagen 1885–1940. Stuttgart 1968

Fersen, Olaf v: Ein Jahrhundert Automobiltechnik (Personenwagen). Düsseldorf 1986

Flatz, Emil: Gedenkrede auf Nikolaus Otto: In '75 Jahre Ottomotor', Cologne 1952

Frank, R.: Mercedes im Krieg

Frankenberg, Richard von/Mateucci, Marco: Geschichte des Automblis. Künzelsau 1973

Frère, Paul/Weitmann, Julius: Mercedes-Benz C111-eine Fahrzeugstudie

Frostik, Michael: The Mighty Mercedes

Gloor, Roger: Nachkriegswagen (Personenautos 1945–1960). Bern 1945

Gloor, Roger: Personenwagen der 60er Jahre. Bern 1984

Goldbeck, Gustav: Gebändigte Kraft. Geschichte der Erfindung des Ottomotors. Munich 1965

Goldbeck, Gustav: Kraft für die Welt. 1864–1964 Klöckner-Humboldt-Deutz AG. Düsseldorf 1964

Goldbeck, Gustav: Siegfried Marcus, ein Erfinderleben. Düsseldorf 1965

Goldbeck, Gustav: Christian Reithmann: Uhrmacher und Motorenerfinder 1818–1909

Günther, Dieter/Hübner, Johannes: Das Große Mercedes-SL-Buch. Frankfurt 1988

Hamburger Stiftung für Sozialgeschichte des 20, Jahrhunderts: Das Daimler-Benz-Buch – ein Rüstungskonzern im 'Tausend-jährigen Reich'

Hanaoka, Komei: Mercedes 300 SL Gullwing – ein Fotoessay

Harvey, Chris: Great Marques Poster Book – Mercedes

Hauf, C. Hennig v/Koester, Ulrich/Scheper, Wilhelm/Schiefer, Gerhard/Csáki, Csaba/ Boussard, Jean M./Tarditi: Forum der

Technik, Bd. I. Die Welt im Zeichen des Motors. Zürich 1962

Heitz, Rudolf/Neff, Thomas: Alles über Mercedes-Tuning: Motor, Fahrwerk, Karosserie. Stuttgart 1986

Herzog, Bodi: Unter dem Mercedes-Stern. Die große Zeit der Silberpfeile. Preetz 1966

Heuss, Theodor: Robert Bosch. Stuttgart und Tübingen 1945

Hoffmann, R.: Daimler Benz AG, Musterbetriebe deutscher Wirtschaft, Band 12. Die Automobil-Industrie. Daimler-Benz AG, Berlin 1930

Hofner, Heribert: Mercedes-Benz-Automobile 2, Vom 'Nürburg' zum 540K

Hofner, Heribert: Mercedes-Benz-Automobile 4, Vom 190 SL zum 300 SEL

Hofner, Heribert: Vom 190 E2.3–16 zum 560 SEL

Hofner, Heribert: Vom 600 zum 450 SEL

Hough, Richard/Frostick, Michael: A History of the World's Racing Cars. London 1965

Howard, G.: Mercedes-Benz S-Class

Jackson, Judy: Eine Jahrhunderliebe. Menschen und Automobile. München 1979

Jackson, Judy: Man & The Automobile. – A Twentieth Century Love Affair. London 1979

Jellinek-Mercedes, Guy: Mein Vater, der Herr Mercedes, Wein, Berlin. Stuttgart 1962

Jenkinson, Dennis: Mercedes-Benz W125 Grand Prix-Rennwagen. Stuttgart 1971

Kimes, B.: The Star and the Laurel – The Centennial History of Daimler-Benz

Knittel, S.: Mercedes 190 SL (Auto Classic 3)

Knittel, S.: Mercedes 300 SL (Auto Classic 5)

Kruk, Max/Lingnau, Gerold: 100 Jahre Daimler-Benz – Das Unternehmen. Mainz 1986

Kubisch, Ulrich/Winkler, Günter. Eine Sammlung historischer Automobil-Dokumente. 1987

Kupelian, Y. und J.: Histoire De Mercedes-Benz

Langen, Arnold: N. A. Otto – Schöpfer des Verbrennungsmotors. 1949

Langworth, R. M.: Mercedes-Benz – Die ersten 100 Jahre

Lewandowski, Jürgen: Mercedes-Benz. 1886–1986 – Catalogue Raisonnée

Lozier, Herbert: The Cars of Kings – The Mercedes 'K' and 'S'. Enclosed Instruction Book No. 6206 SSE for Mercedes-Benz Sports Cars Type SS and Type SSK. Philadelphia 1967

Ludvigsen, Karl: Mercedes-Benz – Renn-und Sportwagen. Gerlingen 1981

Lurani, Giovanni: A History of Motor Racing. (Edited by David Hodges). London 1972

McComb, F. Wilson: Mercedes-Benz V8s. Limousines, saloons, sedans 1963 to date. Osceola, Wisc. 1980

Melin, J.: Mercedes-Benz Supercharged 8-Cylinder Cars of the 1930s, Vol. 1

Monkhouse, G.: Mercedes-Benz – Grand Prix Racing 1934–1955

Nallinger, Fritz: Gottlieb Daimler – Karl Benz, in 'Die Großen Deutschen'. 1957

Nitske, Robert W.: Mercedes-Benz 300 SL. Minneapolis 1974

Nitske, Robert W.: Mercedes-Benz – A History

Nitske, Robert W.: Mercedes-Benz Production Models Book 1946–1986

Nitske, Robert W.: Mercedes-Benz Diesel Automobils

Nitske, Robert W.: The Complete Mercedes Story. The Thrilling Seventy-Year History of Daimler and Benz. New York 1965

Nixon, Chris: Racing the Silver Arrows – Mercedes Benz versus Auto-Union 1934–1939

Oswald, Werner: Mercedes-Benz Personenwagen 1886–1984. Stuttgart 1985

Pascal, D.: Mercedes-Benz Pocket History

Pohl, Hans/Habeth, Stephanie/Brüninghaus, Beate: Die Daimler-Benz AG in den Jahren 1933–1945. 1986

Posthumus, Cyril: Mercedes-Benz Racing Car Guide 1901–1955

Rathke, Kurt: Wilhelm Maybach – Anbruch

eines neuen Zeitalters. Friedrichshafen 1953

Riedner, Michael: Mercedes-Benz W196 – Der Letzte Silberpfeil. Stuttgart 1987

Rowe, Harvey T.: Männer, Frauen und Motoren: Die Erinnerungen des Rennleiters Alfred Neubauer. Stuttgart 1978

Sauzay, Maurice: Mercedes-Benz 300 SL.

Scott-Moncrieff, D.: The Three-Pointed Star – The Story of Mercedes-Benz

Schildberger, Friedrich: Gottlieb Daimler und Karl Benz – Pioniere der Automobilindustrie (Persönlichkeiten und Geschichte, Band 93). Göttingen 1976

Schildberger, Friedrich: Chronik der Mercedes-Benz-Fahrzeuge und-Motoren. Stuttgart-Unterürkheim 1971/73

Schildberger, Friedrich: Gottlieb Daimler, Wilhelm Maybach und Karl Benz. Sonderdruck in 'Von Motorzum Auto'. Stuttgart-Unterürkheim 1973

Schrader, Halwart/Demand, Carlo: Mercedes-Kompressorwagen. Munich 1979

Schrader, Halwart: Mercedes-Benz Silberpfeile 1934–1955. Munich 1987

Schrader, Halwart: Mercedes-Benz 190 SL 1955–1963

Schrader, Halwart: Mercedes-Benz 300 – Limousinen, Coupés, Cabrios 1951–1962. Munich 1987

Schrader, Halwart: Mercedes-Benz Automobile 1: 28/95 PS to SSKL

Schrader, Halwart: Mercedes-Benz 'Heckflossen' – 220 190/200, 230, 300 SE 1959–1965. Munich 1987

Setright, L. J. K.: Mercedes-Benz Roadsters Autohistory

Setright, L. J. K.: Mercedes-Benz SL und SLC

Siedel, W.: Mercedes-Benz – Klassische Automobile in Wort und Bild

Siebertz, Paul: Gottlieb Daimler zum Gedächtnis – Eine Dokumentensammlung. Stuttgart-Untertürkheim 1950

Siebertz, Paul: Gottlieb Daimler – Ein Revolutionär der Technik. Stuttgart 1950

Siebertz, Paul: Karl Benz und sein Lebenswerk – Dokumente und Berichte. Stuttgart-Untertürkheim 1953

Siebertz, Paul: Karl Benz – Ein Pionier der Motorisierung. Stuttgart 1950

Siebertz, Paul: Mercedes-Konstruktionen in fünf Jahrzehnten. Eine Chronik. Stuttgart-Untertürkheim 1951

Simsa, Paul/Lewandowski, Jürgen: Sterne, Stars und Majestäten – Prominenz auf Mercedes. Konstanz 1985

Simsa, Paul: Der Mercedes-Benz 190. Stuttgart

Stein, Ralph-Schnitzler, Winifried M.: Die großen Automobile. München 1971

Stein, Ralph: Das große Buch vom Automobil. Munich 1974

Steinwedel, L. W.: The Mercedes-Benz Story. Radnor. Pa. 1975

Taylor, James: Mercedes-Benz Since 1945 Vol. 1. The 1940s & 1950s

Taylor, James: Mercedes-Benz Since 1945 Vol. 2. A Collector's Guide

Taylor, James: Mercedes-Benz Since 1945 Vol. 3. The 1970s

Tragatsch, Erwin: Die großen Rennjahre 1919–1939. Bern/Stuttgart 1973

Tragatsch, Erwin: Das große Renn- und Sportwagenbuch. Bern. Stuttgart 1968

Walz, Werner: Wo das Auto anfing . . . Die Geschichte einer Weltmarke. Konstanz 1981

INDEX: PROPER NAMES

Index: Car Makes

INDEX: RACING EVENTS

PICTURE ACKNOWLEDGEMENTS

Bacchi, Sandro 136

Bolsinger, Markus/ Autobild 259 top

Daimler-Benz 9, 10, 11, 12–13, 14, 15, 16, 33, 34–35, 36, 37 top, 38, 40, 75, 76, 77, 78, 79, 80, 81, 82, 83 top, 83 bottom, 84, 85, 86, 87 top, 87 bottom, 88 top, 88 bottom, 90 top, 91, 100–101, 104 top, 121, 123 bottom, 124–125, 126, 127 top, 127 bottom, 128 top, 128 bottom, 152, 154–155, 158 top, 158 bottom, 160 top, 160 bottom, 176 top, 222–223,

254–255, 256, 257, 260–261, 263 top, backside

Eisele, Werner 176 bottom, 196–197, 198–199, 225, 262, 263 top, 263 bottom

Fast Lane 258, 259 bottom

Indianapolis Speedway Museum 123 top

Kettler, Ulrich 250–251

Keystone 157
Krähling, Ferdi 224
Kunigk, Klaus/Autobild 218–219

Lindlar, Andress/Autobild 252–253

Lintelmann, Reiner 66–67, 68–69, 89, 217 top, 217 bottom

National Motor Museum, Beaulieu 37 bottom, 41, 65, 122, 132–133, 200–220

Piepenburg, Conrad/Autobild 164–165, 169 top, 169 top, 169 bottom, 193, 194–195

Quadrant Picture Library 159

Reinhard, Daniel/auto, motor + sport 174–175

Seiff, Ingo 42 top, 42 bottom, 43, 73, 97, 134, 135

Seufert, H. D./Motorklassik 72,

103, 104 bottom, 230–231, 232

Seufert, H. P./Motorpresse 44–45, 48, 70–71, 72 top, 102, 129, 130–131, 161, 168, 170–171, 220–221, 226–227, 249

Sommer, Hardy/Auto-Zeitung 228–229

Staud, René 166–167

Zerha, Jürgen 172, 173
Zumbrunn, Michael 90–91 bottom, 92–93, 94–95, 96, 166–167

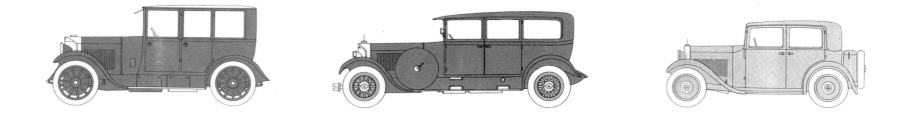